D1217704

THE STORY SPECIES

Our Life-Literature Connection

Joseph Gold

Fitzhenry & Whiteside

All case material cited in this text has been slightly altered as to names and some details of fact in order to protect the identity of patients. For the purposes of this book the cases are stories loosely based on real people I have known.

Fitzhenry and Whiteside Limited
195 Allstate Parkway
Markham, Ontario L3R 4T8

In the United States:
121 Harvard Avenue, Suite 2
Allston, Massachusetts 02134

www.fitzhenry.ca godwit@fitzhenry.ca

Fitzhenry & Whiteside acknowledges with thanks the Canada Council for the Arts, the Government of Canada through its Book Publishing Industry Development Program, and the Ontario Arts Council for their support of our publishing program.

National Library of Canada Cataloguing in Publication Data

Gold, Joseph, 1933-
The story species: our life-literature connection

Includes bibliographical reference and index.
ISBN 1-55041-736-3(bound) ISBN 1-55041-643-X(pbk.)

1. Books and reading—Psychological aspects. 2. Bibliotherapy. 3. Identity (Psychology)
I. Title.

A1003.G66 2002 028'.8 C2002-930680-6

U.S. Cataloguing-in-Publication Data

Gold, Joseph, 1933-
The story species : our life-literature connection / Joseph Gold — 1st ed. [336]p. : cm
Includes bibliographical references and index.
Summary: A discussion of the story form of literature as it relates to the brain's capacity to store and recall, and to selfunderstanding and bibliotherapy.
ISBN 1-55041-736-3
ISBN 1-55041-643-X (pbk.)
1. Literature and science. 2. Bibliotherapy. 3. Psychoanalysis and literature. 4. Mind.
I. Title
6148516 21 CIP 2002

Cover design and layout: Darrell McCalla
Cover image by: Travis Shilling, *Discovery Series 2, Number 2*, mixed media on Masonite, 48x32, 1999.
Printed and bound in Canada

To the masters:
Aristotle; Horace; Sidney; Shelley; Wordsworth; Eliot;
and Tai Yeen Wong, my Qi Gong Master

For the children:
Deborah; Anna; Joel; Naomi; Sarah; Micah; Jonah;
Rachel; Noam; Elijah; Isaac.

Reining in his horse, Sanzang said, "Disciples, can you see where this is?" "You can't read, Master," Monkey exclaimed. "How ever did you get the Tang Emperor to send you on this mission?" "I have been a monk since I was a boy and read classics and scriptures by the thousand," Sanzang replied. "How could you say I can't read?" "Well," Monkey replied, "if you can, why ask where we are instead of reading the big clear writing on the apricot-yellow flag over the city wall?" "Wretched ape," Sanzang shouted, "you're talking nonsense. The flag is flapping much too hard in the wind for anyone to read what, if anything, is on it." "Then how could I read it?" Monkey asked.

— Wu Cheng'en, *Journey To The West*

Macbeth:
Canst thou not minister to a mind diseased,
Pluck from the memory a rooted sorrow,
Raze out the written troubles of the brain,
And with some sweet oblivious antidote
Cleanse the stuffed bosom of that perilous stuff
Which weighs upon the heart?
Doctor:
Therein the patient
Must minister to himself.

– William Shakespeare, *Macbeth*

Ermengarde quite beamed with delight.
"Oh, Sara," she whispered joyfully. "It is like a story!"
"It is a story," said Sara. "Everything's a story. You are a story –
I am a story. Miss Minchin is a story."

— Frances Hodgson Burnett, *A Little Princess*

Contents

Acknowledgements

I WANT TO THANK those who have helped me in the writing of this book. My dear friend and erstwhile colleague, Dr. Roman Dubinski provided invaluable assistance in securing research materials from the University of Waterloo Library when distance made it impossible for me to help myself. The staff at that library were likewise understanding and patient with my circumstances. Elizabeth Bishop of the Haileybury Public Library was also of frequent assistance and was always good-natured about my frequent cries for help at short notice. Dr. Robert Oxlade provided me with plentiful instruction about psychiatric disorders, particularly in the field of post-traumatic stress disorder over several recent years. He also helped me with a number of references and with understanding the role of writing in the healing process. Our frequent discussions provided invaluable feedback for my brain to clarify some of its own ideas. My typist, Johanne Martin, has been unfailingly cheerful and prompt, in spite of language and technical difficulties. Eileen Devaney has also made her time available to assist me with the bibliography, and I am grateful to her. To my editor, Richard Dionne, I want to say thank you for all the support and encouragement, his belief in the project and his careful reading of the text. Finally and most importantly, my wife Brenda has been there whenever I needed her exceptional mind to listen and comment and clarify. She has also passed her hypercritical eye over the text making innumerable valuable suggestions. She has been unfailing in her patience and faith in these ideas. It is really impossible to describe the extent of Brenda's contribution to my work over the last twenty years, culminating in her essential help in the final version of this manuscript.

To all these people and to all those who have laboured so tirelessly and enthusiastically in the realms of mystery arising from that wonder of the world, our human brain, I am very grateful.

Preface

The staggeringly large number of connections in our brains is a hundred thousand billion; however, the number of possible connections among those cells is even more awesome: ten thousand billion billion!

John Taylor

The role of Literature in human biology is to foster diversity, build reader identity, support balance, nurture adaptation, and assist survival.[1] Our human power resides in language and the productions of language. Literature is now the most important of such productions, and Literature is a species specific biological behaviour. This book argues that a biological approach to Literature will restore our connection to language and to the stories that form our view of the world and our identity.

To place our emphasis on Literature as a biological behaviour rather than exclusively as a cultural production is to take a cross-disciplinary approach in preference to the "arts" assumption that has prevailed heretofore. Literature is of course profoundly influenced by and responsive to the cultures where it occurs, but like the language from which it grows, it is a universal human characteristic and represents a sophisticated adaptation for human survival.

Stories are found everywhere in the world and form the basis of a culture, its beliefs, value, and wisdom. Literature must come to be seen as an evolved stage in the transmission of stories and ideas, following naturally on an oral tradition of such transmission. Like syntactical language itself, Literature is a uniquely human production.

On any summer night at the lake, I can hear loons calling to each other, or at least making loon sounds that evoke other loon sounds across considerable distances. There is ample evidence of animal "conversation," or signalling if you prefer. I suppose animals could be said to be "writing" story when they mark territory with urine, so creating a sort of olfactory map. We can also imagine some analogy to an oral record in the "teaching" older creatures pass on to their young, as when cod show their descendants how to migrate if we catch all the larger, older cod the young swim around in erratic and non-productive patterns. The above ideas about animal communication are of course only products of the human brain, designed to see story in everything. It seems fair to say in any case that there is no evidence of non-human animal Literature.

Among the many neuroscientists, biologists, biochemists, psychologists and others who have written fascinating books on brain and mind in recent years, none have concerned themselves very much with the phenomenon of Literature. For me, Literature is the most interesting of human behaviours. It is also, I believe, the most recent of evolved behaviours.

I concern myself in this book with written Literature, but of course I acknowledge that oral literature had its roots somewhere in the mists of time long before writing was invented. What we know about it for certain is that with the advent of writing, oral literature has all but disappeared. Oral literature played the cultural role of transmitting in memorable fashion the accumulated wisdom of human thought. It taught people who listened the origins of their kind, the rules of social behaviour, the nature of human relations to the non-human world, and it provided models for story making, so that others could organize their own thinking. It must also have provided the first windows between unfamiliar groups and peoples, as people exchanged stories to reveal who they were and how they saw the world.

With the erosion of oral story and poem, we are left with written Literature. This change leaves us with a few very big problems. For one, while speaking can be learned passively by listening and making sounds, reading and writing require active, explicit education and hundreds of hours of hard practice. Most importantly, writing, while conferring vast powers of its own, also produces losses for which we must now compensate. Writing creates distance even while it traverses countless miles; it produces otherness even as it creates intimacy; and it is plentiful, so it is often taken for granted. Writing makes it harder to hear the human voice that once carried so much energy and immediacy to the human ear. Writing reduces reliance on memory, so stories do not have to be as well-known as they once were in the oral tradition. And writing, freed from the limitations of the listener's memory and knowledge, and unable to achieve accent, timbre, inflection, emphasis, intonation and dialect, and unaccompanied by gesture and facial expression, can and does become enormously complex in an effort to fill these gaps. A very sophisticated Literature evolves, and along with it a whole industry of critics and experts to explain it, so producing further distance between writer and reader.

But all these problems must be overcome, for strangely enough there is no substitute for Literature in human affairs, and nothing else can do for us what Literature does. Literature still serves all the purposes that oral storytelling once achieved, and remains essential to our well-being. We neglect it at our peril. We must re-establish the connection between Literature in its written form and storytelling, with its human voice and its accumulated wisdom. We must see Literature as a necessary form of language, and we must see language as the means of reconnecting with each other and the world we depend on for life.

Like all the biological behaviours that were victorious in evolution, Literature is a survival adaptation tool. It records, organizes and manages our relations with the world and with our own bodies and their sensations. The many reasons for placing Literature at the centre of human learning must now demand our conscious attention. More than ever, human beings play a role in determining their own evolution, as genetic and social scientists daily demonstrate. We can alter our own biology, the structure of plants and animals, the quality of our air and water. Literature has a critical role to play in shaping what will become of ourselves and our world.
It would be a disastrous mistake to assume, that having lost an oral transmission of story, we have somehow outgrown the need for the role it

played in personal and social life management. In fact, in the blizzard of bits and bites of disconnected information, we are dependent on Literature more than ever. Language achieves its most conspicuous complexities in written Literature.

As a species we are committed to language. We do not have the vision of eagles, the olfaction of pigs, the hearing of dogs. Our brains have evolved large, specialized areas devoted to processing language, and our bodies have developed physical apparatus for human speech. Our vast infrastructures of commerce, communication and social and political organization depend for their success on language. Without a first-hand knowledge of Literature both our language, and our thinking through and by means of language, will rapidly simplify and deteriorate. Along with this deterioration will come a breakdown in the skills we need to manage everything we built with the help of language. Language is the defining power of human beings. If we want to see how people treat each other, or how they see the natural world, look at their language. Unless we recover the sense of responsibility for this human attribute, we are headed for trouble. A second Babel, more devastating than the first awaits us. As a species we have set out on unknown seas guided by the compass of language and the radar of Literature. If we throw them away, or permit their theft by pirates, we are lost.

This book explores another aspect of the impact of Literature on the reader that has not been sufficiently addressed before. As human individuals grow they develop a sense of themselves as agents acting upon everything they encounter. They register the data picked up by their senses and they fit this data into the story of their lives. Human beings both shape and are shaped by their stories. The point is, we are a story species.

The nature and quality of the individual, of the "I," is critically determined by language and by the quality of the story-making skill organizing the incoming data. The individual's richness or limitation of language determines the efficiency of the "I" as autobiographer, how well it can name, fit and expand the accumulating data of the world as perceived.

Individuals with brain damage that destroyed this developing language story, or those whose stories become jumbled or traumatized, may speak words, but they cannot be understood by others looking for the missing story thread.

Nothing aids this "I" making process as efficiently as reading Literature. Stories help children learn to process their world by providing data already symbolically processed. Reading stories is the best training for making stories, especially the one central story which is the reader's life.

It is not easy to shift our thinking from Literature as art to Literature as a biological behaviour, an adaptive tool formed by and for human brains. We are conditioned by a lifetime of culture that has described novels and poems in artistic terms rather than in the functional and biological terms that we apply to other healthful behaviours like exercise and wholesome nutritional intake. Literature is like a species *module*, a brain extension, which serves to make our story-making nature more efficient. We hear and read stories so we can make more stories. And we make these stories to make sense of the world we experience. Human language is inseparable from human story making. Together these features of our brains are the essence of who we are. By means of story all our perceptions, all our emotions are given meaning.

But perhaps the greatest difficulty of all in shifting our angle of vision and the language we use to describe the function of Literature arises from the advent of writing. The book or script has been mistaken for an object. Once language became visible, once oral stories became Literature, the word became a tangible treasure, a political force. Like most treasures it was coveted by those with power, coveted not as works of art are desired and collected for their material value, not as manuscripts are bought and sold for their rarity, but as information — a far more potent means to political control. Literature was not to be given to the masses and has been kept from them by two proscriptions: "You would not understand it, it is not for the likes of you"; and "You don't need it, amuse yourselves with these other things."

Oral story was transmitted by expert storytellers using memorable words and mnemonic devices. It was kept alive over generations by skilled language makers. But there is no evidence that oral stories bred groups of critics and professors. These intermediaries grow and feed upon the body of written Literature as it accumulates. So, along with writing, we find a literary "culture," an industry, a profession, an elite of priests and guardians, keeping Literature and the great unwashed apart. By means of censorship, or the use of Latin, or the failure to provide education, political and religious powers have hoarded the treasure to themselves. We have yet to see a political commitment to the proposition that access to a full understanding of Literature is a human birthright. So on the one hand we lost an oral tradition and, on the other, we are in danger of accepting illiteracy or partial literacy as the global norm.

We are now in danger of forgetting what oral cultures could not forget, that story and ballad make sense because of their essential relation to *ordinary discourse*. Our pre-writing ancestors, Aboriginal peoples, knew that story and poem helped them make sense of their world and helped them survive. They assumed a natural continuum between their daily lives, their language and stories. Writing, however, caused a separation between speech and itself, in effect creating two languages or two modes of discourse. We are gradually losing this link as we speak less and less. Electronics replaces conversation. Written story replaces spoken story. With these changes Literature itself is threatened and weakened. We are in danger of becoming story-less creatures.

Literature is the minds and voices of people speaking to each other, and it must now carry the responsibility once entrusted to oral story. If we lose it through lack of awareness of its function, we do not have the earlier tradition to fall back on. We may take our language gift for granted, but language is reducible. Literature takes us to the farthest reaches of language. Our well-being now depends on Literature to assist us to be maximally functional as linguistic, story creatures.

New dangers threaten our connection to the biological advantages conferred by Literature. Coherent thought and feeling are being dissipated by an endless display of commercial images, advertising, slogans, logos, clichés, icons and visual signs. Reading takes *time*. Time gets scarcer and scarcer in an automated world that advertises automation as a means to efficiency while we spend ever more time enslaved to electronic devices. Video games and trivial entertainment of every kind erode our sense of order, control and meaning. We are endlessly distracted. Our brains and our health are endangered by every such distraction. Anti-depressants and mood altering drugs will not solve the problem of scattered identity, or existential loss of meaning. It is therefore urgent that we renew our acquaintance with the meaning of Literature on a new footing, one that is grounded in consideration of human biology. We must learn what we can do to help ourselves lead whole and balanced lives.

The case I am arguing here for a biological approach to Literature had its beginnings in the book *Read For Your Life*, which appeared in 1990. *RFYL* was my contribution to bibliotherapy, the use of Literature as a healing agent in mental health. At that time I had in mind the eventual discovery of the role, the function of Literature and reading as a human behaviour. I had my own experience, having relied on reading to help me through some very difficult times. I also had thirty-nine years of teaching experience with Literature and university students. As a teacher, I discovered that class after class, decade after decade, students chose to study Literature because their previous encounter with fiction and poetry had become addictive. Whatever the mysterious joys they had experienced from reading — they wanted more, and they hoped academic study of more would help them understand the process of their encounter with Literature. They did not talk about this, probably could not even articulate it properly. They simply liked "English" or were good at "it." What I didn't know until it was almost time to retire from the classroom was how this love affair worked, how it happened. I wanted to fathom the process by which whatever it was that Literature "is," became transfused, like units of blood, into the lifestream, the consciousness of readers. And after the transfusion how did it function to help, shape or alter what readers did, how they lived and behaved? I looked everywhere for answers, for help, for a body of knowledge that I could enter. I quickly learned that I would have to find or form both the questions and the answers for myself. A daunting task, but also an incredibly exciting project.

As part of this self-appointed course of inquiry, I began to frequent the library at the Kitchener General Hospital and spent part of every week reading every relevant thing I could find, including current and back issues of *Brain*. I did not know then (the mid 1970s) that I was entering a new field. I thought brain knowledge was an established science and neuroscientists knew what the rest of us didn't. Since it was not my field, I could not have known, for instance, that in reading everything in print by Wilder Penfield, the great Canadian neurosurgeon, I was working at the frontiers of new information. Perhaps the situation is best summarized by Douglas B. Webster, one of America's foremost researchers on the brain's power to communicate. He points out that until the mid-sixties of the last century, there was no discipline of neuroscience. There was anatomy, physiology, biology, psychology, biochemistry, and many other related sciences studying the brain, but their practitioners did not see themselves working in one domain and their activities had not yet been subsumed under one heading. Since then, and with ever greater communication between disciplines, the study of human brain function has emerged as *neuroscience*, and huge increases in information about brain function have subsequently accrued, so much so that the '90s came to be called the "Decade of the Brain."

The more we know about the brain, the more we want to know and the more humbled we are before the intricacies of this astonishing, evolved organ. As Douglas Webster states:

> The human brain is the supreme organ of the body. Within the brain we perceive, think, know, fear, love, hate, make decisions, and control our actions. The brain defines who we are.[2]

And defining "who we are" is very much part of this book. In the brain's learning curve as it makes sense of the world, it puts together a story of the relationship between itself and its not-self, the "other." The brain's actual physiological structure, along with its sense of being an "I," is formed in the process of constructing this story of the world. When the individual brain successfully creates a fully functional "I," one that is comfortable, confident and consistent, it has also achieved the growth of a person who is efficiently adaptive and operational.

The Decade of the Brain has taught us many things, but as always in our dealings with Nature we uncover more complexity and more mysteries with every new insight. Nothing is as simple as it seems or as we mistakenly hope it will be. To give an example, in the three decades since I started looking into the matter, brain matter that is, it was thought that there were 4 billion neurons in the human brain. (A neuron is a tiny cellular information processor.[3]) I was enormously impressed. Ten years later this estimate had grown to 12 billion brain cells and I was astounded. The last time I looked, neuroscientists were blithely referring to hundreds of billions of neurons in the average human brain. Couple this with the current knowledge that each neuron is blessed with at least one thousand connections to other neurons and you will begin to regard your own super-organ with a lot more respect.

So we have learned to count brain cells with much greater accuracy. So we have made progress. We are, however, still a long way from where I want to go. Studying what was known about the brain was interesting, but it was only part of the picture and at the time a not wholly fruitful part.

Another approach to the connection between brains, Literature and human behaviour was to be found in psychotherapy. Following a clue given to me by Sandra Gold, my first wife and a research librarian of exceptional skill, I discovered that bibliotherapy was a tiny but established branch of library science, and in the U.S., there was in fact a Society for Poetry Therapy. My hope that this path would lead to greater understanding of how Literature connects to and influences human behaviour eventually led to my certification as a Marriage and Family Therapist. Now, I thought, I could merge at least two of the many disciplines involved in the study of thought, feeling and reading.

A lot has happened since 1990. Neuroscience now flourishes. In my view, it is beginning to emerge as the most important and useful of all studies. But of course, my feet are still planted firmly on the rock of Literature and the behaviour of reading. And in spite of every temptation to abandon books, millions of people attest to the fact that nothing is so satisfying, helpful or interesting as a "good read." So this book is about a whole life, and the part reading can play in it; about being born into a language world, going to school and work and struggling to stay healthy, happy and effective.

Read for Your Life was based on a wide knowledge of English Literature and the application of that Literature in a clinical setting. It was rich in case histories and filled with suggestions for specific readings relevant to equally specific situations. In the years since then I have come to see that my patients don't have a "problem" in the way that one has a gardening accident and gets an infected toe, or suffers a broken bone from falling on ice. People are faced with managing, organizing, seeking peace, love and security in a whole life, in family, work, play and community, and this is a continuous process, not one that appears only in crisis. If reading is going to help, it must help all the time, in health and health maintenance as well as in sickness and distress. The Literature people choose must apply to various aspects of their worlds, to relationships, to conflict, to problem solving, to sexuality, grief and being alone. For Literature and reading to merit a pre-eminent place as a biological ingredient to surviving well, it must be relevant to all aspects of human experience, and it must do so across time.

Nowadays I find myself urging patients to read whatever appeals to them and I am prepared to discuss whatever emerges for them. I realize now that the very act of reading an engaging story is such a massive brain activity that its consequences are very far-reaching. Now I understand better the role reading plays in identity formation, and I see that reading certain books alters the world my patients inhabit. I have for some time felt that the questions only theoretically touched upon in *RFYL* deserved deeper treatment. I felt new understandings of brain function and the role of language and emotion in human behaviour could now be applied to those questions that had driven my interest all along.

I believe now that beyond its personal value, reading has social and political consequences that merit consideration, and these also deserve more than the passing nods they received in my earlier work. In fact, the overwhelming presence of television, and the avalanche of electronic entertainment and its consumption of time has social and personal implications for our culture that make me wonder if there will still be a place, a time, an audience, for reading anything as slow and thought-provoking as a Dickens novel.

So this book attempts a form of synthesis and integration. It is not a guide to neuroscience and I am not equipped to write one. But it does use my understanding of the knowledge of language and brain processes. Here I explore and propose connections between Literature and its neural origins. I suggest that reading Literature is a biologically evolved species resource. I describe the social and personal results of practicing reading consciously to *assist* ourselves; and I follow the connections and implications of the choices people make between reading and other uses or abuses of their brains.

I also take the position here that there is nothing neutral or inherently benign in any of the electronic "progresses" we are witnessing. Instead, political and commercial forces are at work to shape every technological step to specific ends. I am very conscious that these developments, in technology and its applications, happen without debate, vote, or consumer or user input. And they happen virtually free of government involvement, so that elected governments become more and more irrelevant to what happens to the people who elect them. Governments are simply being swept into the service of those who produce and control media. Information was never more widespread nor ever more threatened by ominous controls of one sort or another than it is now. The minds of young people are the battleground for a conflict already underway between identity and depersonalization. Commercialism and electronic teaching are entering our classrooms. There appears to be no political will to resist this trend. But the consequences for our children's brains are profound.[4] And many of us remain to be convinced that such consequences are beneficial. I for one believe that these trends are not inevitable. They are a matter of social will, social policy, political power and who has it. So there are chapters on education and on politics.

I am aware that any one of these chapters could be a book-length essay in itself, but I want to at least touch upon some of the ways that Literature functions as a biological resource for human well-being; the social implications of this if I am right; and the threats to full literacy that now appear. It is not enough to survive. We want to survive well.

Are there connections between reading (or the lack of it), and economic fairness, social conscience and decency? We know that the rate of literacy is much lower for prison populations in North America than for the population at large. Is this only because being unable to read results in economic hardship, or does this handicap stretch to self-image, self-knowledge, inability to organize a world view and failure to form personal identity? How can we restore and reclaim the quality of our water, soil and air, create peace and justice, improve the complexity of civil discourse? Are the connections between reading, the implications of reading and the quality of our social, environmental and personal lives any less important for not being obvious? There are numerous fears and lamentations published in recent years about the loss of complex literacy among our students. Several are cited in the bibliography. I do believe we are entering the crisis phase for reading and risk losing its unparalleled power as an aid to being fully human and fully aware. But this is not one more such lamentation, or part of a debate to which I made my contribution in 1975.[5] No, what I am arguing here is much more worrisome than the loss of a decorative or pleasurable human amusement, like the loss of horse-and-buggy rides because cars came along. The loss of the ability to access the complex language of Literature is an alteration of the process of evolution and a threat to human well-being, even survival. I believe we have a choice, but only if we understand what the choice entails.

If reading is both a sign of and a means to human biological well-being, then we would do well to re-examine our relation to it. It is said that fish to water and birds to air are indicators of environmental quality. This book argues that language and reading behaviours are indicators of the quality of human life.

I am inevitably asked, directly or indirectly at various public lectures, whether my claims for reading Literature are not extravagant in the face of our knowledge of oral cultures, where pre- or non-literate peoples live adequately, even happily, without writing and reading. The question is a romantic and nostalgic red herring. Oral cultures survive only in rapidly disappearing pockets on this planet. We can never go back to some garden paradise where print disappears. We must remind ourselves that in pre-literate cultures the same limitations applied to everybody. Once writing and reading appear, the control of information becomes a means, the most powerful means, to absolute control of minds. Move to mass media, then gradually remove widespread literacy and the picture is complete. Concentration of press ownership and media distribution can turn us into puppets or parrots. We will always have just enough literacy to read the instructions. Such low levels of literacy threaten to enslave us. Is this what we want? If the answer to this question is "no," then we had better begin to understand how our brains work, how they incorporate Literature into the lives we lead, and what is at stake if we allow reading to slip into the history of human culture, by inadvertence. I hope this book will convince you to read for your *self*. We are rapidly reaching a time in human history when reading Literature as an antidote to depersonalization could become a subversive activity. Those who want to control populations have been in the habit of suppressing Literature. If they do not ban and censor we must start to worry that it may be because it is not necessary. If we do not read, we do the work for them.

Why Biology?

A biological approach to Literature is the best way to prevent its being marginalized, or lost altogether. While Literature remains an "Art," it is subject to the colonization of politics and professionalism, victim to those who would brush it aside as decorative fringe, or those who see themselves as the only ones able or worthy to absorb its mysteries.

In *The Lopsided Ape*, Michael C. Corballis goes to some pains to point out that humans have a cultural history, or at least a modern, Western history, that denies their animal nature. Indeed, much of our religious tradition has focused the greater part of its energy on persuading us to overcome our bestial, that is animal, nature. We want to be angels, or close to angels, and free ourselves from Earth. Socially and environmentally this has obviously cost us dearly. To deny that we are animals, albeit with large and peculiar brains, is to twist our study of ourselves out of shape.[6] When we study the biology of animals, insects, shellfish, we study their genetics, diet, habitat and, most important, their *behaviour*. And once we start studying their behaviour we must study their social interactions, their motives, their relations with other creatures and their conflicts and co-operation.

In this book I treat literature as a human adaptive behaviour. I discuss it as built upon a brain process for managing and transmitting information. I see this process as an evolved brain strategy that uses story sequencing as a management tool for organizing vast amounts of information. Those who specialize in Literature have called themselves critics and professors of literature. They have never called themselves biologists of Literature. To pursue their profession they have gone to extraordinary lengths to separate the word construct, the novel or poem, from the human animal itself, including and especially its adaptive behaviours. I have referred to Literature as a tool. Now it is possible to study tools from many points of view, say historically, or for their artistic qualities, or as pieces of engineering, or as examples of the qualities of various materials used in their construction. But to do any of this while separating the tools from their makers and from the thinking and ingenuity that produced them would be willful blindness. Not to mention refusing to look at their purposes, or their adaptability, which would seem peculiar in the extreme. Yet this is precisely what we have traditionally done in the study of Literature. We have managed to regard Literature as a collection of art pieces divorced from the biology that gives rise to the product. We have failed to see these language constructs as extensions of human brains designed to achieve specific ends and existing as bonds between people, across time and space. There is a notable gap in literary theory, a gap to be filled by the biological approach.[7] To fill this gap requires a new kind of thinking about Literature, a paradigm shift, a change in the language we use and in our ways of reading and teaching. There are pioneers who have given us clues from time to time, but they have run into resistance from those who prefer angels to animals.

As, and if, we proceed to examine Literature as a human behaviour we would be well advised to avoid the unbounded quagmires of the false dichotomy of Nature versus Nurture. Genetics obviously shapes environment, as when beavers make dams, but environment also shapes genetics through the process of adaptation, or what Darwin called the "survival of the fittest." We know that certain toxins cause cancer and biological change. So genes determine some things, predispose most animal forms, while environment composes. We are predisposed neurally to learn language, but environment will determine which languages we learn, and of course which customs, social behaviours, beliefs, tastes and diet, to mention only some observable human characteristics. We might then refer to something which I shall call the Geneviro Loop, whereby genes and environment act upon each other in a process of continuous reshaping and change.

The old debate between nature and nurture has outlived its usefulness and is now a distraction, a hindrance to our knowledge of human behaviour. Obviously we are dealing with systems and subsystems of enormous complexity. It is the very interconnectedness of human brains and bodies, of individual humans and the group, of groups and the Earth, and the whole with the efficiency of all its components, that must concern us. Literature is part of a language system occupying a large part of human brain function.

In none of the brain damaged patients that are relied on by neuroscientists to establish models of normal working brains, and described in the scientific literature, can I find one case of a person who had not previously formed an identity, a set of beliefs, values, feelings and attitudes with the help of and along with language, prior to the injury. All of them had learned to speak, gone to school and otherwise been normal members of Western society before a lesion, disease or surgery had damaged their brains. In other words it seems clear, at least to me, that human brain development, both phylogenetically and ontogenetically, takes place with consciousness and language forming at the same time.[8] Consciousness and language have boosted each other in an upward spiral to more consciousness and more language. To look for primary cause in this realm will only confuse a complex enquiry.

The consequences of this boosting process are not confined to the areas of the brain specializing in language. The entire brain is affected by this development, in spatial, visual, auditory, memory and reasoning functions. It is important to bear this in mind if we are going to change our casual and take-it-for-granted attitudes to language, and to the tool of Literature that most efficiently records language. Language and Literature don't just change people in a single skill area; they change the entire functioning organism that is a human person.

Human beings are supposed to use Literature to assist them to create a personal identity and to help them manage this identity's encounter with the world. That's what evolution is telling us. The human brain, the Literature it writes and the Literature it reads are a systemic feedback loop, continuously self-generating and cumulatively growing.

A biological approach to Literature requires an understanding of its roots in, and connections to, language, from which it has become separated in our minds and beliefs over time, probably beginning with the advent of writing. This, then, is where we begin our story.

Notes to the Preface

1. I use Literature with a capital L throughout this book to signify my reference to the body of stories, poems and essays that constitute the cultural reservoir of creative writing about human experience, as opposed to literature meaning anything printed, as in government documents or in medical journals.

2. *Neuroscience of Communication*, p. 4.

3. I hope this book will adequately convey the sense that process is everything. Knowledge or information does not exist as a lump sum sitting somewhere and doing something. It achieves function only in process. The best analogy or example of this is the print on the page of the unread book. What is it?

4. See Jane M. Healy, *Failure to Connect*, 1998.

5. See Joseph Gold (ed.), *In The Name Of Language*, 1975.

6. "The close resemblance in DNA structure between humans and chimpanzees even suggests that a hybrid species would be viable—a chastening thought." Michael C. Corballis, *The Lopsided Ape*, 1991, p. 35.

7. Those who wish to read further about the theory directions I propose may choose to turn to Appendix III at this point.

8. In other words from birth. Taylor (1991) for instance assumed the presence of language in proving consciousness. See pp. 14-15.

Part One

Origins

Chapter One

The Beginning is the Word

Poetry is the first and last of all knowledge — it is as immortal as the heart of man.

— **William Wordsworth**

We can read reality in as many ways as we can make theories.

— **Bernard J. Baars**

Literature is a form of language that humans have evolved to help themselves cope with the world they inhabit. Creating and sharing complex stories is an adaptation of language to help humans survive well. And language itself is an adaptation of our brains to the Earth's environment, our home, and the human interaction with it and with each other. So before this can be a book about Literature, it must first be a book about language.

In *The Symbolic Species*, Terrence Deacon faces a problem similar to my own. He wants to describe a process by which, as the brain evolved, it gave rise to language, and as language evolved it led to increased brain adaptation for language. He conceives of a continuous, circular, mutual prompting of brain and language, an incremental mutuality of development. He opts for the subtitle, "The Co-Evolution of Language and the Brain," giving precedence to language, and arguing that language proved to be so advantageous that the brain shaped itself to make more language possible.

I have a similar problem with language and story, or Literature as story becomes. No sooner does human language proper begin to develop, than it forms itself into the story shape familiar to us. Questions and answers, maps and descriptions, instructions and requests all take this story organization form. The simplest children's sentences, "Mama shout," "Joey eat," have the story features. This too then is a co-evolution, language and Literature are mutually reinforcing and become biologically intertwined. If we ask questions about Literature we are at the same time always asking questions about a form of language.

I began asking questions about Literature, this certain form of language, half a century ago. The ears they fell on were so deaf that I gave up asking for a couple of decades. Then in despair at the games academics were playing I started asking them again. The questions go something like this: What is story? What role does Literature play in human evolution and in individual lives? What role do the transferred words play in the biological and social life of readers? How is the product of reading stored in the body of the reader? Why is it that if a painting is burned it is gone forever, but a poem (or a letter) can be memorized intact, unaltered and transmittable as long as a human brain retains it? What has taken place in the event that you take a novel off a shelf, read it, and return it? What "being" does the book (or rather its words) have, there on the shelf while not being read? — for clearly it is not just a material object to us readers, yet to a creature to whom it is a "closed book," a novel is less useful than toilet paper. Where does the power of a book lie? How is the process of transference achieved when it is being read? Why is some particular arrangement of words more effective to a particular reader than other arrangements? What makes Literature different from say, memos from head office?

I am taking the position here that answers to these questions are not readily found, and even the questions have never been precisely formulated. As we embark on this journey into Literature as a biological behaviour, I ask you to remember that we confront these questions, not only as if they were new, but buried also, obscured and made more difficult to get at following centuries of literary criticism, after millions of commentaries on and reviews of innumerable writings, and in spite of the efforts of untold millions of dedicated people to "teach Literature." Not that such efforts have been fruitless in themselves. They have disseminated Literature to millions of people who have loved and been rewarded in their lives by reading. But there are millions of others who have never seen the point of reading, and this is a huge human loss. The *Industry of Literature* has been preoccupied with other questions, questions of *art* and *morality* that have either become dead ends or will prove to be irrelevant, so that this Industry will quietly eliminate itself unless we can demonstrate that writing and reading Literature is necessary. Otherwise, "teachers" of Literature will become "teachers" of film, report writing, memo composition. Maybe.

As far as I can make out, teachers of language and Literature have not conversed with, or professionally consulted biologists, physicists, biochemists or neuroscientists in any effort to answer some of the questions I have asked above; and the scientists in their turn have not explored the varieties of form and the complexities of neural storage of Literature as they have mapped the workings of human brains. Oddly enough, linguists, neurolinguists and psycholinguists have virtually ignored Literature in their researches into language. For them, the utterances of a three year old, or even a chimpanzee, are as interesting, even more interesting, than Dante's *Inferno.* This situation will have to change if we are to make any headway in understanding the role of Literature as we read it into our lives. The answers to the sample questions I have posed above will only be found in a multi-disciplinary effort.

In order for us to utilize and fully realize the far-reaching and powerful human resources that can result from reading Literature, we will have to change our thinking. We will be required to shift our assumptions about Literature. Even our language and our educational arrangements for transmitting Literature will have to be re-thought. This will include changes in the training of those who teach it. We must stop thinking of Literature as *art*, in the same sense and lumped along with other works of art. The assumption that a "work of Literature" is an art "product," an artifact, will get in the way of our understanding. We will need more precision. We need new terminology to move our discussion onto new and more useful ground so we can take a fresh look at Literature and the relevance of reading to human survival. Literature is important, indeed vital *information*, and will lose nothing of its wonder and beauty for being so regarded. On the contrary, it will gain in status, respect and usefulness for whole populations.

Human brains have evolved themselves to be linguistic. Language, even in its form as Literature, never becomes the thing itself, in the same way that paint becomes the picture or painting. For this reason, you cannot quote painting as you can, say, "sleep that knits up the ravelled sleeve of care," before snoring on your pillow. You can of course try to visualize or imagine a painting from memory, but you can't describe it or transact its relevance without language. There is no value comparison intended here. I am trying to convey the difference between the medium, the tool of language, and the art object. Moreover, we must remember that even the painting does not represent an object out there, but an image, registered in the brain, of "out there" sensory stimuli. We paint brain versions of received sensory impressions.

Language however is not an image of anything. It is a symbolic code for referring to *everything* out there and provides a *means only* to creating images stored in the brain. So no matter what form language takes, it always remains a code only. We must imagine language as a code kit, like Meccano or Lego, whose pieces are pulled out to construct something, but can then be dismantled to construct something else. Except of course that since the pieces are codes, not things, they can be used infinitely without being used up or in short supply. The word "brain" for instance remains available at the molecular storage level no matter how many times we use it in sentences. I have a magnetic notice board at work that limits what I can display to the number of small magnetic letters available. If I have five small magnetic letter "b"s, I can only use "b" five times. But as long as the "b" in my brain *does not become a material thing*, I can say or write it as often as I like.

So language alone of human products is devoid of all materiality. And it is precisely in this freedom that the power and the glory of human language resides. For this reason human brains have devoted a great deal of their function and mass to language.

Now if we turn to Literature it becomes crucial to remember, and to teach, that the arrangements of words by Shakespeare or Hemingway never become things. Northrop Frye wrote a book about the Bible called *The Great Code*. But all books are codes, and their greatness is only a matter of opinion and allegiance. Perhaps it is the *I Ching* to the Chinese or the *Iliad* to pre-Christian Greeks, but for now I don't care as much about what the code represents, so much as I do about persuading you of the need to get used to the idea that language is a code *per se*. We need to recognize and accept that language is a biological code that achieves molecular change in brain tissue;[1] that organization of this code into stories is created by selection, transfer and association of data through immensely complex brain processes; that this happens both internally in one brain and in transfers from one brain to another; and that we need to consciously work for the expansion of this code in the service of our own selves.

Works of Literature are coded models of experiential patterns in the brains of writers. They are specialized forms of neural potentials and never achieve physical mass, weight, dimension, colour or texture as do other works of art. Such words, of course, *are* used to describe literary works, but these words can mislead. A book is not the words, the marks on the pages, and the marks on the pages are not "things" either, but symbols of sounds. The sounds behind the words are, in turn, a code for sensory registers of data, data being the brain's responses to neural signals of incoming "out there" information. It is easy to be deceived by the "thingness" of a book, but "the map is not the territory."[2] We will have to realize that qualities attributed to Literature, but borrowed from objects, are metaphors describing the *mind of the reader decoding the text.* Such a radical shift in understanding the human biology in decoding the signals of Literature will not be accomplished easily. Not only are we dependent on neuroscientists who are themselves only at the threshold of understanding human brain processes, but they are usually too obsessed with their own questions to talk to "humanists." We must overcome habits of thought and the politics of institutions, vested careers, "artsy" prejudice; add to this list the contemporary commercial and ideological goals of simplifying everything and diminishing all independent thought and creativity — and it becomes clear that before us we have an uphill battle.

Embodying Information

Life is a process of continuous learning. This learning is stored in the body as a coded form of information. Indeed, it may be said that the brain stores all its information as cellular codes, though we think of these stores of information as words and pictures because of the speed with which the codes convert back into sounds, pictures, smells and textures. Most of this translation of sensory data is done by means of an evolved coding device we call language, which is in its turn converted to molecular codes in brain cells. Language, story, writing and reading, which is the evolutionary sequence that leads us to the present, will all be inextricably bound together in the following pages to describe a bundle of uniquely human behaviours. In other words, the human organism is a collection of information made flesh, organized and energized into cellular activity, and continually modified by more and more information. The individual arrangement of this information is called *identity*. Identity is never complete because it is a process of response to, and accommodation of, new information which cannot stop until sensory activity itself stops at death. We must learn to remind ourselves continually that language is at its root metaphoric. I mean language is the best we can do to represent body experience, our physical encounter with the world. We need to refer back to that body experience to test the language and its fit to our own experience. This produces a reflective and reflexive response, a sifting of emotion and memory. This process becomes developed with the growth of individual language knowledge. Terms like "identity" and "information" are themselves metaphors for our awareness of internal change, our sense of being someone and knowing something. When we learn or know something new we have a mental and body sense of owning, internalizing that "something." We call this neural registration "information." Such "knowings" are not "things" but biological changes in our own bodies. Information then, is a bodily adaptation to sensory experience. It is helpful to get used to this if we are to change our thinking, as we must.

Sound Language

By language I mean words and syntax, the mysterious human code system for describing and recording the world and the experiences that the human organism encounters. All other uses of the term *language* are secondary metaphoric applications of its fundamental meaning, whether we speak of body language, dance, photography, "statements" of dress, interior design, architecture or landscaping. Language is so basic to human behaviour that it naturally lends itself to metaphor, especially given its characteristics, namely that it communicates meaning in a pattern of connectable links between the world "out there" and memory, and so affects the reader's (listener's) perception. Since all other human behaviours, like watching ballet, also affect the perceiver, language seems like a handy way to describe everything. But true language is grounded in the lexicon, our store of words and their organization, and must be reclaimed as such if this book is to have any meaning.

Human language originated as sounds and then evolved. Animals make sounds and humans, who are very sophisticated animals, also still make sounds. We express cries of pain, howls of pleasure, grunts of effort, growls of anger, screams of fright, whimperings of fear, squeals of delight, hisses of surprise and sighs of satisfaction. These sounds are not language, but reflexive expressions made at some level where thought does not exist, from which we call on our animal origins, still alive and well in our brains, I am happy to report. Such non-lexical noises are releases of emotional energy.

The difference between these sounds and the conscious choosing to utter deliberate language implies some intention to utter controlled and result-seeking communication. We must imagine that over huge tracts of evolutionary time, the sound-making animal, who is to emerge as *Homo sapiens*, becomes conscious that the reflexive and emotive sounds he makes can be turned into deliberate signals consciously made about the world and about himself, how he is feeling and thinking. The sound maker would have to realize that sounds can be uttered that have meaning and can be understood to refer to something. This change would of course require new levels of consciousness. We can invent a symbolic story that compresses this long time span into one illustrative event, something like this: A biting animal, maybe a human, but not necessarily, is surprised when he bites to hurt and produces a scream from the victim. He, the biter — that is the evolving species, as this whole process took hundreds of thousands of years — eventually becomes conscious that his action is the cause of the sound the bitee makes. Now the same biting animal is capable of "love" or play bites, as animals still are, and here the sound that the bitee utters may be a moan of pleasure or a purr. At some point the biter makes the connection that the sound feedback is information, giving him the results of his actions. If sound can do that, why not voluntarily and consciously make sounds that will convey information about what is going on in the bitee's mind. In this process, the biter then becomes the speaker. What has happened is that sound uttered by the speaker can be made to point to thoughts and images in the mind: "That small animal over there (rabbit, lapin) looks yummy, let's eat it," or "I love you." It is also likely that prelinguistic humans copied the sounds animals made and so learned and evolved the consciousness that they could control and apply language in a variety of situations, for instance by luring animals to the hunt. In reality it is very probable that there were many sources and promptings for prespeech hominids including copying animal sounds for a number of practical as well as playful reasons.

Sounds were designed to be symbols for things first, and were later designed for abstractions, feelings, body states, social concepts. This process took a long time because it required the construction of special brains and unique voice apparatus to give full range to human potential, but it was worth the effort. Animals that could make such sounds could reveal the connectedness of themselves to the "not-selves" and control what they could describe. They could possess something represented in their brains by naming it, move it from *out there* to *in here*, carry away in their brains a code of the named thing, and thus free the object from its *out there* location. Then they could move it from one brain to other brains. So humans, like magicians, could turn a real rabbit into a brain-word rabbit, then transport this word to another brain. At this point both brains would know what they were talking about and thinking, so they could plan. In fact, these brains didn't even need to see a rabbit any more, they could just plan to go and find one: "Let's go find a rabbit and eat it." The power to name things is the quintessential power that has given humans dominance over the natural world, at least as far as it can be dominated, or managed for good or ill.

Language develops with the realization that co-operation is more efficient than silence and isolation. If Adam had not been presented with Eve, he may not have been driven to speak. Over millions of years, as language changed brains and brains in their turn evolved to grow more language, language became increasingly complex. In fact, it was able to free itself from immediate objects so it could operate independently. It became possible to internalize environments that did not then have to be in the vicinity of the senses. It became possible to speak of the remembered past and to plan for future action, since language symbolically replaced the material world. Similarly, language could now describe felt experiences and thoughts that never were material and yet were very real as experiences in the brains which language helped form. Body states like grief, sexual desire, anxiety and hunger, abstractions like freedom, forgiveness and sympathy could now be expressed, deepening and broadening the bonds between people.

But far more happened than improving social efficiency and overcoming personal isolation. Human beings are not limited by the language they learn; they recombine and reinvent language continually. Consequently they teach and learn from each other all the time, and they are altered by this process. The human exchange of language relentlessly expands the knowledge base of the whole community. More thought and action and more language become possible. So for hundreds of thousands of years this process has continued until we find ourselves today turning our awareness to an exploration of the *process* itself, precisely because our language and language brains have led us here. The next stage of evolution, the one we are now in, has developed our brains to the point where we can examine our own brain functions and invent the tools to make that possible.

More important, we *must* do so as a matter of survival, for without more self-knowledge and understanding of these processes we must inevitably fall victim to the forces unleashed by those very brains. We are very clever, but are we clever enough to control the products of our cleverness? We cannot leave our brains to their own devices. We will have to discover how we think and feel and therefore, what is in our best long-term self-interest. We must seek to enable our "minds" — the whole of us — to manage our brains and bodies — the parts of us. The consciousness of this whole is not limited to one "I" but involves our entire human heritage and awareness of our place in the broader human and natural community. We are one species, whole and indivisible across time and space. We have no time to lose learning this and coming to terms with its implications. We know already and for sure that we will not survive by destroying our habitat, slaughtering each other and forgetting how to read.

Let Me Tell You a Story

Gregory Bateson, whom some call the father of family therapy, liked to tell his students during the early days of computers the following story:

> A man wanted to know about mind, not in nature, but in his private large computer. He asked it (no doubt in his best FORTRAN), "Do you compute that you will ever think like a human being?" The machine then set to work to analyze its

> own computational habits. Finally, the machine printed its answer on a piece of paper, as such machines do. The man ran to get the answer and found, neatly typed, the words: THAT REMINDS ME OF A STORY.

Bateson goes on to give his definition of story:

> A story is a little knot or complex of that species of connectedness which we call *relevance*. In the 1960s, students were fighting for "relevance," and I would assume that any A is relevant to any B if both A and B are parts or components of the same "story." Again we face connectedness at more than one level: First, connection between A and B by virtue of their being components in the same story. And then, connectedness between people in that all think in terms of stories. (For surely the computer was right. This is indeed how people think.) Now I want to show that whatever the word story means in the *story* which I told you, the fact of thinking in terms of stories does not isolate human beings as something separate from the starfish and the sea anemones, the coconut palms and the primroses. Rather, if the world be connected, if I am at all fundamentally right in what I am saying, then *thinking in terms of stories* must be shared by all mind or minds whether ours or those of redwood forests and sea anemones.Context and relevance must be characteristic not only of all so-called behaviour (those stories which are projected out into "action"), but also of all those internal stories, the sequences of the building up of the sea anemone. Its embryology must be somehow made of the stuff of stories.[3]

Bateson is telling us that the quintessential characteristic of human thinking is narrative. In fact, in this extraordinary passage, Bateson goes much further, suggesting that everything in nature is structured on a narrative basis: the rings in tree development, the shells of oysters, the stones so beloved of geologists, to him they all tell a story about time and origin and identity. Now if Bateson were not the great mind I believe he was, I would call this a fanciful, metaphoric stretch. If there is, however, any genetic connection between the minerals and proteins that make up the origins of human life, and the minerals and proteins that make up the origins of plant and animal life, and the formation of rocks, gases and liquids that are so familiar and comfortably part of our earth home, then perhaps the story form that Bateson sees everywhere is not so outlandish after all. Perhaps the organizational structure of the world's material is inherent in the human species that grew from it. Perhaps the storying principle is buried so deeply in our genetic structure that it is indeed part of our very cellular make-up.

Various writers who focus on language and consciousness recognize this quintessential story-making character of human brains and struggle to describe it. Terrence Deacon, for instance, sees this language story making as uniquely characteristic of human brains, and a behaviour essential to our nature:

> We tell stories about our real experiences and invent stories about imagined ones, and we even make use of these stories to organize our lives. In a real sense, we live our lives in this shared virtual world. And slowly, over the millennia, we have come to realize that no other species on earth seems able to follow us into this miraculous place.[4]

Certain it is that no sooner did humans evolve the language parts of the brain than they simultaneously and inevitably began thinking and storing information in narrative forms. At the same time as brains were evolving in favour of language and syntax, so this language was instantly enlisted into the construction of narrative. We can assume, safely I think, that language once acquired served the same purposes always: to negotiate intimate relationships, to describe (map) space, to express personal and social states, that is, the condition of one's own mind, body and emotion, and to organize the condition (politics) of family, tribe and intertribal relations.

So I am arguing here that the form this language assumed, and the thinking that resulted from this form was, and still is, narrative in design. What benefits would narrative confer on human thought? What are its core characteristics? There is something enormously congenial to humans in story. From our earliest days we have loved to hear a story. It provides comfort, security and order. Humans are extraordinarily good at making and interpreting stories. Story is the most effective form and the oldest form of teaching. What makes story such a good fit for human brains? Or why should brains have preferred story above all other forms of language storage? I think the answer lies in the sequential nature of cellular formation and how cells are assembled by their responses to information genetically encoded. In other words, the sequential assembly of human bodies at the cellular level seems to bring with it an imperative that carries over to human behaviour, the story-making behaviour. It will help us to think of all interactions, reactions, attractions and repulsions as sequences of information: rain or sunshine is information to life forms; light, dark, food, vibration are information, even for the most primitive organisms. When information is received, it produces various biochemical and electrochemical consequences. In nature most activity is going on nonstop without language, but not without information. Likewise the human organism has come to depend on a continuous flow of information, for instance whether something we put in our mouth is bitter or sweet. This is biochemical news to our taste receptors, and whether good or bad, is registered as temporary change to microscopic hair-like membranes (microvilli), which then alert neurons along a pathway to the brain by means of electrochemical signals. The news about taste becomes information awareness in the brain and is registered as body sensation — a like or dislike of what we are tasting. Action is the goal of all information that we pay attention to, so the next step is decision — whether to eat more or spit it out.

Information registers like this all the time in nature without the need or benefit of language. The process certainly went on in our remote pre-hominid forebears before they could name these tastes or write cookbooks. There is undoubtedly a story in the three-second experience of sucking a lemon, but we should note that by the time we have come to the story of the Last Supper (Passover), and the symbolism of eating the body and blood of Jesus (the matzo and wine had already become drenched in layers of symbol), we have increased the complexity of story by many orders of

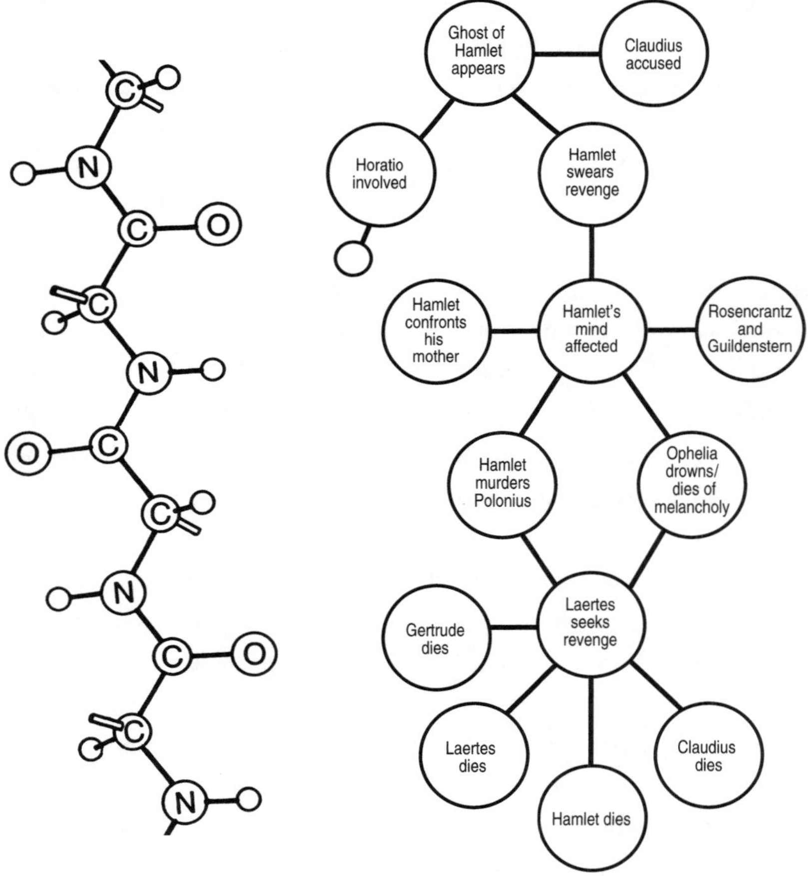

Stick-and-Ball Protein Model and My Model of Hamlet

magnitude. My point here, however, is that whatever the magnitude of change achieved by language in creating story, *the links to molecular organization and sequence are maintained.* I refer you to the preceding figure where I have made comparison between the stick-and-ball model of proteins, and a stick-and-ball model of *Hamlet.*

Each ball is an element, chemical parts of the whole protein in one case, and events of the whole play in the other. The sticks are bonds joining the elements together, molecular in one case and words or strands of meaning in the play in the other. These models convey representations in the minds of the scientist and of Shakespeare respectively. They are thus transferred to the mind of the reader where they remain, constituting ideas or forms of a reality that is part of the world construct made by the brain.

Each of the proteins may be regarded as a "story" (a model *is* a story), in that it contains various elements assembled in a fixed sequence and organized in an invariant pattern. If changes occur in these arrangements, the protein becomes something else. To operate properly, the story must be reliable and constant, in the same way that a story familiar to a child must be retold as she remembers it or she demands that it be corrected to conform to her previous understanding. Similarly, the ball-and-stick model of *Hamlet*, which we know as a story, is presented here as a "model." It now has a system of events and characters that occur along a time sequence. It should be noted that this timeline only exists in the reading or watching of the play. It does not exist as part of the printed pattern of the connected elements. The character elements and subplots are organized and assembled in association with each event, in various patterns that are fixed in relation to those events and to each other. I have arranged *Hamlet* like this to show that there is not much difference *in kind* between these models/stories. I do not believe that seeing *Hamlet* this way twists it out of shape to fit my purposes. The point here is not to show that *Hamlet* is like a protein molecule, but that human brains have a built-in preference for organizing data into models or stories like these *no matter what data brains are constructing*. We know who wrote *Hamlet*, but a more interesting question might be what, or who "wrote" Shakespeare?

Science proceeds by making models; Literature proceeds by making models, in fact it is the largest collection of models that the species has produced and managed to preserve. Humans function by making models, so it is not far-fetched to assume that there is something like a model-making disposition in our genetic structure.

Formed out of words and syntax, narrative is sequential. It builds, snowballs upon itself. It is cumulative and it organizes experience. It is a map, a pattern that takes the data acquired by our senses and seeks to store it in kit form ready for re-assembly. This re-assembled story is then available to sensory memory, to be re-visioned in the brain as though it were the original. In other words, we are building a mental model out of our experiences, a model basically constant but continually modified in its role as part of the larger narrative life story, the personal epic, modified again and again by new experiences. So in this way the reader is also always the writer, always writing pieces into the life story. The personal diary is precisely the model for this kind of life writing, which goes on in everybody with or without pen or paper. The collection of kits we acquire through life experience, including the experience of our reading, becomes the "I" we carry around with us and into which we try to fit all new experience.

It is this model version of ourselves made up of stored, coded experiences that seems to take on a powerful life of its own, *our life story*. This is our identity, and on the basis of this identity all our thought and behaviour take place. All its parts must be connected, and this drive to connect the parts forces us to work continuously to organize and reorganize the parts into a whole, a whole that is ever changing. In fact, the principal activity of human minds, moment to moment, is the fine tuning, the adjusting of this narrative. In the words of Terrence Deacon, "At the level of what an individual knows, a language is very much like one's own personal symbiotic organism."[5] What he means is that though we begin life with a self, we create as we live our "I," a language creature that has its own dynamic energy and its own rules and functions.[6] I would add that this "language" Deacon refers to is a narrative, that its form matters crucially to the individual, and that this narrative "organism" is a second self that *we create*, layered over the first.

And here is the good news: in the freedom to create this second self, this "I," lies the key to our well-being. It is this freedom that is the source of all effective therapy. Threats to our identity are the source of what we call noxious stress, experiences we live through that are difficult to incorporate into our "I." As I will show in Chapter 6 (and Appendix 1), problems with the construction of this model "I" will lead to mental, emotional and social dysfunction.

But for now, discovering that we have the power to shape, alter, and manage this narrative, that we can change ourselves to be more effective, healthy and successful, is part of the evolutionary process. Making this "I" function smoothly to accommodate whatever it encounters is also called *adaptation*, and story is the very special form that human adaptation takes. This book is dedicated to describing the role of reading as it contributes to this process.

I have referred above several times to the ways in which humans use their experiences by creating a working "I" built out of stories. But we must now shift our emphasis to writing and reading which for the last, say, four or five thousand years, have extended the range of personal experience virtually without limit. We must first remember that reading is a choice. To be motivated to do it we must increase our awareness of its value to us, just as we do when we choose to exercise in an age of sedentary work and automobiles. In my view, Literature is the best tool we have for helping ourselves develop a fully functional "I."

Notes to Chapter 1: The Beginning is the Word

1. This is the working assumption of John Taylor in *The Race for Consciousness.* See also Cairns-Smith, *Evolving the Mind.*
2. Alfred Korzybski's famous dictum means that mental representations of things perceived are all we know of them; these mental constructs, however, are not the same as the things themselves. This is also true of course of maps of the brain, the human attempt to represent the architectonics of brain structure in visual terms. This is the brain doing its best to draw itself, to represent its own representing organ. Suffice it to say that the brain's knowledge and representation of itself is subject to the same limitations with which brains represent all perceived data. There is no escape from human subjectivity. Though this teaching of Korzybski's is about seventy years old, and has been endlessly quoted, it has still not entered general consciousness. We really do need to come to terms with the fact that human brains are continuously constructing and exchanging information about their "maps" — and not about their territories.
3. Bateson, p. 14. Our computers are a long way from the humanized machine in Bateson's little parable. In fact, rather than enjoying the company of story-composing talking robots, we are in danger of altering our own brains in adapting to what computers can now do. In other words, there is plenty of evidence that, because we have committed ourselves to the "efficiency" of the computer, we must reduce and shape our work and our thinking to what the computer can manage, from exams to spelling, from curricula to inventory, from diagnosis to prescription.
4. *The Symbolic Species*, p. 22.
5. I interpret Deacon to mean that a "personal symbiotic organism" would be something like an organic, modular, brain extension that is uniquely one's own. A kind of organic robot perfectly fitted to the self. This "other self" would have grown along with oneself in life, like a language alter ego that interpreted your every linguistic need, and did whatever you wanted it to do, within the limits of its own organic development. Its powers to be an assistant would therefore grow as it grew, the more of language there was, the more it could serve your needs.
6. See also Damasio, 1999

Chapter Two

Arithmetic, Writing and Reading

And the Lord God formed man of the dust of the ground, and breathed into his nostrils the breath of life; and man became a living soul.

— **Genesis 2:7**

Study, in Judaism, is a sacred rite, a devotional act informed by creativity and imagination, ideally practiced with others who are committed to listening to the past and to one another and in the process adding their voice.

— **Lawrence Fine**

I am writing this sentence in the year 5761. Almost six thousand years ago the world and humankind were created by God, according to the reckoning of the Jewish calendar. Even if we assume that our ancient ancestors did not know about the fossil record, about the cave drawings at Lascaux, about archeology and anthropology, we must still somehow account for a creation date as recent as 5761.

There are hundreds, perhaps thousands of creation stories around the world. Everyone has one because everyone wants to know where we came from and how we got here. We must have a story that explains our origins. Humans must have an answer to every question because we must make sense of our relation to the world in which we find ourselves. This is part of the biological imperative of our story brains. Yet most creation stories do not worry us with a date. The ones that do, though, tell us something about the meaning and mindset of those that selected the date. For instance, Christians adhere to a calendar that started just over 2000 years ago. This tells us that for Christians, the world was in some sense re-created at that time. It is not exactly a creation story but it is a re-creation story — which means Christians are not much interested in what happened before Year 1. Christians decided history began with the historical event that they pin their faith to, the birth of Jesus. Jews, on the other hand, have chosen a different event: the invention, or in their view, the divine gift of phonetic writing. In my view the Jewish creation date coincides with the writing of their creation story.

Jews have been called the "people of the book." They have a special attachment to writing and they place a scroll at the centre of their worship. The God of the Jews is represented, manifested, made present in language, in a text, not in the flesh. Writing marks the start of History. Writing does not indicate the start of creation but it does make possible the transmission of a record of stories and that record includes a creation story. The point is that the actual date of creation cannot be known, but a date for the origins of the record of what can be known is what matters.

The Bible is the history of a people and it includes a creation story, but 5761 represents a date for the origins of the record. For Jews, that date is the mark of *their* origin — that is, when they were created by means of the record, and that has become part of Judaism. Language and creation were brought together in the Jewish story where creation and clay become inextricably associated. First there was life and breath; from breath came language; from language came writing; from writing came reading. This all happened in "seven days" because the story had to account for the Jewish organization of time. Jews work for six days and rest on the seventh; according to the story, Jews do this because God did it. That is the Jewish story, and we know this only from the Jewish story. Story is the most powerful agency for human behaviour there is. What we can learn from the creation story of the Jews is how they came to view the importance of writing as a shaping force of human behaviour, and the beginning of history.

Whatever is written in the Bible, or anywhere else for that matter, is the result of human experience. Jewish experience in the Near East from five or six thousand years ago, for instance, involved an intimate acquaintance with clay and agriculture. Clay was the primary building material and the source for most utensils and commonplace decorations. Clay was easily obtainable, malleable, and could be hardened to keep its shape and stay waterproof. It was cheap, or free, fairly durable, easily replaced, and lent itself to both art and utility. It was almost the stuff of life itself and could be shaped into virtually anything. It was, in fact, inseparable from human culture throughout Mesopotamia. But where others made images of clay, Jews made writing on clay. It is hardly surprising then that humans should think that just as they made everything from clay, so God made them. They were merely transferring their own experience. The human person was simply a more wonderful creation than anything they could make from clay, but an appropriate work of art for God. Put clay into His hands and look what He could do! In fact, since humans were God-made they invariably took on some God-like qualities, just as the clay men and women handled became imprinted with aspects of the human. Humans were so God-like (though only made from clay), that they too would discover that they could make clay come to life, make it speak and make it powerful enough to govern human affairs and contracts.

We know that creationists and evolutionists still disagree on whether humankind was made overnight or over a billion years. But whether Adam is *Homo erectus*, *habilis*, *sapiens* or *sapiens sapiens*, he was certainly *Homo narrator*, the storyteller, and only after his creation is the world we inhabit shaped by story. But creation, biological creation that is, has been part of an extended process, and story and writing have been integral to it. This chapter, then, concerns itself with the invention of writing and its consequences.

Humans did not invent language, which is often regarded as a gift. Many stories around the world testify to a belief that language is the most powerful attribute accorded to humans, and as far as we can see, it is not found elsewhere in the natural world. But humans did invent writing, again a tool of such import that it is widely attributed to God. Writing is an example of culture impinging on biology, the very biology that gave rise to the culture in the first place. Writing, which is language made visible, is one of those extensions of language that alters the history of the language-making species.

We are faced with a number of questions that lie between myth and history, the answers to which may help us understand how language and story work. Myth is story designed to explain what is not accounted for in history. There is no history before writing. The mysteries of natural origins, including human biology, give rise to many myths. We do not know how much of the written record is simply a writing down of the oral record of myth, oral history and legend. We can be sure, however, that the recording of myth was coloured by the existence of writing in human consciousness. Once the writer lives in a writing world it is impossible to write story or myth as though writing has not altered thinking. For instance, the myth that God breathed life into clay to create Adam may have predated the invention of writing, but once it is written down the writer cannot *not* be thinking of how humans write on clay. The connection between God the creator of a language creature and *Homo* the writer now becomes inescapable. The myth is now charged with writing awareness.[1] History produces myth by looking backwards to explain what lies outside its purview.

Since writing is the most important single invention created by the "symbolic species,"[2] and since it appears to have changed everything, for better or worse, and since there is no voluntary turning back from where it has led us, it might be useful to have an explanation of the origins of writing. This should help us, the writing descendants and inheritors, to understand how our minds are affected by the medium of written language.

So far, the most convincing description of the path that led to writing has been put forward by archeologist Denise Schmandt-Besserat.[3] Her extensive archeological researches in the Near and Middle East led her to a fascinating thesis that covers a critical period of change from the nomadic era to the time of agricultural settlement. She describes writing as a cultural accompaniment to a social and economic structure that continues in a fairly straight line to the present.

Dr. Schmandt-Besserat's story begins about 10,000 years ago. The place is Mesopotamia, Modern Iraq and the entire area stretching from Israel to the Tigris and Euphrates. It is a long story that I will make very short. Crucial to this thesis is the prehistoric transition from hunter-gatherer lifestyle and nomadic herder tribes, to settled agricultural practices and finally to urban communities. According to Schmandt-Besserat, writing has its roots in book keeping, in accounting, in arithmetic. Prior to settlement, which has its motivation in the cultivation of cereals, and therefore a reliable food supply, we know that people had few possessions.[4] They shared what they killed or gathered. They could not preserve or hoard or transport large quantities of food. They did not transport much in the way of shelter.[5] They could not hamper their searches for food by carrying many things. With the change to farming communities came completely different societies. From then on we see the development of classes of citizens with a ruling elite. Individuals now breed herds of animals, acquire stores of grain and oil, require a good and reliable water supply where they live. Owners of property, crops and livestock can't go roaming around the continent, as today's farmers and even dog owners know. They must stay and feed and protect their property or get someone else to do it. They must trade with neighbours who become more and more settled and known, and also rely on visitors to bring what is not available locally. All this will require record keeping. With the growth of rich and poor, and eventually temples, states, kings and bureaucracies, more and more records become necessary.

So 10,000 years ago, in order to keep track of possessions, trade, taxes, tributes, profits and losses, it became necessary to invent an accounting system. This began with the making of small clay shapes, cones, balls, discs, triangles, rectangles etc. designed to symbolize commodities, previously traded on a one-to-one basis (e.g., one oval of clay = one vessel of oil). Schmandt-

Besserat calls these small objects, excavated in huge numbers, "tokens." Later on these tokens, by means of impressed marks, became more complex, but at first they were quite simple, primitive geometric clay forms. In various guises these token-based records of goods prevailed for about five thousand years and grew more and more complex before being replaced.

As the number of tokens increased, it became necessary to organize them in some way and store them. So they were placed in "envelopes," that is cylindrical or spherical hollow clay containers, which were then sealed. It was understood that no one could remember the contents of these envelopes. So to check the records the envelopes had to be broken open and the tokens counted or changed as the property they represented changed, following trades or the death of livestock. After a time it was discovered that marking the containers to show their contents, like putting a list of "contents" on the outside of an envelope, meant you did not have to break open the containers to examine what they contained. This was the next step toward writing. Even though you could describe the contents of the envelope by writing on the container, you would still have to break open the container to change the contents themselves. The third step must have followed fairly quickly, for once you had written on the container it was no great leap to the idea that you did not need the token symbols at all. *The record engraved on the envelope replaced the three-dimensional symbols inside.* All you had to do to make changes in the record was replace the clay tablet with an updated one, or cross things out like keeping score in a game of darts.

This discovery may have taken a thousand years or two to spread and be learned. But what a lot of time and trouble was saved. If you did not need the token symbols themselves, you could simply flatten out a piece of clay, like the sides of the original envelope, write the commodity signs on it, fire it and you would have a clay tablet record of goods: goods to be paid as tribute, to be exchanged in barter, or paid as wages and eventually paid and received as taxes, all of which had to be recorded. But the implications of this "writing" realization, from the point of view of brain activity and communication, were enormous.

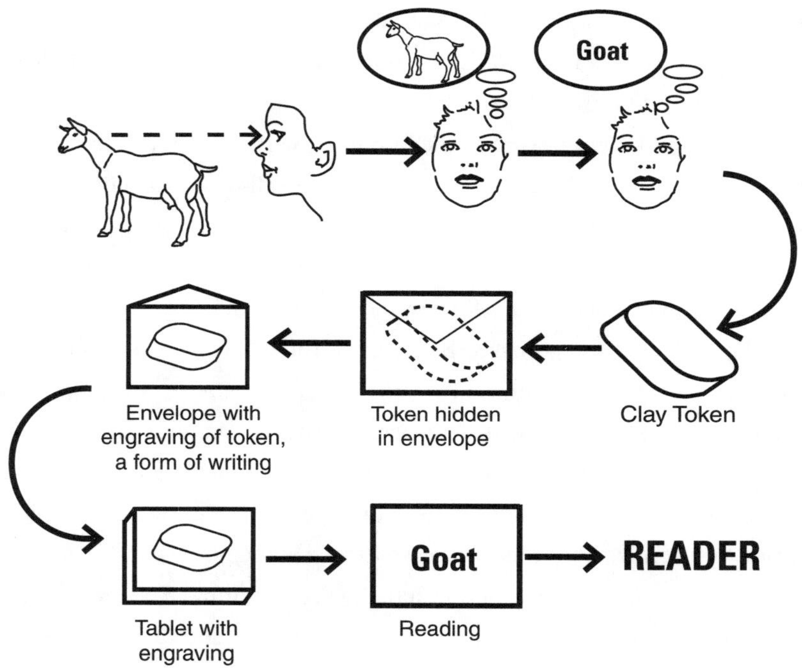

You will see that writing has taken us quite far from the world of objects, into the world of purely symbolic exchanges between brains. Clay has been made to speak. To arrive at the position of the reader you must reverse the diagram above and start at the end. The writing or language on the tablet is now visual and has displaced the vocal and the auditory. The voice behind the writing has become internalized. The writing and reading process is silent, with far reaching consequences. Non-human animals recognize and identify various objects and people. To a dog, the couch means a good place to rest and the leash means "walk time." The dog makes associations. We do not know how these object-activity connections are represented in the dog's brain. In the human brain, though, they are represented by words. "Couch" and "leash" are sound codes that produce images and associations in the brain, or they are words called to mind by seeing the actual objects. The calling to mind of words from objects is essentially an intricate two-step process. The object goes through sensory assessment, category identification and naming. Adam looks the animal over and then to God's amusement invents a name for it. Writing, on the other hand, is a whole different matter. The *written* word has now introduced an exchange of information process between parts of the brain, but without immediate reference to the object world. Writing, reading and decoding into sound meaning before we arrive at "real world" imagery is a purely mental process and can take place with thousands of written words organized into sentences, read inside a lighted cubicle, shut off from the "real world."

The reader must go from the word, to the flesh and blood object, *via* her own mental representation of the object awakened from her own memory through a sensory (usually visual) process, reading. From a neural point of view this is a very elaborate and uniquely human process. Writing has introduced a further step away from the material, natural, or object world. Written language has increased the distance between "inner" and "outer" worlds that human brains actually seek to unite. Spoken language was much "closer" in a neural sense to non-lexical sound, and therefore closer to emotion, the grunts and cries and squeals I mentioned earlier. You can verify this easily for yourself. Music, birdsong, the call of the loon, a growl or roar near your campsite, a scream of pain on the street — all of these produce immediate emotional responses in the hearer, in a way that written words do not.[6] Writing can enter and alter the consciousness of a culture, as it did for instance with Charles Dickens's *A Christmas Carol* and H.B. Stowe's *Uncle Tom's Cabin*, but spoken oratory can, in the short term, move large numbers of hearers to emotional frenzy, social action and revolution. Winston Churchill, Huey Long of Louisiana and Fidel Castro produced many modern examples of such oratory. The list of history-making orators is long: Moses, Cicero, Augustus Caesar, Jesus, St. Paul, Milton, Sydney "Silver Tongued" Smith, Abraham Lincoln, Tommy Douglas and so on. Even softly spoken, personal words, expressed on stage, or in bed, are much closer to emotional evocation than words that must be read to be decoded, and so add an extra but significant thinking, cortical, and non-emotional, distancing process.

The most interesting thing about this view of the origins of writing is that it vaults us at once to the present. Writing reinforced, and is probably the source of the Western schism between emotion and reason. It led in philosophy to what Damasio, a prominent American neuroscientist, called *Descartes' Error.* His next book, *The Feeling of What Happens,* is, as its title indicates, an attempt to reunite emotion and thought through a discussion of brain function. The need for such a reunion arises because we have become lexical creatures, we have all become people of the book.[7]

Since the origins of writing and especially since print, an endless proliferation of written information, data, and stories have flooded our human world. Solomon knew this would happen: "Of the making of many books there is no end." Since the invention of phonetic writing there has been very little change in communication behaviour and the attendant cognition, in spite of the blossoming of technologies for transmission. Brains evolve much more slowly than the machines they create. The information content however, and the complexity of the information has increased a thousand times. Now there is no turning back. As you read this book I hope you will see that I am arguing that Literature has been the product of the species' struggle to overcome the very distance writing creates between the human and himself, between the human and the other. Literature will have to be the means to release us from the double bind: we can't return to the infant state of the non-reading oral; and we cannot survive as split personalities, treating the world as a schizoid projection of dissociated brains.

The history of writing begins with lists of things, as the early tablets and tokens suggest, but very soon it becomes clear that it is conceptually possible to write anything. It must be possible, for instance, to write thoughts and stories. This would be too complex a process for sign language in written form, and required the invention of the phonetic alphabet, which could represent actual speech and the language thought that precedes it.[8] What was important about the earliest cuneiform clay tablet writing was not the lists of goods or chattels represented, but the process of language representation itself. This would lead in an unbroken pattern of development to written and therefore visible and recordable speech. The radio and tape recorder of today are a return to pre-writing stages of cognition, but they were possible only after the concept of recording spoken words had entered human consciousness.

It seems to me that the recognition of the power of writing to represent the mind's structure of the external world had an effect far beyond the practical, beyond the convenience of having shopping lists and book keeping. It altered consciousness, the way language itself did. For instance, Jews reckon human history from the beginnings of the knowledge of writing. The written word altered the concept of time. Time could now be managed in terms of historical record, as in the list of generations we find in the amazing series of "begats" in Genesis. If this list is not fiction, and I think it is not, then it must have been memorized by and eventually recorded with some relief when writing became available. It was memorized by Tannaim, the scholars of phenomenal memory, living archives, who kept alive holy commentary and text up to and through the writing period. Revealingly, once it is written to be read, the list stops being compiled and the generations and population become too numerous to record. We are left then with an instance, evidence of tribal origins, history in short. So it is that writing actually creates whereas memory records the passing of time and creates a continuous present. What could not be written about as historical record, being too complicated or distant, like the pre-writing experience of early cultures, or the unseen realms of spiritual or felt experience, diminished in importance, to be replaced by law and ethics, philosophy and politics.

From this point of view, creation could be seen as *what can be created by writing*. Year 1 — 5761 years ago based on the Jewish calendar — is just about right for the spread of phonetic writing, according to Schmandt-Besserat's timetable. Token recording and then tablet stylus writing prevailed for about four or five thousand years, after which phonetic writing spread throughout Mesopotamia for another two thousand. It is also entirely possible that Jews invented phonetic writing evidenced by the twenty-two letters of the Hebrew language. This would explain the quintessential link between God and language that caused Jews to enshrine language in their Holy of Holiness. For Jews, language replaced images and the word could be sanctified without risk of idolatry. The word was the path to the Divine, but not the Divine itself. Jews treated their discovery as if they were "chosen." Their role on Earth was to safeguard the "word." As we see, once language could be *seen*, it entered the brain as "consciousness-of-language."

Phonetic writing produced the next stage of complexity. Phonetics made it possible to actually mimic speech in written signs, which could combine to convey grammar, sentence and long, complex, linked thoughts in visible form. Writing could convey sentences and complexity not possible in speech. For both the speaker and the listener the limitations of short-term working memory made intricate thoughts and reasoning almost impossible to follow. A series of dependent clauses and parallel references and lists could not be retained while waiting for the verbal conclusion. Seeing language made extended, qualified thinking transmissible, as Henry James and William Faulkner proved. After writing, two languages developed, one spoken and one written, and they were not the same. Different characteristics distinguished each. Feelings too, and thoughts and abstractions could now be symbolically represented as visible text. Likewise, inevitably, emotion, thought, sincerity, truth, complexity have gradually eroded from speech and have become the preserve of written language. For instance, once upon a time a man's *word* was his bond. I heard this first from my father who, sixty years ago, believed it. Now the written contract has virtually eliminated verbal contract, except in some time-lapsed corners of the world. I am arguing that the gap between speech and writing has widened at an accelerated pace. *The written text has become the repository of story, careful thought, complex language and personal sincerity.* As we shall see in my discussion on politics and advertising, the spoken word has also become untrustworthy.

The other thing to note about the evolution of symbolic writing is this: what took five or six thousand years for the group to develop, learn and pass on, we expect a child to master in its first few years. From birth to Grades 1 or 2, our children must learn speech, symbol formation, abstract thought, grammar, writing and reading. Before writing, children learned only speech without apparent struggle. Dyslexia was unknown. We now regard not only thinking but symbol making itself as part of being human, and in literate societies our social and cultural expectations are treated as a biological imperative.[9] Hardly surprising then that things seem to have speeded up.

Revising the Past

One of the significant effects of written history is to assist in the construction of group identity and so enhance the life story formation of the individuals who form the group. We require a flexible but reliable history, against which background the individual forms identity from personal experience. If the history is too rigid and exclusive, or if it changes too constantly, stability for the individual story becomes difficult if not impossible to construct. The cognitive ground is too shifting or too non-adaptive. It is also possible to falsify history in order to undermine group and individual identity and so in a sense invalidate the life experience of those one wishes to disempower. Holocaust revisionists would be a good example of this practice as political policy. George Orwell warned in his novel *1984* that totalitarian government could both authorize and change history on a daily basis in order to have total control over the thought and identity of the citizens. Kept off balance by not having a reliable group story, people lack stability, confidence and therefore power. Writing used in this way undermines faith in personal experience and eventually any trust in language itself. Those who write have the luxury of making choices. Those who can read a story from only one source have serious limitations on their freedom. Once it is possible to record stories, it is possible to create and even distort the past. Writing gives permanence and authority to the record; for this reason many stories from varied sources are necessary to provide an antidote to writing tyranny.

But whatever writing did with the past it inevitably drew attention to language with the same compelling reality as a photo does to the process of recognition. Written language continually proves its reality, its existence, its presence as an existential force. Let's look at some examples of how writing changed the attitudes of cultures to language and its role in human affairs, so changing human civilization itself.

The Chinese still believe the Four Treasures of civilization are writing tools. It was once believed that a person's brushmanship was a measure of overall accomplishment and an indicator of moral rectitude. To be educated and worthy of respect one learned to write elegantly. A few years ago I bought a personal seal in China hardly knowing why. It was one of the things tourists did. Now I know that my elaborately carved jade seal is a curtsy to the most ancient form of printing in the world. I speculate that some form of printing existed between four and five thousand years ago. The Chinese had ink during that period and they had bas-relief carving. By the Common Era they had paper, no one knows for how long. They certainly had brushstroke writing earlier than anyone else. I think it very likely, given Middle East dating, that at least four thousand years ago the Chinese were transferring carved symbols to paper by means of ink. The art of paper making was not learned by the Arabs from the Chinese until twelve hundred years ago, and reached Europe less than a thousand years ago.

But for our purposes we must look to the Middle East, about fifty-five hundred years ago, or the creation date of the Jews, 5761 years ago. It is here we find the story of the Ten Commandments, or Decalogue. These rules for social conduct became the core of written law, the entire codification of civil order. But as the story tells, it is the writing on the clay tablets that marks the significance of the occasion. Did God give Moses the first set of inscribed clay tablets in the world? It seems very doubtful. What would have been the point in His doing that? Who could have read them? Only after writing was invented by humans could God *write* the law.

Having already acquired writing and law, the Jews attributed its origin and transmission to their God. Even more interesting, it could be argued that the gift of the two tablets of the Decalogue says more about the gift of writing than about the law itself, if we presume that the Jews were already functioning under laws, rather than in social chaos. Moses actually smashes the first set of tablets given to him and must return for another copy. Why could he not have simply memorized the rules and taught them orally? Because the story marks the point in history when human *consciousness moves from image, icon, to word*. And this awareness, the essence of the story, is only possible after language becomes visible in writing. Moses' anger at the people's calf worshipping is very much connected to the clay tablet and the markings on them. "If you cannot or if you will not read, then you are not worthy of God's greatest gift — (written) language." This watershed moment in history follows the invention of writing. Though language was there for half a million years at least, it was only six thousand years ago that it came to occupy centre stage in human thinking. To this moment in the mythic history of the Jews we may attribute a shift from the worship of nature and fertility, to the study of texts. It was at Sinai that the Jews became the "people of the book," not because they acquired law, but because they transferred their worship to the non-material word.

The earliest written stories were the oral stories that preceded writing. The history of Scripture shows precisely this editorial process, for both Jews and Christians, as for instance with the inclusion in Genesis of two creation stories. With the advent of writing it was now possible to revise and shape the past and choose what to record. The role of story was suddenly (in evolutionary time scales) given unprecedented momentum. Following the invention of writing we find sacred accounts of the power of language. In fact there are five major Biblical references to the awareness of language power after the invention of writing. One, God speaks the world into being: "Let there be light." Two, Adam names the animals. Three, the Hebrews invent the story of Babel, or at least think it worth recording. It says that if everyone were to speak one language they would threaten Heaven itself. Such is the conception of the power of language *after the invention of writing* that it represents a threat to Divinity and to the natural order of the universe. The story of Babel, which seeks to explain the existence of multiple languages in the world, occurs only after human consciousness of the power of language has been heightened by seeing language in writing. Four, God hands over the model of writing as tablet inscriptions at Sinai. And finally, St. John asserts that God and the Word are one and the same: "In the beginning was the Word, and the Word was with God and the Word was God."[10] Beyond these landmark references to the role of language in the history of human story, the Bible is simply filled with references and metaphors to speech, language and writing; it is the most outstanding characteristic of the Hebrew scriptures.

For instance, one book of the Bible, The Book of Esther, alleges that at one point in Jewish history, the fate of the people hinges on the King reading the palace log during a bout of insomnia. The modern feel to this familiar idea of getting up to have a read when he can't sleep is amusing to us, given its antiquity. But to the Bible editors it must have seemed novel and significant in the extreme. To them, it suggested that in the Hansard of the day lay justice and authority, and in this instance validation and survival. Their enemies could bear false testimony, but the official record would not lie, could not be allowed to lie because somewhere some reliable version of events must provide the foundation of stable and thoughtful government. The written record has become part of the apparatus of monarchy. It is also noteworthy that the king can read, a rare but obviously critically important accomplishment necessary to the good ruler. Here too we see the seeds of the great palace libraries that were to culminate in the ancient world at Alexandria. These huge collections of handwritten manuscripts were to be the forerunners of the world's great modern book collections, The Vatican, The British Museum, The Library of Congress to name but three.[11]

We have seen how breath and speech are associated in folklore and human experience itself. When writing becomes widespread it joins this set of associations and takes on magical life-giving properties. For instance, in the tenth century there was a European belief suggesting that by placing a paper with the name of God on it in the mouth of a dead person, that person would be brought back to life. There was also a story that credits Rabbi Loew of Prague, one of the great Jewish religious leaders of history and legend, with inventing the Golem of Jewish folklore.[12] Under the great stress of religious persecution in the sixteenth century, the Jews of Eastern Europe needed a hero to fight their enemies. So, long before Mary Shelley invented Frankenstein and his monster, Rabbi Loew invented a huge figure of clay, as God had made Adam out of red earth. This giant could only be activated by placing in its mouth a piece of paper on which were written some holy words. Thus it is said that through the agency of this creation and that of other Golems were the Jews of Eastern Europe saved from genocide; surely another way of saying that the Word of God, in writing, is what saved Jews from extinction.

I think there are some valid reasons for thinking this may be true. The Jews are a good example of a people who moved from an oral culture to a written one. Those that did not make this change have not survived as well. Many have perished and left no trace, like the Philistines, whose reputation in history rests on the record of its former enemies. It is a curious fact that Jews as a "people," that is as a cultural group with an identity, customs, beliefs, rituals, language, and dietary habits, managed to survive exile in Egypt; defeat, captivity and exile at the hands of the Babylonians; dispersion around the world and absence of a homeland; and the devastation, both in numbers and in psychological trauma from the Holocaust. I think it very likely that this durability can be attributed to the Jewish attachment to a written text, called the Torah. This unaltered, handwritten, parchment scroll sits at the centre of every Jewish shrine, or Ark. It is always in Hebrew, which kept the language alive through every move to every land, amidst every language. It is portable, so that the destruction of one shrine does not mean the end of a centre of worship; it is never altered by a jot or a tittle, so it remains a constant and reliable bond in every congregation; it remains unaltered no matter what schisms or subsects adopt it; it is always handwritten by specialists so no digital printing process can corrupt or alter it; and it contains stories and rules, history and myth to which every Jew has access. Being able to read it in Hebrew is the coming of age ritual in every congregation. No other example of writing illustrates as clearly the power of the written word to keep a culture alive, to ground people in their traditions and origins, to provide stability through chaotic disruption and to provide bonding between humans across time and space.

It is also important to be aware that the Torah is based on a long oral tradition that precedes it. In a real sense this oral tradition is kept alive by traditions of study and commentary on Torah, which are regarded as contributions to it. There is an essential lesson for us here in our public education systems. Readers are empowered to share thoughts and questions, comments and feelings in response to text. Readers are connected to texts, to Literature that they share. Thus writing becomes alive and present. It might be said that the contemporary popularity of book clubs is based on the need to be involved in stories. People who attend these clubs find themselves bonded by sharing responses to texts. They are keeping alive an oral tradition by elaborating on texts. They are reintroducing voices to story. Yet the words of the text, as with the Torah, remain more constant and authoritative than any priestly or professorial commentary on them.

For a long time the writing of words was accorded magical properties, found in spells, in signs over doors, in wills and in laws and decrees. As I have said, I believe this recognition of the power of language came only after writing forced us to *look* at language. Once this happened it became possible to see that symbolic language, possessed only by humans, could manipulate and control people and social economics. Language first, and then with greatly accelerated speed, writing, freed humans from the attachment to the material objects themselves. But it also meant that people could become numbered and categorized just like livestock. You could take a census, conscript an army, monitor taxes. We had embarked on a trajectory that would lead to the virtual elimination of privacy and anonymity.[13]

So powerful is symbolic language after it becomes written, that it could encompass the existing world and create new ones. With it, people could dream and plan, organize the past, design the future and make sense of the present, and pass all of this on to others.

Writing for Better or Worse

Given the huge time scales of evolutionary change, and the thirty thousand years of brain work required to move from pictures to truly symbolic writing (where the sign is pure symbol, not visual similitude), what happens next is very rapid indeed. Prompted by the social circumstances of the new agriculture, it takes a mere four thousand years to move from sign writing to phonetic writing. And phonetic writing spread at an even faster rate. By 2000 BCE it was common in the eastern Mediterranean and throughout Mesopotamia.

The Indo-European languages were very friendly to phonetic writing. With a mere twenty or thirty letter set of alphabetic signs, all possible speech combinations of sound could be represented in visible form. It was now theoretically possible to write whatever could be said or thought to be said. It was even possible to skip the speech step entirely and go straight from thought to writing. It is hard for us to imagine a time when this was not so, when in order to communicate or even articulate one's thoughts even to oneself it was necessary to speak, to give vocal utterance. There are far-reaching consequences of writing that we must look at because they are determinant of everything that follows, both for social and individual outcomes. A mere thirty-five hundred years after the generalized acceptance of phonetic writing, we are in possession of mechanical printing with movable type. After that nothing will ever be unaffected by the written word.

The more obvious rewards of writing in trade, commerce, travel, and law include the shrinking of distance; the transmission of news; the moulding of politics and the arts of rhetoric and persuasion; the recording of history; the spread of learning and education — these are well-known and cannot be analyzed here. What we can and must consider, however, are the consequences of writing for the transmission of story. Since there is no turning back to a pre-writing state, what imperatives do we face in this world of written language?

Writing had an effect on how we think. It altered our relations to ourselves and others. It imposed certain requirements on our behaviour even as it freed us from limitations of time and space. We are all familiar with the old adage, "out of sight, out of mind," which means that in personal relations people often manage to forget and ignore those who are not physically present. In the case of writing, however, the opposite seems to be true. We might say that when language becomes visible, in sight, it no longer needs to be kept in mind. There have been many psychological benefits from writing, but there have also been enormous costs to our world and how we manage it. Writing gave us better control over our own thought processes and increased the development of personal identity. But it also created much greater distances from our natural world. Writing and reading produced disconnections. In order to overcome these disconnections, we need to better understand them.

Once words can be written, and especially written phonetically so their sound is represented, then brain information becomes extrasomatic, outside the body. Memory space is saved. Writing becomes an external memory module. Writing the word "goat" increases the distance from the real flesh and blood goat. The owner is now free to forget about the goat and get on with something else knowing that the goat is stored somewhere on a piece of clay. I use pen and paper in exactly the same way. Last night I got up to jot down a few thoughts on paper so I could leave them there and get to sleep. I had temporarily removed them from my mind, into extrasomatic storage. In this way, writing overcomes geographic and temporal distance between people: I can share with others who are not in my presence my extrasomatic storage information; while at the same time, writing increases separation from the world of the "not-I": my extrasomatic storage information does not require my presence to be read and understood, nor does the person reading it need to be in the vicinity of the goat, or whatever else is being discussed in writing. Computers have greatly expanded the storage of this day-to-day, out-of-body memory module, and just as surely distanced us even further from the natural, sensory world.

It is well-known in clinical therapy that if patients can be persuaded to write about their negative emotions, thoughts and experiences, they feel better and become healthier.[14] Many fiction writers attest to the therapeutic results of writing. Some even become professional writers as a result of writing begun in therapy.[15] Why is this? My answer seems so obvious I hesitate to offer it here. It has been generally assumed that the answer to this question lies in the "insight" gained through verbal expression. I believe that the answer lies in "outsight"; the writing step increases the sense of having externalized, put aside, filed away the negative emotional material carried in the body. Expression in writing is purgative. This is one more example, a benign one, of how writing creates distance between first-hand experience and memory. The negative experience and its consequences are not forgotten, it is distanced and "objectified." It can now be viewed by neocortical processing, managed and integrated as part of a "filed" narrative. From a cultural perspective there was a downside to this result of writing. Putting the language of thought and feeling "out there" also involved a generalized sense of dissociation. The language and its speaker were not as close as they were before. While this can be useful for dysfunctional mental states, it was problematic for the species.

We assume that humans could speak before they could write. I also assume that since speech and gesture carried with them all the meaning, thought, feeling and intention of language transmission that was available, both speakers and listeners paid special attention. They surrounded speech with formal structures and signals. They were sensitive to nuance and inflection. Since speech is merely a disturbance of air it cannot be seen. It is heard through the auditory canal, interpreted in the midbrain as "sound of special significance," and sent to a specialized area of the cortex, for language decoding. This decoding will activate many other parts of the brain, depending on the meaning and association of the words for the hearer. The speaker on the other hand calls upon another part of the brain also specialized for language. This part requires involvement of the motor cortex, since forming and shaping words with vocal apparatus requires physical movement. It may also be said that words can be tasted because of the use of throat, tongue and soft palate in speech utterance.[16] All of these vocal areas are also brain areas: taste connecting to motor cortex, also to speech and also to breathing. In using them for one purpose we elicit other felt associations, including echoes of memory laid down from associated sensory record, as in olfactory hallucinations upon hearing, reading or seeing an appropriate trigger. The cry of a gull might elicit the taste of the sea-salt air and spray.

With the arrival of writing much of this auditory sensitivity to nuance has been lost. The burden of utterance and interpretation has now shifted to the visual. Here a third area of brain is conscripted, as well as the cortex involved in seeing (or in touching, the tactile sense, if reading is done by Braille). This third area becomes crucial to our discussion, because it adds what I might call a third dimension to our awareness, our self-awareness of language, and ourselves as language creatures, first and foremost. This 3-D or stereo effect of awareness happened because some critical threshold of information had been crossed by the brain.

I must enlist here the concept of *feedback.* Feedback means putting out a signal and examining the responses it gets. Physiological feedback machines seem to be effective in helping people control their own visceral responses. They can, by seeing their heart rate, slow it down. Seeing or touching language in the form of written symbols that could be read, added a level of consciousness to human brains. This happened because by means of writing and reading the brain could *feedback thought to itself.* It had made one part of itself visible to another part which could then examine what one part was thinking or feeling in language terms. The brain, through writing, had learned to project itself out there, for internal review.[17] Writing was a reflexive technology that altered the brain's own thinking processes. At the same time the brain had *externalized* its thoughts and feelings which, in the case of the environment, produced a sense of detachment.[18]

The emergence of this language self-consciousness through writing is glimpsed in the story of Helen Keller. This famous American had multiple sensory deficits and told the story in later years of how she discovered language. What is remarkable about this story is that along with learning language itself, she had the extraordinary experience of being aware of the magnitude of the discovery of how language works *in her own brain*. What she learned was the functionality of language. The rest of us, those not so handicapped, do not have the opportunity for such a discovery. We gradually and naturally learn to speak, read, and write, as though there is nothing wonderful or remarkable about it. For Helen Keller, discovering the secret of how language connected her to her sensory world was like being born into a new and magical universe. I discuss her story at greater length in the next chapter, but I mention it here, because I think it gives us a clue as to the impact that writing must have had both on individuals and on cultures five thousand years ago.

Humans began to think about language as a power separate from themselves but under their stewardship. I credit writing with an increased human awareness of the wonders of language power, a power made conscious through a feedback loop into the neocortex by means of seeing language represented in visible signs. Language and its various forms required writing before it could register on brains as a mysterious attribute to be cultivated and pondered. It could be studied, analyzed, parsed and described. Other consequences of this objectification of language are immediately obvious. It could be translated into other tongues. It could be sent like traded goods over great distances. And so in a very real sense written language became a means to achieve the preservation of thought, feeling and wisdom, a means to achieving immortality of that part of the human that is worth preserving. The words, the feelings and values, the thought, the parts that can influence and germinate in others — these are the real person, the real identity. For better or worse we are remembered, if at all, for what we said and wrote, not how we looked.

Hearing Voices

According to one theory, European and Near Eastern people once upon a time lived by hallucinating, functioning with two separate brains.[19] One of these brains heard messages from the gods and told the other brain what to do and think. Something happened and these two brains became one and the voices of the gods stopped. I think the reverse of this more likely. What happened is that agriculture and writing emerged on the human scene and changed the thinking process, but rather than giving rise to unified connected thinking, writing led to schizoid behaviour. The history of humanity for the last four thousand years suggests very strongly a breakdown, not of the "bicameral mind," but of the perception of connectedness. I am speaking not of the connectedness between the two cerebral hemispheres, though this may be implicated, but of the cognitive relations between the human and its environment, and the human and its membership in a single, biological species.[20]

The advent of writing effectively destroyed oral culture. Obviously there was no need for oral tradition, or transmission or the memorizing of rules, beliefs, rituals and wisdom when it could be written down. True, orality has hung on for a long time and can still be found in pockets of isolated people in various corners of the world. Essentially, though, it has all but disappeared. This has meant a number of serious losses which concern us directly as we plan our survival and examine what Literature can do to assist us. For one thing, the written text freezes the form of story (and the rules), so it takes on a fixed and unchangeable life of its own. Stories become fixed in the time of their context, long after that context has passed into ancient history. The Jews have tried to compensate for this "written in stone" quality by encouraging something called Midrash, a never-ending commentary on Torah that tries to keep alive the flexibility of text in the face of writing. Others, however, have picked and chosen bits of text to live by as though nothing has changed. This then is a loss of adaptation that oral culture enjoyed, for it could weave new events and discoveries into its stories and so remain relevant and adaptive to change. For us the context is gone but the story lives on, often irrelevantly, often requiring a denial of contemporary reality.

Another serious loss is the fading of human voices. In the oral culture the voice took on supreme importance. It informed the story and it was inseparable from its human origin. The voice became the link between teller and listener. It humanized story. It guaranteed relevance and it ensured engagement. The voice was a person who could be questioned, what it said could be learned, it could be known, the voice was a part of what it said. With the loss of the voice there has been a separation between people. An element of the impersonal has come along with writing. A middleman has stepped in and in the case of political writing, perhaps there is no voice, only a team of managers and handlers. But readers still hunger for a voice and flock to readings by authors to find that voice.

Human brains need other human voice responses *in order to form themselves.* The cement of human bonding is language, and the need for the bonding is in the service of growing our individual brains. Parents who are bonded to their infants talk to them even before they get any response. Parents who don't do this are not so bonded. The effects of speech on brains is profound:

> The neurological foundations for rational thinking, problem solving and general reasoning are largely established by age 1.... Furthermore, new studies are showing that spoken language has an astonishing impact on an infant's brain development. In fact, some researchers say the number of words an infant hears each day is the single most important predictor of later intelligence, school success and social competence ... the words have to come from an attentive,

> engaged human being. As far as anyone has been able to determine, radio and television do not work.[21]

The sound of the human voice may be the most fundamental of stimuli. Without this sound we can experience not only the loss of the personal but also a loss of empathy, a deterioration of that pre-frontal part of the brain that recognizes the self in the other. Not only loneliness can result but I suspect also psychosis and violence. Writing has made us more bicameral, not less.

Another outcome of the loss of orality, is that since the written is a memory module it can be taken for granted, it can be shelved. I don't actually have to remember or even think about what is in my hard drive or the books on my shelf. I can refer to them as needed. For this very reason I may in fact pay less and less attention to what the books can do for me. I can simply assume that the information is out there somewhere, then give my mind over to undemanding and trivial, effortless entertainment. Such a view might in fact be encouraged by the unimaginable proliferation of books and information. Or I might cease to think holistically and participate in a specialty, the study of a disconnected "field." Further, since writing has now become "objectified" it can itself become a "field" controlled by those specializing "in it," so making Literature less accessible.

Where does this leave us? We must now recognize that Literature has replaced the oral tradition and all the purposes that storytelling served. While the forms of transmission have changed with profound consequences, our needs have not.

What were the needs that the oral satisfied? Humans have needs far beyond those in Maslow's hierarchy. Humans have privileged language above all other specializations of their brains, and in so doing have become the communicating animal. The need to communicate has become biologically necessary in order for the brain to understand its own thinking. What and how do humans communicate? The form that brains selected for the organization and transmission of vital information was story. What destroys a culture, a religion, the bonds and identity of a people, is the loss of its story. When the oral was eroded and replaced by the written it shifted the burden of story to Literature. This did not mean that the human need for story was diminished. On the contrary. Without the speaker's voice, without the closeness of community and group, the need for story increased. We are now in the position that having lost the oral source of identity we are dependent on stories, in writing, to make us human and give us identity. *If we do not have one or the other we are lost.*

What we face now is a hegemony of unintelligible homogeny. Only Literature can make life intelligible, unified, organized. Without a tribal story we must have the riches of Literature to help us select and form our own story for shaping the world. If you doubt me, you must answer the question: What else is there? Where can we turn for the voices and shaping perceptions, the experience and wisdom that once came from the accumulated memory of oral story generationally transmitted? Literature is cumulative, adaptive, continuous, sensitive to context and change. It is the carrier of varied and complex and regenerated language. To be human is to function in what was once talking but is now found in reading groups.

Having acquired symbolic language, humans acquired yet more needs than other creatures, needs that have to be satisfied for them to survive *as human.* This is not merely a liberal or romantic notion. A creature who has devoted a large part of its brain to symbolic language over millions of years of adaptation, to the thoughts, ideas and exchanges of information compelled by that linguistic brain — such a creature must satisfy its needs or be less than the definition of itself.[22] Human needs will include a very powerful curiosity drive; an insatiable need for new information; the need to hear the sound of human speech; the need to talk; the need for the company of other language animals. Most of all we require story, and we must overcome the idea that story is some frivolous or childish entertainment that distracts us from the serious business of, say, making money. We are biologically driven to function in the story mode.

I am trying to establish here the degree to which the exchange of language (and reading Literature as the best aid to that exchange) is a biological imperative to being human, not potentially human, not humanoid, but fully human. The development of language brains took place so that individuals could make sense of the world, and at the same time, share and exchange that "sense" with others to the mutual benefit of all. Human brains are designed to function interactively. But this is not only because "many hands make light work" or, "two heads are better than one." Most wild animals and insects survive in groups, in schools, herds, flocks, swarms and packs. The survival benefits of this are obvious and well recognized. Your dog gets excited when he sees another dog because he is genetically programmed to want the company of dogs. He does not know or ask why, or what they can do together. But human brains need information and particularly other human voice responses *in order to form themselves.* The cement of human bonding is language, and the need for the bonding is in the service of growing our individual brains.

Because writing was language visible "out there," it quickly developed a life and magic of its own. It obviously conferred powers never seen before, but it also produced some distance between spoken language and speakers, between the writing and the origins of the writing in human biology, the speaker's own central nervous system. Once writing became phonetic it began its long cultural career as an art, as an act of creation, as something to be wondered at and studied. Writing began elbowing out an oral tradition wherein speaker and listener, teacher and student, message and receiver created a loop without the middleman to create further "noise." It weakened the human awareness of the *connection*, the symbiosis of language and brain. The very residency of language in the body could now be more easily forgotten. Language could now, like good Victorian children, be seen but not heard.

But along with this loss of the spoken word we have substituted four thousand years of compounded written Literature. It is our reservoir of support. It is our language anchor and the means to our own brains, our health and our survival. We must return to the notion that we are a story species. How are we helped as a species to pick our way gingerly but persistently through new experiences? How do we make the best use of past experiences? Help used to come from storytellers. The storyteller, sometimes balladeer, was valued before writing, as one of the most important, esteemed, honoured, sought after, and useful members of society. Through his skills and knowledge, the wisdom of the tribe, the news of the day, the best of the language itself was passed on. In most parts of the world today the storyteller has been replaced by the book, by reading. The storyteller spoke as one to many listeners. Now the individual reader seeks, among the thousands of voices from books that span time and space, for what interests her and what she needs. Fiction, or at least narrative, in print form, is the principle source available to us of translated experience in its most accessible form.

Many forces have combined over the last few thousand years to break down community and to isolate and alienate individuals. Communities and tightly bonded groups used to cultivate individual identity in their members, through the process of identification — "by my membership I know who I am." Now, we live in dense, mostly urban environments, our cultures and identities submerged into an undifferentiated mass of homogenized participants. We have become in the West, and especially in North America, a generic consumer culture. As a result, electronic media and advertising have supplanted most of the carefully preserved stories and traditions that the oral tradition kept alive.[23] Writing created huge benefits and many problems. We are in danger of missing the principle benefit and being destroyed by the problems. No one among the audiences of ancient storytellers doubted the importance of what they heard. They did not mistake the spoken stories for mere entertainment. They knew that they were learning valuable lessons of history, religion, medicine, parenting, morality and they felt, at some level in their central nervous systems, stronger for being members of a group, a tradition, a continuity. In other words, they were learning not only who the "people" were, but who they were, the listeners, as individuals.

The role of the oral, with its wisdom conveyed directly in spoken storied form, has been transferred to Literature. The trouble is, Literature is one more remove from the storyteller's voice. Literature can be taken for granted, left on the shelf. And reading Literature requires more active learning than listening. It is hard work. It requires educational commitment. But Literature matters. For having destroyed and then replaced the oral transmission of what we need to know, Literature now remains the great repository of the wisdom of the past, and *the* means to personal identity. We must be trained to understand and value our Literature, as our forebears were trained to survive in the bush, in the hunt and by means of the ordeals of coming of age. Our Literature is the most important aid we have in forming identity. If we ignore it, we risk living formless, disconnected lives, slave to every manipulative wind that blows, whirled about passively like a page of yesterday's newspaper on a dangerous street in the City of Zombies.

Notes to Chapter 2: Arithmetic, Writing and Reading

1. The Hebrew name for Adam is Adom, the name for red clay. There has always been a recognition in all cultures of the physiological connection between breathing and speaking, and therefore between life and language. A loss of breath prevents speech, and a certain level of energy is required to expel enough air to create speech sound. To give life to clay tablets is to write on them and so give them the power to speak.
2. Deacon, 1999.
3. See *Before Writing*, 1992.
4. There is also strong evidence that cereal carbohydrates are addictive.
5. I have recently seen a group of resourceful people erect a substantial shelter in an hour or two from saplings growing nearby. All necessary building materials were presumably available in ample supply to our ancient forebears, along with clean water, good hunting and fruits and berries. These people, for whom there is archeological but no written record, had perfect diet, good physical condition and few environmental toxins. They seem to have lived a lot longer than we do, in spite of large animal predators, who were clearly less dangerous than automobiles and smoking.
6. See reference in note 20.
7. Those who predicted from the 1970s the end of reading and books, strongly influenced by Marshall McLuhan and his love of television and Global Village imagery, have proved themselves wrong, or at least wildly premature. And even if we did stop reading we would still be a story species, albeit, without Literature, significantly handicapped. Our wings would be clipped. It should be remembered that I am not speaking of the book "thing" made of paper. That may go. It does not matter how the book may come to be represented. The paper or the screen or whatever is just a vehicle for the written language. I should add that so far nothing promises to come close to the efficiency, economy and portability of the book as we know it, whatever science fiction may predict.
8. These comments apply to Indo-European and Semitic languages. They do not apply to Chinese, which works in ideograms, a complex form of representation of objects, ideas and parts of speech, but not sounds. Perhaps Chinese psychology and Chinese Buddhism determined this way of writing thought and helped Chinese culture avoid the dissociation from the non-human that characterizes Western thought since writing.
9. See Gold, 1981.
10. This assertion that God and the Word are identical is the very essence of the shift from Judaism to Christianity. In this union lies the key to understanding the nature of Christian historicism and literalism.

11. I recall that the most distressing discovery I made from reading history as a youth was that in the third century A.D., the library of Alexandria, reckoned the greatest collection of manuscripts in the ancient world, was burned to the ground. It made me sick to think of that loss of information and it bothered me that no one but me seemed as shocked by it or grieved as I did. The Great Library of Alexandria "had been burnt in the Caesarian war, and the queen [Cleopatra] began a new collection which she attached to the Serapeum. Here for four hundred years was the most learned spot on the earth. The Christians wiped it out." The quotation is from E.M. Forster, *Alexandria.*
12. An excellent modern treatment of the Golem in the context of the post-Holocaust era is found in Mordecai Richler's *St. Urbain's Horseman.*
13. It is now possible to disseminate almost endless amounts of useless and unconnected information. It is also possible to reach more and more people with the same information, however inaccurate, partial or toxic it may be. And it is now virtually impossible to block out such "information."
14. Pennebaker, 1997.
15. Two examples are Vale Allen, *Daddy's Girl* and Danica, *Don't: A Woman's Word.*
16. The connection between language and taste organs is ancient. See for instance Ezekiel, 3:3, "So I opened my mouth and he gave me the scroll to eat.... Then I ate it; and it was in my mouth as sweet as honey." Jewish tradition has it that parents used to form letters of dough and bake them and coat them with honey as rewards for children learning their alphabet. I remember playing games with my children by identifying and naming pieces of Alphagetti when they ate it, and playing word games with the pasta letters.
17. This effect of seeing one's thoughts and feelings written down, expressed and made visible, has powerful consequences in human awareness, as in formal therapy, where journal making becomes an effective tool for increasing self-awareness. The sense of controlling thought and feeling is greatly enhanced by this act of creativity which enables the "reader" and "writer" parts of the journaler's brain to communicate, like writer and editor. Another benefit is that the therapist is greatly facilitated by joining the dialogue as a third party.
18. The next stage of consciousness must be the restoration of the connection to the rest of the natural world, if our survival is to be accomplished, a task that Wordsworth deliberately set himself.
19. In 1976 psychologist Julian Jaynes published a book on consciousness which claimed that in about 1200 BCE, humans, or some of them, became conscious because some sort of "catastrophe" initiated single-minded consciousness. Before this, people had "bicameral" minds. The "two brains," left and right hemispheres, were more separated than they are now, with the right telling the left what to do in the form of hallucinated divine instructions. As I explain in the text above, con-

sciousness did change, and revelation and number of gods did diminish, and history was altered, but because of the brain's invention of writing. I believe consciousness developed in stages along with brain changes, and a lot earlier than three thousand years ago. I cannot imagine the invention of writing without consciousness, an invention that Schmandt-Besserat places some 10,000 years ago. New forms of neural looping of thought developed from this along with a shift in consciousness.

The invention of writing was not an unmixed blessing on the species. It led to detachment from the natural world, the rise of capitalism and the secularization and cynicism of Christianity, which in turn led to the brutal genocide of non-literate peoples and the stealing of their goods and lands. It was the evolution of language specialization and social change that led to writing in the first place. The writing was then used to *explain* the "divine" origins of language after the fact. This is not proof that language and consciousness had not existed before writing. Neither writing nor anything else suddenly produced consciousness; it just expanded an existing consciousness and moved power from muscles and objects to language and communication.

This power shift has never been altered. We have to remind ourselves that language prior to this was limited to the same area of influence that a spear could be thrown. Language, voices became super-powerful, and eventually and very quickly travelled round the world, but only after the moment writing was invented and perceptually brain processed. The "word of god" became much widespread *after* writing than before, contrary to Jaynes's thesis. In fact, I think it can be argued that the last 3,000 years has shown a steady decline in human consciousness and that people are behaving more like automata than they once did. I envy Jaynes his sanguine view of modern humanity.

I trust Schmandt-Besserat's time frames more than those of Jaynes. But I do sympathize with Jaynes's unstated preoccupation: how can we explain the sudden and astonishing acceleration and shape of human history and the almost sudden shrinking of the planet in a mere 5,000 years, after millions of years of slow and painstaking evolution? My answer is that writing quickly and forever altered the human relationship with everything extrasomatic. It's not that amazing things were not going on in pre-history, it's just that there are no written minutes to summarize what they were and who said what. The historical record of the last 5,000 years hardly covers everything, but it makes it seem like a lot happened in a short time.

20. Racism is absurd in the face of human biology, in spite of various racist attempts to prove "scientific" grounds for practicing it. We can look to political and economic forces for explanations of our brutal and alienated history for the last four thousand years, but we will look in vain for a scientific explanation for the motivations for so much destruction and cruelty as we have recorded. The theft of continents; the practice of genocide; the destruction of our human and animal habitat; the tyranny

of the literal: all these suggest that humans have mastered the art of doublethink and are determined to lose touch with reality. See Ronald Wright, 1993.

21. Report on the work of Dr. Patricia Kuhl and others in *Science Times Book of the Brain*, p. 152.

22. Prominent brain researcher, Michael S. Gazzaniga and his colleagues, recently came to this conclusion: "That a lowly mouse can perceive perceptual groupings, whereas a human's left hemisphere cannot, suggests that a capacity has been lost. Could it be that the emergency of a human capacity like language — or an interpretive mechanism — chased this perceptual skill (found in mice) out of the left brain? We think so, and this opinion gives rise to a fresh way of thinking about the origins of lateral specialization." *Book of the Brain*, pp. 137-138. This gives new meaning to the question: "Are you a man or a mouse?"

23. See my chapter on Media and also Klein, 2000.

Chapter Three

"I" Openers – The Word is Your Oyster

Language may not be the source of the self, but it is certainly the source of the "I."

—Antonio Damasio

Philosophers, even as far back as Aristotle, used to think that humans were born knowing nothing, their minds blank, what they called a *tabula rasa*, or "clean slate." On that slate would be written everything the person would learn, until he or she died. We now have plenty of evidence for believing that a human is born with considerable amounts of information. At birth, for instance, we can distinguish human voices from other sounds, even mother's voice from other voices. We know how to suck; we can distinguish what tastes good from what doesn't; we can cry and make sounds that send signals. We very soon know how to grasp with our fingers. We can distinguish light and visual patterns and move our eyes to find sources of sound, at least very soon after the shock of birth. What we don't have at birth, though, is experience, or very little of it, there being not much experience gathering in the womb where our senses are not required for growth, and we are cocooned from experience by layers of insulation.

But no sooner do we experience the separation of birth than we begin learning the world. We take in information and convert it into a personal construct, the "I." This "I" is given a name, and this name becomes the title of a book that each of us will write for the rest of our lives.

The self is the individual's arrangement of cells with all their genetic programs, predispositions, strengths and weaknesses, skin, eye and hair colours, gender, height potential, immune systems and so on. Life experience may modify some of this. Nutrition, for instance, or air quality or injury can effect the genetic potential. Basically, though, some things are in the cards dealt from birth. Exceptional creative talent — in visual or plastic arts, language arts, or mathematics for instance — is certainly evidence of a pre-set arrangement of brain preferences. But given all this, once we appear on the world scene, environment, and especially language environment, start to shape who we are. What good old mom and dad think and say about religion, politics, the people next door, and assorted races and foreigners is almost certainly what we are going to think and say for a very long time, often for life.

When we come to the formation of the "I," we have moved to a level of information processing that leads to the construction of who we are in relation to the world. A non-narrative organism might experience a moment-by-moment set of disconnected responses to sensory data. A human story creature constructs out of such data a story model of itself as an active, aware, influential, choosing, recording, planning, organizing and aware-of-feeling "I."[1] The "I" is a combination of the self and language, language used to construct a running record of personal experience that creates identity. We can't do much about the self our ancestors passed on to us, but we can do a lot about our language and the stories we shape from it.[2] We can become aware, for a start, that we are story creatures and make everything including ourselves into stories that we then live by. The only freedom from being captive inside a story, like a Genie in a bottle, is the knowledge that it is a story — and it can be changed. The realization that we are a story species is the most liberating knowledge of all.

How do children acquire language? How can they learn it so quickly and effectively? Why are children better at learning more new or foreign languages than adults? We know all too well how hard it is to learn a new language as we grow older. What gives children this advantage?

The attempt to answer these questions has led to a long and heated debate. One of the "big names" in this controversy, Noam Chomsky, argued that humans are already pre-wired with the rules of grammar, grammar being so complex that young children could not possibly learn it as they do from scratch, for children don't just mimic words (like parrots), they quickly learn to speak in grammatical sentences. To read a skillful objection to Chomsky's theory you will have to turn to Terrence Deacon who says that children learn by trial and error. Children are continually corrected and rewarded for grammatical correctness by adults. Many other linguists and psychologists have participated in this academic fray. I suspect there is a partial or kind of truth in all these learned arguments. Clearly, humans have some language readiness in their brains and just as clearly they have some deeply vested interest in getting the language right enough to be understood by those who are teaching them — those who have power over them and control the food stores, along with the rewards and punishments, praise and humiliation.

What strikes me as most plausible however, is that learning joins with genetics to generate the child's facility with language. I enter this debate, not as a neurolinguist or a grammarian, but as a student of Literature and a family therapist. Neonates, "newborns," arrive with incomplete brains. The weight of the newborn's brain is one-fourth of what it will weigh when full-grown. And yet this growth will not take place in neurons, the billions of minute information terminals of the brain, but in the neural pathways, the wiring, the linkages connecting neurons. These come to number thousands attached to each neuron in the adult brain. The growth then is not in the number of information containers but in the assembly power for organizing and recombining information, as well as in the routing, transmission and exchanging of new information.

Now the most interesting thing about this brain growth is that it takes place in the world outside the womb, in the world where information is being received by the human organism at a steady and unrelenting pace. This information is sent for processing to brains as they are forming. In other words, human brains are experience dependent and form in the human body *as they learn.*

Deacon's idea of the symbiotic co-evolution of the brain and language can help us here. He proposes a kind of circular evolution for the brain as language processor, by which the brain generates some language which proves so advantageous that the brain biases its evolution toward more language-making tissue, which in turn produces more language, which in turn continues this process. We now know that brains in modern humans do a lot of their growing as language processors. There is no reason why Deacon's theory should not apply equally well to modern infants as they learn language and come to recognize the social power language confers. The child who is nurtured in a language-rich environment will presumably "grow" its brain with active and enriched language centres. The evidence is clear that the years from birth to six, especially prior to the age of four, are critical to language learning and literacy skills in later years. Brain and language foster each other's development in a symbiotic collusion. There is not much point, or much justice, in blaming teachers for a failure of schoolchildren to read, write and speak effectively when children do not start school until after the critical language learning period is over.

As the newborn quickly discovers, the most important information to be learned in the world is received in the form of language. Most interactions between speaking people and the infant are attended by language, so the child learns to babble and learns what a rattle is long before it can say "rattle." Likewise, the child learns its own name long before it understands the use of the "I" pronoun. Though it refers to itself by name in the third person, it is still very conscious of being an active agent in its own survival. "Debbie want cookie," or "Me hungry" work well enough. Being fed and given attention become at once associated with its own name, its presence and reality as a sentient being, with identifying features. Food and comfort also get associated with names Mama or Dada. Since the neural pathways are forming even as the language is being learned, it seems safe to conjecture that language is shaping the brain and teaching it how to function linguistically — within this language dominated world.

The great English artist and poet, William Blake, wrote two small poems that illustrate a number of these points forcefully. Below he portrays two newborns and their birth receptions:

Infant Joy
"I have no name,
I am but two days old."
What shall I call thee?
"I happy am,
Joy is my name."
Sweet joy befall thee!

Pretty joy!
Sweet joy but two days old,
Sweet joy I call thee:
Thou dost smile,
I sing the while,
Sweet joy befall thee!

Infant Sorrow
My mother groan'd! my father wept.
Into the dangerous world I leapt:
Helpless, naked, piping loud:
Like a fiend hid in a cloud.

Struggling in my father's hands,
Striving against my swaddling bands,
Bound and weary I thought best
To sulk upon my mother's breast.

These birth stories reinforce several ideas I am trying to convey. First, identity begins at birth, not because of what the human child brings with her, but in response to the environment and reception accorded her. Second, language plays no small part in producing infant joy — this baby is welcome and is told so in very clear and oft repeated terms. She starts life feeling good about herself. In contrast, Sorrow is not welcome and, meeting animal sounds and human tears, not language, this child begins to form the self-image of the unwanted child that, "hid in the cloud" of its life, will later be miserable and so become dysfunctional, perhaps even criminal. Legislators, criminologists, and all those who want to punish the population of "Infant Sorrows" we daily deal with, should start their training with a course of study in Blake.[3]

Brains grow in a language environment. Many have wondered whether children would speak spontaneously in the absence of adult modelling. The very scarce evidence for answering this question suggests drastic mental and linguistic deficits in the absence of language nurturing. King Frederick II, Emperor of Germany, conducted his own experiment in the thirteenth century. He ordered a number of foster mothers and nurses to suckle and attend to infants, but otherwise never to speak to them. He wanted to know which language they would speak when it came time for them to talk. Unfortunately, the experiment was never completed: all the infants died "for they could not live without the petting and joyful faces and loving words of their foster mothers."[4] The most famous case of a language deprived child who appeared otherwise neurologically normal was the Wild Boy of Averyon. It is believed that this child grew up in the forests of southern France. He appeared in 1880 when captured like a wild animal at the supposed age of twelve or thirteen. Thereafter he was held captive and "taught" language but never learned to speak.[5] The other case that is widely cited is the story of Genie, who was raised by her father as a dog from the time she was twenty months to the age of thirteen years. Although various remedial efforts were made to teach her to speak, she never managed to master simple grammar.[6]

Once we know that brains are still growing continuously as grammatical language is "radiated" at and around them most of the time, and almost all the time they are awake, I believe the need for controversial theories fades. Brains form in an environment to which they adapt, adaptation being the key to human development and survival. Since they will have to function in a language environment, it seems evolutionary fitting that children should do seventy-five percent of their brain formation taking that environment into account. Language shapes the growth of the brain the way yeast acts to shape bread. Like the yeast in a loaf, language becomes indistinguishable from the brain that incorporates it in its growth.

So we begin to see how the individual *is* his or her language. So it is that professional writers convey distinct voices that can be detected by practiced readers without knowing the author's name. Only damage to the cortex itself will diminish the activity and transmission of language, but then such damage will alter many other aspects of the individual and make him into a "different person."

Now since language helps form the brain after birth, it should follow that the more language being transacted around the new brain, the more language will be produced as part of the forming brain; conversely, a scarcity of language heard will diminish the amount of language learned. Silence produces silence. Nothing will come of nothing. Birds whose mothers don't teach them to sing, don't sing. It now becomes clear to us that the primary advantage of talking to children (not yelling at them), and reading to them, is the teaching of grammatical language, words, sentences, expression, intonation, accent, inflection and reflection. (Of course, talking also teaches ideas, order, conversation, dialogue, social behaviours, attentive listening, and narrative formation, but more of this in the next chapter.)

In spite of the genetic past, and the tremendous shaping power of the present, we are not merely passive dough in the hands of impersonal forces. By means of language, and the identity it helps form, we can acquire a significant degree of freedom, independence and individuality. With the first word learned we begin to realize a sense of our individual power. By virtue of our own language-self, each of us shapes and creates our own personal world. For one thing, the two forces of past and present interact with such complexity that they produce individual uniqueness. This is achieved by different parts of the brain joining forces, so that the one part that has processed and recorded past information is called into action to compare, sift and organize new information.

Both past and present experience combine into information that is recursively embedded in the ever forming "I" (recursively meaning a recurring pattern with special properties).[7] Human brains make Russian stacking dolls. They add clauses to sentences in great number without violating rules of grammar or violating sense. Both these activities are recursive.

Imagine that two of us form a club. We have two rules. One is all members of the club must agree on who can be a new member. The second is that each new member must go and find another to join, subject of course to rule one. Now the addition of each member is governed by the same two rules, and as each member passes the screening test, the club changes by virtue of its increasing membership and the different personalities that have been added. Also, the screening process gets more rigorous and more difficult to administer. This is analogous to what happens when we screen new information to test its fit with the "I" we are forming. New information must join with the old. In the process, the whole "I" package is modified to accommodate the new information. The "I" grows but must stay consistent with the "I" being formed. While the old information shifts, the new information is more rigorously sifted according to its suitability. The requirement is that this multitude of information must be integrated into the brain of the individual so that he can operate as though instructed by a single command centre, *of his own making.*

Reading Literature constitutes a very efficient behaviour for acquiring experience. It is of course relatively risk free and energy saving. More importantly, reading story as experience is to realize experience imaginatively, in a pre-formed, pre-managed package. Literature is peculiarly suited for integration into the "I" formation by virtue of its story format, which is congenial to the brain's need to assemble experience material into story form anyway. Literature is akin to an experience kit, ready to assemble and adapt in order to augment the reader's own mental "I" structure.

This nonstop, "I"-forming action also gives clues as to why we cling so tenaciously to our hold on who we are and what we think. We have invested vast effort and time, we have founded a great deal of our life choices on the results of these efforts, and we have come to rely on the "I" we have formed to take us forward. We have made thousands of choices. Some of these choices are actions, but the most important are beliefs. At this point in the history of our species, I don't think we are going to be able to afford any more *unexamined* beliefs. In the encounter between the self and the world, the "I" is created out of necessity, out of the need to adapt, to be effective. Success for human identity is really success at adaptation.

In the realm of acquired information we have the choice to make influential and significant changes to who we are, how we behave, what we think and believe and how we manage our lives, including our mental and physical health. Please note that I am not saying we always exercise these choices. For various reasons lots of people just don't bother. They don't want to change or they don't want to work at it. But everyone has the potential to change and acquiring language by reading story is the most powerful method for assisting change. It is true that even without conscious effort, humans are going to get some form of an "I" simply by processing unique experiences by means of their own unique genetic arrangements. Animals have selves, and no two dogs are identical. But human beings have "I's" that form in a world where experience is mediated by language, and this alone should tell us that language is a means for controlling experience and therefore our identities. And language is something we can cultivate — or neglect. The popularity of animal stories is instructive when we see how animals must be given an "I," a recognizable character, a language, history and a set of beliefs, attitudes and plans for action. Readers do not want a scientific treatise on the life of the otter. They want an "I" they can identify with, like Tarka. They want an animal person. Consider the body of work by Charles G.D. Roberts, a modern pioneer of the animal genre of fiction, and the novels *Watership Down* and *The Plague Dogs* by Richard Adams. Here animals think in human language and even speak such language. Where they don't behave like this we get stories like *The Red Pony* (John Steinbeck) or *Black Beauty* (Anna Sewell), which are less about animals than about their owners, or at least relations between the two.

So humans form an "I," but how do they do it? What are the structural pieces that form the jigsaw of the "I" story? Oliver Sacks, the noted brain specialist, gives us his view:

> We have, each of us, a life-story, an inner narrative whose continuity, whose sense, is our lives. It might be said that each of us constructs and lives a "narrative," and that this narrative is us, our identities. If we wish to know about a man, we ask "what is his story — his real, inmost story?" — for each of us is a biography, a story. Each of us is a singular narrative, which is constructed, continually, unconsciously, by, through, and in us— through our perceptions, our feelings, our thoughts, our actions; and, not least, our discourse, our spoken narrations. Biologically, physiologically, we are not so different from each other; historically, as narratives — we are each of us unique.[8]

"Not least, our discourse, our spoken narrations," and I would add to this that we are also very much a product of our written narratives, and those of other people we read. Our fascination, no, our compulsive attraction to other people's stories, is explained by our need to use these stories to structure our own identity. That we face an identity crisis in our culture is evidenced by the cult of celebrity, the fascination with other people's lives that function as substitutes for our own (see Chapter 8). Thinking, feeling and examining our own lives, minds, behaviours, aided by reading Literature, plays very little part with an increasing number of people.

The "I" is our living, breathing, ever changing autobiography, the story of our lives. What we need to learn is that we can actively participate in the construction of this narrative of who we are. In composing this story each of us is inescapably an author and each creates the one living "book" that is our guide to everything. This guide gets "written" by taking in information assimilated by all our senses and converting it into a complex language code by our brains. This code is sequenced into stories of incidents, experiences, and responses involving both emotion and rational thought. Feeling and thought are in turn woven into a larger running narrative that creates identity, a composite account of the thoughts and feelings that become a filter through which we see all new experience. We come to rely on the stability of this filter. We count on the fact that we will wake up each morning with this narrative intact. A serious violation of this structure, as in the case of violent trauma, is a source of horror to human imagination. Nothing is more frightening than trying to imagine the loss of this "I." The gradual erosion of the "I" is basically the process we witness in progressive Alzheimer's disease.

Many writers have played with the loss of "I." Franz Kafka turned one of his characters into a cockroach who views his family from the corner of a room. Dorian Gray was given a double "I," his depraved secret self gradually unveiled as he furtively looks at his own beautiful portrait. Hamlet is driven to the edge of madness and assumes a false "I" when he discovers his father has been murdered by the uncle who has usurped the throne. Dimmesdale, in Hawthorne's *Scarlet Letter*, is driven to his death by his refusal to integrate his adultery and desire into the story of his public persona. On the political front, Orwell's *1984* tells us that the real goal of the totalitarian state is to destroy individual identity so that it can be replaced by the language and beliefs of the State. The real life experiences of political prisoners and concentration camp survivors is grim testimony to the reality of this struggle for identity survival. When individual identity is gone, our enemies have effectively eliminated who we are, our consciousness. So writers, if we will read them, help us understand the necessity for taking the construction of our narrative seriously.[9]

We refer to this narrative construction, this brain-book we continuously write for thoughts, comparisons, beliefs, responses, tastes, and feelings. There are smells that we like or dislike, sounds that alarm or soothe us, textures that are pleasing or disturbing and sensations that we welcome or avoid. All of these are rooted in experience. All can change or be changed by new experience, if we are willing to encounter it by new insight or new information. They are also changed by aging and reorganization. But all of this new material must be integrated into the existing narrative, even if it means changing the narrative. Our well-being depends on this integration. And this integration depends in turn on our being aware of the shape, and sources, of the existing narrative and the impact on it from new information. Reading is the best *tool of consciousness* for assisting this process.

It should now be possible to see that language is part of the actual formation of the individual brain, and by means of language the "I" experiences its early sense of power. This power is the growing ability of the "I" to manage, control, change and where necessary, to adapt to its environment, and in so doing take care of itself. Language in children quickly replaces crying as the means to getting help. With words the child will command adults. Calling "Mama" can summon her from some invisible world, like the power of a magician to call up invisible spirits in fantasy Literature.[10] Language, its questions, answers and arguments, feeds back to the "I," to the knowledge of its own reality, its ability and its influence.

We can learn a lot about the relationship of language, "I" formation and the world of the "not-I" by returning to the instructive and remarkable story of Helen Keller. Born in 1880 in Alabama, she suffered an infection that left her at nineteen months both deaf and sightless. For the next five and a half years she lived in darkness and silence. Her world was apprehended only by feel and touch, by vibrations as doors closed, by sun and wind on her skin, by pure sensation. As she grew so too did her frustration.

Her behaviour was rapidly deteriorating. Crying, hysterical, violent outbursts that left her exhausted were occurring several times a day. Fortunately for Helen, and for us, her parents had enough love and sufficient means to seek what help was available. Just before Helen turned seven, Anne Sullivan came to live at the Keller home to tutor the child. Annie, as she came to be called, taught Helen words by spelling them into her hand with finger touch. While Helen could repeat this process she had no real sense of what the words meant. They triggered in her mind no accompanying imagery or representation of the world they described. What follows is one of the most famous passages in biographical literature — a description of nothing less than the dawning of consciousness.

Helen describes the moment when language crossed the threshold between the "I" and the world. For most of us this experience is so gradual that we could never pinpoint when it happened, but for Helen Keller it was indeed a moment, an incident, that she was to recall in her autobiography, written fifteen years later when she was a student at Radcliffe College. Annie has been trying to teach Helen the word "water." Helen has learned the word, but she has no concept of its referent in her brain — she can't make the connection between the word and the thing to which it refers:

> We walked down the path to the well-house, attracted by the fragrance of the honeysuckle with which it was covered. Some one was drawing water and my teacher placed my hand under the spout. As the cool stream gushed over one hand she spelled into the other the word water, first slowly, then rapidly. I stood still, my whole attention fixed upon the motions of her fingers. Suddenly I felt a misty consciousness as of something forgotten — a thrill of returning thought; and somehow the mystery of language was revealed to me. I knew then that "w-a-t-e-r" meant the wonderful cool something that was flowing over my hand. That living word awakened my soul, gave it light, hope, joy, set it free! There were

> barriers still, it is true, but barriers that could in time be swept away.[11]

This passage never fails to move me with its momentous consequences for little Helen. Reading this unique experience is like watching her change from a tormented animal into a human being. I quote it here, however, to illustrate a crucial point about language and the formation of an individual. The quality of coming awake, of thought and feeling coming alive, of the sense that "I" am knowing, feeling, registering sensation and am present in the world — all this is the beginning of identity. Immediately following this catalytic moment, Helen returns to the house:

> I remembered the doll I had broken. I felt my way to the hearth and picked up the pieces. I tried vainly to put them together. Then my eyes filled with tears; for *I realized what I had done*, and for the first time I felt repentance and sorrow. [My italics]

Looked at neurologically, her teacher has hit upon a remarkable experiment. Ms. Keller does not say which hand was under the water and which was receiving the word but I am going to guess. By placing Helen's left hand under the water and spelling the name into her right hand, the hand controlled by the left language hemisphere of her brain (we call this contralateral meaning on the opposite side, assuming the child was right-handed and not ipsilateral or same side, which is rare), her teacher activated massive connections across the corpus callosum connecting the two sides of the brain, so that space, sensation and language were united. The two hemispheres of Helen's brain could now work together, one supplying raw data (the feel of the water), and the other registering the word code and interpreting the finger spelling as a sign, a name for water-feel. Her left brain was calling into activity an area known as Wernicke's area, after the German physician Karl Wernicke who worked with brain-damaged patients and identified the speech reception area in 1874. It is now clear through fMRIs and PET scans that no matter how the words are transmitted, visually, orally or tactually, they will finish up at the Wernicke area for processing.

With the neural connection now active for Helen, the connection between words and non-verbal sensory experience becomes clear. Now she understands how the process of joining language to experience works. Henceforth she will look for that "kinship with the rest of the world" as she later calls it, between her "I" and the "not-I" that will inform the rest of her life. But as she points out, now that her brain information is explosively re-routed, she will also experience many feelings that accompany actions, she will "realize what she has done" as felt emotion, regret, sadness, joy or guilt. Now she can build up a store of words so organized as to form a mental representation of the world, and her associations with it. Now she can learn to read and with the help of Braille she goes on to become a scholar, a published writer and a wise philosopher. I invite you to consider what would have become of Helen Keller had "dear Annie" not managed to break through the silence and isolation with the word "water," and then to think about the role of language that we take for granted in the lives of the rest of us, who live without language disability. Shouldn't the Helen Keller story, with appropriate commentary on it, be part of every teacher's education?

Listening to a story, a hearing child is still faced with learning challenges and must decode the words into meaningful syntax and images. This passage from *The Wizard of Oz* will help us understand what happens to a child when she hears a story.

> While Dorothy was looking earnestly into the queer, painted face of the Scarecrow, she was surprised to see one of the eyes slowly wink at her. She thought she must have been mistaken at first, for none of the scarecrows in Kansas ever wink; but presently the figure nodded its head to her in a friendly

> way. Then she climbed down from the fence and walked up to it, while Toto ran around the pole and barked. "Good day," said the Scarecrow, in a rather husky voice. "Did you speak?" asked the girl, in wonder. "Certainly," answered the Scarecrow. "How do you do?" "I'm pretty well, thank you," replied Dorothy, politely, "How do you do?"

First the listening child must decode the words into grammatical units, while at the same time assign meaning to them. If there are words not understood, not known, they must be translated by the reader, using analogies from the child's existing experience. For instance, if the child does not know "earnestly" the reader must demonstrate. In the case of "scarecrow" there may be a book picture to help, but in the twenty-first century an explanation of old farm practices will be necessary. Pictures, along with words, increase the child's vocabulary and become part of the child's real life experience. For most of the text the listener must produce her own mental pictures and feelings stored in brain and body. The sequence of the text events produces narrative so the child learns how a story is made. Since the child is required to form a life story in her brain, this skill takes on importance. To imagine the scene and the conversation, the child must identify with the speaker, or principal actor, and in so doing adds to the construction of her own identity. Dorothy, and indeed the entire novel, will become part of the child's mental landscape, a reference point, in confronting new experiences.[12]

It is not a very big move from having books read to you, to wanting to read them for yourself. All independence feels empowering. Reading for yourself is a big step in growing up. It is part of taking over some power from parents.[13] Now the magic can be made when you want, and with the materials you require. The "word" is your oyster. At this point the "I" takes a huge leap in its formation. Not only is the power to decode text, use a dictionary, go to the library extremely reinforcing to the sense of "I" as controller, but by consulting the self, the "I" can pursue those interests that lead to growth in its areas of strength. The "I" starts to specialize. Escape from narrow mental confines is possible. Travel and adventure are possible. Social skills can be learned. By the time adolescence is reached the "I" is well on its way to formation, but it will never be so fixed that it cannot be changed. Indeed, life events, joys and sorrows will ensure that it changes, modifies, refines and hones itself, adapts itself to new experiences, not the least of which will be marriage and adaptation to another and very different "I" — and, of course, the formation of a new family. Woe betide the marriage where the "I's" of the partners don't or won't change. In every instance, and at every stage, be it a crossroads or merely a milestone, reading Literature can be an instrumental help.

The formation of identity is an integrating process and it assumes a story form in human brains. Stories are the word shapes that brains make to assemble and integrate information. For some collections of information these stories are called models or theories. In encountering the moment-to-moment impressions of life experience, a human story creature is equipped with a very highly evolved battery of receptors. A large part of this equipment is emotional. We experience a great deal of emotional sensation that we identify as "feeling" and to which we try to apply meaning. There is however a lot of cultural and social interference — or "noise" as it is called in communication theory — designed to relegate emotion to some forbidden realm of mystery. But a well-integrated identity must take account of and accommodate its emotional experience. Literature, born from the process of integrating thought and emotion, can be important to readers who can use it to assist their own such integration.

NOTES TO CHAPTER 3: "I" OPENERS — THE WORD IS YOUR OYSTER

1. For one neuroscientist's recent attempt to describe the brain's role in this process see Damasio, *The Feeling of What Happens.* He does not of course address the role of Literature in the process.

2. I am making a distinction here between the self as the genetic composition of the individual, with all its predispositions, strengths, weaknesses, and physical characteristics, and the "I" as a composite of learned responses to environment. In this learning of the world, language plays an indispensable role, and through language we learn beliefs, attitudes, and the quality of relations. In computer terms we might see the self as hardware, and the "I" as software. This is only a crude analogy of course, given the infinite variability and complexity of the organism.

3. In North America there is no educational, intelligence, or moral test for running for public office.

4. Cited in *Parabola,* Vol. 17, no. 3, 1992, p. 6. From *A Portable Medieval Reader,* NY. Viking, 1949, p. 366, ff.

5. Shattuk, 1980.

6. Cited by Corballis, 1991.

7. Recursion is discussed at length in Hofstadter, 1979, esp. pp. 131-135.

8. Sacks, p.105

9. Two classics of modern literature that describe surviving this assault on identity are *Darkness at Noon* by Arthur Koestler, and *Prisoner Without a Name, Cell Without a Number*, by Jacobo Timerman.

10. I am reminded of the pithy exchange between Hotspur and Glendower in Shakespeare's *Henry IV,* Part 1, Act 3, sc. 1: *Glendower*: I can call spirits from the vasty deep. *Hotspur*: Aye, so can I, or so can any man, but will they come when you do call for them?

    Any child can do better magic than Glendower by yelling "Mama."

11. Keller, p.18.

12. The construction of an adaptive, functional identity ought to be much more prominent in psychotherapy than it is. The therapist would then function as an editor to the writing of the patient's story. Literature has a major role to play in this process, as I mentioned in my earlier book, and *The Wizard of Oz* is one of the most useful texts. It speaks to many women through Dorothy and her friends about endurance, courage, self-reliance and assertiveness. It illustrates to adult readers that they have power they have not realized and can tap into it (Dorothy's magic shoes). First the reader can be in Dorothy's shoes, then in her own shoes. Real life experience

often results in an “I” that is not working well. If a person has grown up with rejections, insults, abuse, failure, any of the endless and repetitive forms of negative feedback, she incorporates this learning as part of the “I,” so the “I” comes to view itself as inadequate, unattractive and useless. It can be very difficult to change this self-view. It is the therapist’s job to help the “I” change, precisely because some “not-I,” the therapist, is outside the patient’s world and can look in on it and see how it handicaps her.

13. I venture to suggest that children who read a lot of fiction will have much more success in leaving home, becoming emotionally independent, and coping with the world on their own. I am unaware of any research to confirm this and it would require lengthy follow-up studies, but if and when it comes I predict it will show the results I am claiming here.

PART TWO

Process

Chapter Four

That Inward Eye: The Emotional Reader

I gazed — and gazed — but little thought
What wealth the show to me had brought;
For oft, when on my couch I lie
In vacant or in pensive mood,
They flash upon that inward eye
Which is the bliss of solitude;
And then my heart with pleasure fills,
And dances with the daffodils.

— **William Wordsworth**

Among the many recent and exciting insights into the workings of the brain and of that larger awareness of ourselves that we call mind, none are more significant than those that relate to emotion. Information about where emotion originates, how it functions to affect our thinking, and how it is central to human memory, decision making and belief continues to grow, confirming what poets and lovers always knew: emotion is an integral, essential, inextricable part of the process of human thought and human survival.

The biochemistry of emotion is located in the brain, but connected to our viscera, gut feelings, so our bodies know and register emotion that the brain can identify. Emotion constitutes a primary filter for sensory data that we record or register from the outside, not-us world. Emotion is the watchdog over the junkyards of our mental accumulation of random information; but it does its barking so quietly and quickly that we are not even aware of most of what we filter — those emotional checks and balances — unless we are paying very close and practiced attention. If we really don't experience *any* emotion, then the information is not affecting us in a personal way and is not connecting to memory of past experience. This tells us that even the absence of emotion provides important information to our moment-to-moment life management. The presence of emotion increases our attention to various degrees, from mild pleasure or interest, such as I felt this week when I saw the first of my tomatoes in the garden turning red, across the spectrum to panic, if I let myself dwell on my failure to meet yet another publisher's deadline. We need to know that emotion provides us with information crucial to our well-being, and we need to learn to pay attention to it as part of our thinking apparatus. We need to become aware that emotion is laid down in memory and helps us record what pleases or frightens. Emotion guides and shapes the stories of our lives, the organization of our experience, and the choices that we make. We need to know that the control centres for emotion, like other parts of the brain, are connected to everything else about us.

Arousing emotion along with thought is the real goal of good fiction and poetry. Avoiding the arousal of emotion may, on the contrary, be the aim of most scientific articles or academic writing, because such writing is meant to convey a depersonalized version of "the truth." But artists like Charles Dickens, George Eliot, Jane Austen, Shakespeare, Tolstoy, Walter Scott, William Faulkner — in fact all the great and not so great writers — regard the evocation of emotion in readers as their highest achievement. Whether it is anxiety (suspense), pity, fear, happiness, curiosity, anger, or sadness that the reader feels, these emotions are what engage and recompense the reader for the effort of reading.

Why is emotion so important to the act of reading? How does it add to the value of what we read? How can we enhance the usefulness of the emotion we experience? "Emotions are not a luxury," we are told by Antonio Damasio, a prominent professor of neurology and author of *Descartes' Error*, an influential book on emotion and reason. What he means is that emotion is a crucial part of the human brain's thinking process, or perhaps more accurately, its knowing or feeling process. Feeling may be regarded as awareness of emotional states. Feeling is emotion that has been registered at a higher level of consciousness. I have felt fear many times but have only known I felt it after the experience. Emotions or affects are very hard to describe because they occur at such basic levels of our central nervous system. Describing the feelings that follow recognition of emotional response requires considerable language sophistication. People often find it easier to simply deny their emotions entirely. In terms of identity, balance, health and relationships, it becomes crucial to be able to both acknowledge and describe how we feel. Emotions like fear, anger and joy, and the feelings that accompany them, are powerful sources of information that can tell us about who we are, what we believe, and what we think can heal or hurt us. Emotions shape and alter our behaviour and affect our responses to future experience.

Because emotion has been so elusive, and far from words, it has been ignored as a subject of scientific inquiry until only quite recently. Emotions are neural processes, not organs, and use pathways and networks in the brain that are not reserved exclusively for them, much as various vehicles with different destinations use the same roads, or some use different roads to get to the same destination, and yet all might be part of the same car rally. I mean that along with our beliefs, values, life experiences, and factual information, emotions are essential to the management of our lives and steer us through countless interactions with our environment. Emotions are thus a vast extension of thinking ability, and deliberately complicate what we know about our relations with the world, in the hope of giving us the best possible outcomes.

There is a long history of hostility to emotion in the West. Plato preferred philosophers to poets because they avoided emotion and appeared, at least, to work only in the realm of thought. The reason for this lay in the language used.[1] Poets and playwrights delighted in words that aroused emotion. Aristotle noted this and approved. But in the West, there has been a long bias toward reason. Reason was male, emotion female. Reason was the voice of God in Man, and using reason would lead to God. Emotion leads astray, to Sin, to the irrational and failures of duty, and so to corruption. Love, passion, has been the most suspect of all emotions, and is regarded as central to the Fall of Man in Christian readings of Hebrew Scripture.

But emotion also leads to compassion, empathy, self-knowledge, affection and imagination. It is interesting to note that in political culture, reason has been the darling of those that advocate the greatest degree of self-interest and have the least faith in compassion and empathy. We have been urged to ignore our emotions as misleading. The celebration of reason and the dismissal of emotion can, and has lead to strategies aimed at mind manipulation and thought control. People are persuaded to believe arguments from their churches, governments, and places of employment that their own feelings directly contradict. The denial of emotional "truth" is a big part of the social and economic chaos growing around us. Compassion, the most important of all emotions, and compassionate government that would result from compassionate public policy, have all but disappeared from official public policy in North American society.

Yet reason and emotion are not at war. They are not even located in different parts of the body, but in fact are forever working together in an interactive neural system to help us survive. Thought and emotion combine in a systemic organic balance to produce a well-regulated person that can think. Such a person uses thought and emotion in a cycle, thought leading to emotion and emotion leading to thought.[2] Such a system produces a double check on the individual's responses to the environment. It makes possible a multi-variant analysis of the best and most productive responses. The combined neural estimate of what is going on, and what to do about it, has a better chance of accurately sorting the data and leading to higher success rates than the use of only one type of analysis and reference. The emotion part of our brains is thought to be much older in evolution than the thinking part, more related to our animal instincts and buried deeper in our brains than the immensely complex cortex systems

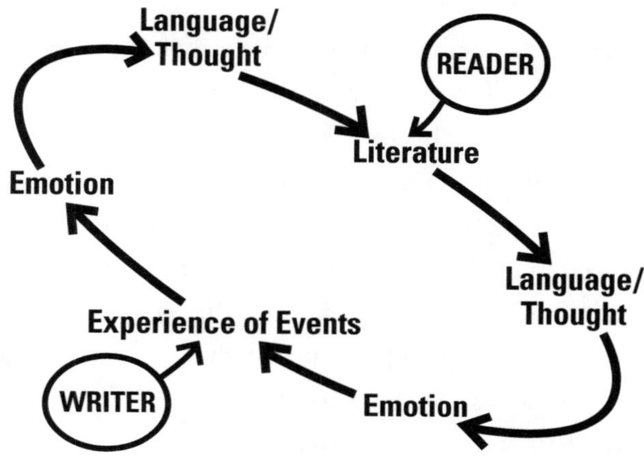

The Relations of Reader and Writer on a Cycle of Experience and Language

that evolved later and gave us our brain size. Fear, anger, joy, curiosity we readily recognize in our doggy friends. We are less able to identify them in ourselves. The better we get at paying attention to emotion, the more highly developed we will be as coping individuals successfully dealing with a variety of situations. In other words, emotion is part of our thinking and can be used to enhance our adaptation and survival.

Because the emotional centres are situated beneath the cortex, and joined to the cortex by a complex pattern of pathways, the brain can be said to have a vertical structure as well as a side-to-side, right-and-left connection. It is now clear that this entire structure operates as a single information processor when it is healthy and functioning normally. We might have assumed, you would think, that the unity of the human brain would have been obvious, given its slow evolution over millions of years. It seems intuitive to believe that as thought and language organs grow over time they would build upon the essential emotional guides to environment that preceded them. What has interfered with this "natural" view of the brain's functioning is the politics of reason; the bias of Western religion to rules, laws and writing rather than ritual; our alienation from the natural world;

and the *Homo*-centric determination to see people as a non-animal species, when in fact we are animals, animals who make stories and live inside them. The split between reason and emotion is an example of the dualism of Western thinking which I treat in the next chapter.

We can hardly imagine a creature that is all reason, unless it be a robot, an android, a computer. And a person who is all emotion would be seriously psychotic and would have to be restrained or sedated. Yet for hundreds of years, at least, we have tried to keep these aspects of our humanity separated, relegating emotion to the dark underworld of our forbidden "animal" selves. Nothing could be more irrational. Not even science — with its much touted neutrality and courage "to boldly go where none has gone before" — has been immune to the social prejudice. Emotion has been the Cinderella of cognitive science. Only recently have serious researchers turned their attention to it as worthy of investigation.[3] This research and its conclusions have not yet entered into popular consciousness.

Children are for the most part still not raised to respect their own emotions or to screen emotional response for information that can be used to help make decisions. We still don't have a good language for the discussion of emotion. And emotional response to science, art or data in general is not encouraged.

Many of my patients bring stories that illustrate the repression of emotion in their family life. One patient told me she was not even allowed to grieve at her grandfather's death. We are taught that curiosity killed the cat. Boys who are afraid are sissies. Anger is wicked and we must love and forgive everybody. Sadness shows ingratitude for what we have. I have heard all of these in my office time and time again. What happens to all this unexpressed, unrealized, unacknowledged emotion? It becomes toxic. It can turn into depression. It can turn into violence. It impairs our thinking. It damages our powers of discernment and judgment. It limits the effectiveness of our behaviour and action. It puts us in conflict with ourselves and our situations. It makes us unhappy. And of course unacknowledged emotions cannot be processed and resolved because they are not supposed to be there.

Novels and poems provide a two-stranded connection of thought and emotion between writer and reader. The writer of interesting, intriguing, gripping, useful, engrossing or stimulating Literature is the one person we rely on to combine emotion and thought in language. The writer sifts and sorts, organizes and describes her life experience into a narrative that comes to new life in the reader's mind. In decoding the writer's language the reader is forced to use personal memory to make sense of the story. Story is meaning.

Emotion is intimately involved in storing memories. Emotion makes events important and ensures that what is remembered best is stored along with its emotional associations. Stimuli, perhaps from reading, may evoke emotions related to past events. (The most frequently quoted example of this is found in Proust's *Remembrance of Things Past.*) The power to recall is inexorably linked to emotion, and memory is crucially important to the management of our lives. Memory is the source of our orientation to time, space and identity. It gives us the store of learned information that helps us manage the present, know what to do and how to do it, know what to avoid and seek, and know what we don't know. We plan our future on the foundation of our past. We could not anticipate or be safe without memory. Memory includes, of course, what we have read and remembered because it was relevant and impressed us. The stories that were important to us have blended with our lived experience and become part of our own experiential record.

Emotion, then, is critically involved in two aspects of our lives that are immediately enlisted when we read Literature with emotional relevance. First, emotion is essential to memory. We call up mental images from the past when we are emotionally prompted to do so. Armies of memories are conscripted to make sense of our reading; and because they are revisited and reorganized in the emotional context of the reading, they are probably not demobilized exactly as they were before the text was read. The process of decoding another's experience, say Anne's in *The Diary of*

Anne Frank, has altered our arrangement of our own identity. Our language and the perception it creates has been modified.

Second, reading turns us inward as well as outward. We learn awareness of emotion by having and recognizing feelings. Feeling may be regarded as the link between emotion and thought; a feeling is a stage in the transition from emotion to thought and the expression of emotion. Reading trains us to join emotion to thought and so helps us become whole. Literature helps us understand the world we must deal with; and it helps us calibrate our own biological system for the most mindful and therefore efficient encounter with our environment.

To summarize then, we monitor our well-being by using emotion to test what is good or bad in the environment. We sense what is sinister, violent, menacing, hostile, hurtful or pleasure giving and beneficial. This might be true of weather, terrain, words or human gestures. We filter most important incoming information with our emotions. But we don't just survive passively. We take arms against a sea of troubles. People are motivated to do things because their thoughts are associated with emotion — not just the big events like getting married or divorced, relocating, or adopting children, but everyday things like turning the news off or on, planting gardens, refinishing furniture or collecting things. Acts of charity, protests of anger, phone calls to inquire, most of what we do with conscious deliberation is rooted in emotion.

The world is sorted out for us by our emotions, and the thinking we do about the world and our place in it depends on our emotions. The words we read are a coded description of the world we inhabit and the bodies we live through, so it is not surprising that we should read with our emotions. It will repay us to pay attention to what our emotions tell us as we read. And every reader will experience a different configuration of emotions that combine with their thoughts and memories in a unique response. The goal of reading Literature is not merely to experience the pleasure and excitement of emotion, but *to cultivate an awareness of the emotion and what it can tell us about ourselves.*

You would think then, that Literature might have been a powerful antidote to the suppression of emotion in a literate population.[4] I think it is true that Literature has helped millions of readers recognize their own emotions. It has also helped them re-examine past experiences in light of these emotions and trained them to be more aware of the intricate weaving of emotion in their own responses to life events. Yet so widespread and entrenched is the fear of emotion in our culture that it has entered into the very teaching of Literature. Emotional response to novels and poems has not been encouraged in our classrooms, so a kind of schizophrenia has evolved in dealing with Literature. When I tried to introduce courses in English that would explicitly invite emotional, personal responses from students, the idea met with astonishing hostility, not only from my colleagues in psychology, but even from my own colleagues whose "field" was Literature. They feared I would unleash storms of disturbing emotions in students, and presumably the Counselling Centre would soon be overwhelmed. We were supposed to teach Literature as though it had no life relevance. This is akin to banning all knives from kitchens rather than teaching household safety. The failure to acknowledge the central place of emotion in understanding the role and uses of Literature has had the effect of greatly reducing its potential for helping people deal with their own lives. Only very recently has this truncating of the usefulness and indeed the very purpose of Literature begun to change.

My academic experience taught me that to "study" Literature, to make criticism a *profession*, it was required, it was politically correct, to distance the text from the emotions of the critic/student/teacher, to turn the literary work into an *object*, to surgically remove the personal, the subjective. I imagine this is not difficult to do in physics, or geology, where the objects of study are objects. Even in biology students try and sometimes manage to steel themselves so they feel as little as possible when they dissect live frogs and worms, or in medicine where students dissect cadavers. And we would probably not fish with worms if we could not suppress our fellow feeling for them. But to do this with the reader's interaction with fiction and poetry is truly to distort the process that is in reality going on. We finish up with results that alter and misrepresent the very activity of reading. For the truth is that life and Literature are not separated by even a fine line, not even the thinnest of membranes. Reading and writing are human behaviours. Creating and enjoying Literature is a biological process. We must learn to think about reading as a life activity, a form of coping action, an interactive brain/body/mind exercise. *The books on the shelves are potential energy modules that become activated when we plug them in and read them into our minds.*

When we speak of reading we are describing a way of acquiring information. Information has no weight, no mass. But it is recorded somehow, somewhere inside us, presumably by means of a molecular code which can be activated into consciousness by the appropriate stimulation. Computer information, in words or pictures, is recorded onto a compact disc by means of electromagnetic signals projected onto a receptive surface. But whereas the compact disc is unaffected by the kind of information recorded on it, whereas it is indifferent to what it receives and can even be erased and used again without harm to its receptive character, living organisms are affected, and can, and do alter with the information they record. Information codes are moved around as necessary by neurochemical and neuroelectrical transmitters in our bodies. These processes alter our living tissue. Pain causes muscle tissue to shrink and contract. Anxiety causes changes in metabolic process, increase in heart rate, increased secretion of gastric acid, and these in turn can cause more radical tissue change, ulcers, heart attacks etc. Yet pain and anxiety are information. It is important for us to pay attention to information.

When you read you acquire bits of information by decoding language symbols into life equivalents stored from experience into memory, mostly by means of language but not exclusively. Let me diagram this so we can keep it straight. I'll tell you a story. The other day I knocked over a glass of water and it smashed on the floor of my bedroom. By "word store," I include all the syntactical devices that can be enlisted to assemble words

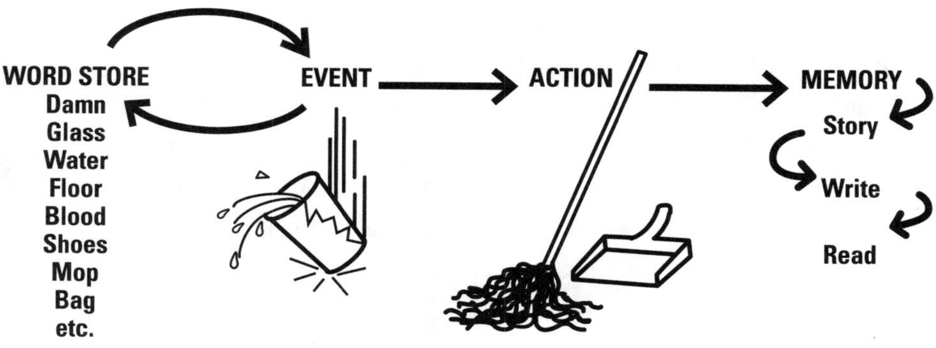

Broken Glass Story

into sentence structured narrative. So here's what happened to me. First I cursed. The curse word expression worked like a pressure relief valve for mini-shock, breath holding and anger. This cursing business is virtually reflex and requires no thought, but even startle reflexes in humans tend toward language. Then I went into the word store and assembled a hasty story of the event to make sense of it and deal with the remedy. There were two circumstantial spurs to fast action: I was afraid of cutting my feet; I did not want my wife to know how clumsy I had been. My reaction was regressive, my guilty inner child suddenly appeared. I went and got equipment. I cleaned up like an adult. I then stored away the whole event until just now when I wrote the little story. Now you enter. You read the "story," meagre though it is, and you go into your word store to find the words we share and for you to "ingest," that is, reassemble your words, match them to my words and "screen" my story and maybe turn it into your life experience. You may know *exactly* how this event feels, or you match *similar* accidents from your memory to make sense of this.

Reading uses and adds to a pre-existing word store. This word store has been forming simultaneously with life experience since birth. Your reaction to the words you read will vary in emotional intensity depending on the emotional associations laid down with your own word store and its various story organizations. Obviously, the word store in the diagram above is not confined exclusively to the glass breaking event. It is called up and assembled to fit that event. Its parts could be used quite differently for some other event. These bits of language information are almost invariably organized into narrative for storage and transmission in both the writer and the reader. The language narrative simulates the actual life experience *because the life experience has already been narratized.* In other words, language and life experience are continuously, and virtually simultaneously, interacting in brain activity in a cycle of energized neural firings with input from the body.

Let's try out this story response idea together. We'll use a passage from a brilliant novel by a Canadian writer.[5] The novel is a complex and riveting narrative, too rich to summarize here, but this passage is simple enough. I'll tell you how I read it and you can see what it does to and for and through you and your unique central nervous system. Let me set the scene. The story is founded on an historical event. The date is June, 1873, and we are pulled into the lawless frontier, the Canadian West. A small party of white men, American wolf bounty hunters, slaughtered an undetermined number of Assiniboine men, women and children and destroyed forty lodges. This event is known as the Cypress Hills Massacre. In the novel, the Boy has left his dead master the Englishman, and joined a roughneck gang of drifter cowboy adventurers in pursuit of some stolen horses that have been mysteriously spirited away by Native people. This scene, a little story within the longer story (which is how novels are often assembled), shows the cowboys at "play." The details of this scene are explained in the passage itself.

> As he [the Boy] closes, he can hear shouting, wild cries, sees rifles bristling, horses stamping and wheeling. He reins his lathered horse in beside Scotty, stands in his stirrups to view the shivaree. Thirty yards off, Hardwick is on his horse, head to head with a big bull buffalo.
>
> "Vogle was scouting for Indian trace when he spots this lone bull," a man called George Bell tells them excitedly.

"Hardwick bets Vogle he can't take him down from back yonder, one shot with his Sharp's buffalo gun. Vogle lets fly and misses clean. The buffalo breaks and Hardwick snaps off a chance shot. Lucky son of a bitch hits one of his legs and cripples him." He points to the buffalo sidling and backing, shaggy head swinging slowly from side to side like a church bell tolling as Hardwick edges a nervous pony towards him.

Bell grins. "Tom's just hazing that old buff. Playing some kind of bean-eater Mexican bullfighter, I reckon."

Hardwick spurs his fidgety horse towards the bull. The bull lowers his head, lunges. Hardwick skips his horse to the side as the buffalo's leg buckles, crashing him into the dust. There are war-whoops, rebel yells, shrill whistling.

The bull struggles up smeared with ashy dust, panting, maddened, drool hanging like tinsel from his beard. Hardwick slaps his horse forward with a rifle barrel along the flank and the bull bawls, hooks his horns into the earth, gores and rips the prairie, showering dust and dirt over his back, his blunt head.

The men are all bawling, answering the bull. Deep, sonorous bellows. Shouts. "That buffler is in a fine pucker, Tom! He's a looking to hook you up Salt River, he is!" "fix his flint, Tom!"

And Hardwick, heeling his horse on, a cold, arrogant look on his face, rifle-stock planted on his hips. The bull dashes for the horse, the smashed leg crumples again and the buffalo capsizes, a blur of flailing legs. The wolfers guffaw, trumpet and bellow. Hardwick steps his horse daintily around the buffalo while the bull strains to rise, great hump and shoulders pitching, wrenching himself up to totter on three legs, fractured foreleg flapping like a broken branch only held together by a shred of bark.

> Hardwick presses the jibbing horse to where the bull waits with black, distended tongue and blood-red eyes, shaking his huge head, flinging threads of slobber into his dirty, matted wool, massive shoulders bridling, the curved, polished horns hooking the air. Hardwick, erect in the saddle, eyes on the bull, rowels the horse on. The musk of the bull flaring the mare's nostrils, lifting her head higher and higher on a twisted neck, turning her eyes crazed and white, firing her hind legs into an executioner's drum roll.
>
> They are all shouting now, some in English, some in French. To the Englishman's boy, the Frenchies' gibbering is crazy folks' noise, the babble of the county madhouse. Beside him he can hear Bell shouting frantic encouragement to Hardwick. "Go it, boy! Take him by the tail!"
>
> The heavy head rises, the red eyes stare.
>
> The Englishman's boy ducks at the sudden explosion beside his ear. Hardwick's horse is rearing and Hardwick clinging to her back. An acrid whiff of gunpowder sweeps like smelling salts through the head of the Englishman's boy. The bull is slowly dropping to the earth, a mass of meat and bone sinking slowly under its own weight, hindquarters slumping, head lolling. He subsides into the bunch grass with a groan, a whoosh of dust squirts out from under the collapsing body.

Members of this gang then proceed to cut and tear at the steaming carcass and eat it's brains, liver, heart and muscle raw.

I consult my body, my visceral reactions, my emotions and their associated thoughts. I am not very good with lawlessness, with physical violence or brutality, with mindless sadism and bloodletting "sport." There is too much of the Nazi in this scene, too much of the depraved, partially human horde that became authorized, uniformed and armed to conquer the Europe I grew up in.[6] I am repelled by the picture of human cruelty, the sadistic. This is the white man in North America. The quiet natural dignity and bravery of the animal contrasts painfully with the mad savagery of the European invaders bringing "civilization" to this land. The bull seems like the very last of the buffalo, wiped out in shooting practice by horsemen, or men in suits lounging in trains, firing from windows. There is no beast like a human beast. This scene frightens and appalls me. I am physically uncomfortable. How can learning, reading, thought and compassion survive, let alone prevail, against the dark, demonic side of our species? There is no distance at all between this baiting of an animal and the same baiting of a person, of people. We see it in schoolyards. We see it in the racist bloodbaths of recent history. We see it daily in cruelty against women. Part of us seems intent on wiping out all the complexity, compassion and decency we have evolved. Only the merciful execution of the great buffalo redeems this scene at all. This is how I really feel and these are the thoughts that arise from my feelings, calling on my memories and experiences to inform what I have just written here.

Okay, now it's your turn. Perhaps I can induce you to read the entire novel. If you feel at all as I do, then you may find that this novel is a complex capsule, metaphor, an apprehensible, storable *language experience*. And what this powerhouse of a magic language pill does when you swallow it is *clarify and consolidate* other thoughts and language in your mind. A "well digested" complex narrative, or very often a poem *that matters to you*, provides a model, an identifiable shape, for an accumulation of thoughts and feelings scattered around the workshop of your mind. *The Englishman's Boy* weaves together two narratives that reveal very persuasively the connections between modern America, Hollywood America, the white racist falsification of history, and the greed that drives modern society. Rather than try to explain the complexity of these connections I would simply ask you to read the novel. Only story and metaphor can encapsulate and make apprehensible as a revelation so much complex information.

Buddhist tradition uses the lotus or water lily as a symbol of the potential beauty of the fully realized human life, the struggle to enlightenment.

Rising from the mud of watery depths, this unlikely, humble green plant struggles toward the sun until, surprisingly, it flowers into stunning golden radiance on the surface of the water, victorious above all its humble origins. For those who understand the meaning and power of symbol and metaphor, it is sufficiently eloquent to point to the lily, or the novel, to reveal a world of meaning.

Literature is just such an evolved collection of models of experience, experience too complex to be organized and managed without assistance; too complex because the species has evolved neural systems formed in conjunction with other minds and the world that nurtured and tested it. Our brains demand feedback. We crave models and analogs and we are not healthy without them. Therapy is principally about providing feedback and models. But for most readers, Literature is the best therapy. Just like a map that provides "models" of terrain, models you can hold, read, pocket and remember to help guide you across the land or help you imagine the country you must traverse, so Literature is provided by the species, for the species, to further our cognitive and emotional management of the human species. Literature is designed to assist us in the space or interface, where the "I" meets everything else, the "not-I." Literature is not an accident.

What We Half Create and Half Perceive

About 200 years ago the English poet William Wordsworth wrote an essay to introduce a collection of poems that he regarded as an experiment.[7] While this essay is not cited or noticed by psychologists or neuroscientists as far as I know, it is in my view one of the most important documents in the history of theory regarding Literature and its place in human biology.[8] Wordsworth proposed a very convincing and I think still valid interpretation of both the process of composition and its effect on readers. He explains what he sees as the connection between emotion and thought that produces poetry. Both the writing and the reading derive their effectiveness from the experience of pleasure that links the two and originates in the stimulus that prompted the writing in the first place. The pleasure emotion is important not only as motivation, but because it produces a kind of emotional health. Pleasure can take many forms, and though Wordsworth does not use the language of neurochemistry or neurohormones (serotonin, endorphins etc.),[9] he does point out a process that seems to be as accurate now as the day he proposed it.

> I have said that poetry is the spontaneous overflow of powerful feelings: it takes its origin from emotions recollected in tranquillity: the emotion is contemplated till, by a species of reaction, the tranquillity gradually disappears, and an emotion, kindred to that which was before the subject of contemplation, is gradually produced, and does itself actually exist in the mind.

And he elaborates:

> For all good poetry is the spontaneous overflow of powerful feelings; but though this be true, poems to which any value can be attached, were never produced on any variety of subjects but by a man [human being] who being possessed of more than usual organic sensibility had also thought long and deeply.

This is the first explicit account of the psychology and neurology of literary composition. It remains a rare, perhaps unique attempt by a poet to explain the process by which language becomes the synthesis of feeling and thought. Once this feeling and thought have taken the form of poetry, they can be transmitted to another human brain where the poem is reconstituted as thought and feeling akin to the neural origins of the poem in the poet. So it is that the poet's "more than usual organic sensibility" can be used in the service of the ordinary reader, who "must necessarily be in some degree enlightened, his taste exalted, and his affections ameliorated," which is the health of the organism I posited above. I hope you begin to see how language in a particular form, taking shape in a responsive brain, and relating to a particular subject, can affect the host organism — the reader. This happens in beneficial ways that might be described as calming, exciting, enlightening, or satisfying by showing order and connection, and validating compassion, sadness, joy, grief and so on. That all this occurs in a language form that is subject to rational, neocortical, and prefrontal lobe processing is a critically important feature of Literature, making possible the integration of emotion into the life story, world account and "I" formation of the reader.

This process and the relations of writing and reading, thought and emotion are illustrated below.

Whether you enter these circles via thought (reading) or emotion (stimulus) you will arrive at the other. This process can now be put in neurological terms. In the case of heard speech, the auditory pathways of the brain are immediately enlisted so that the brain can decide first whether the sound is in fact human language. A filtering process in the midbrain interprets sounds and sends them on to other areas for the application of meaning and action. If we hear screams of "fire" in a theatre, the emotional response will be so rapid that we will have no consciousness of having gone through the interpretive stages: 1. This is a sound 2. This is a human speech sound 3. Send this to associated areas for meaning 4. Feel fear 5. Take evasive action. The yell "fire" would seem to produce instant emotional response. The point about brain processing may be better illustrated by

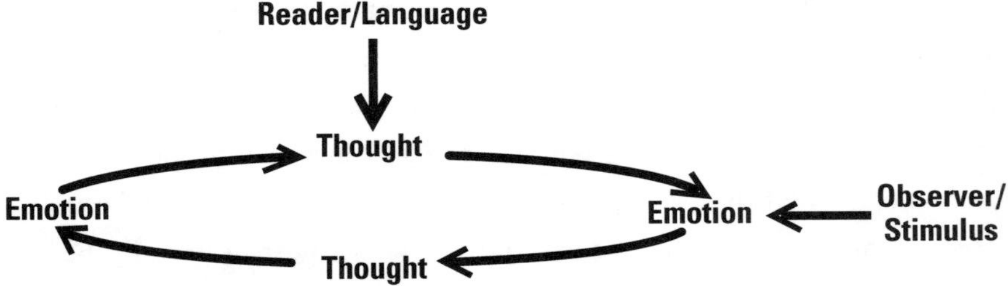

omitting the language cortex altogether. Say, for instance, I am walking home late at night on a deserted, dark street and I hear a scream from quite close. My auditory response will still require some processing: Is this a human or animal scream? Where is it originating? But the scream will not require language processing. The emotional response from the midbrain will be almost immediate and unfettered by language, not neocortical, but virtually and primally instinctive, like panic, startle, fight or flight. This is a good example of a trigger response. Soon after this, however, I will almost certainly arrive at language as I try to story and make sense of what is happening.

Now you will recognize that you cannot hear a scream in reading. If you read that someone screamed and startled someone else, you will have to imagine it with the help of recall from your own memory store, you will somehow have to produce a scream, and you will arrive at emotion only after decoding and interpreting language text. This textual filter that must be passed to get to emotion should be regarded as a protective barrier, producing enough processing to enable the reader to manage and control emotion arising from reading, in the case of non-psychotic readers, at least. I will return to this thesis when discussing media and visual entertainment. For now the important point is that Wordsworth taught us that the language/stimulus/emotion circle is unbreakable and, wherever you enter it, you will go round and through all of it.

When Wordsworth speaks of "affections" he means emotions, what modern psychology calls "affects." On the following page is one table of affects from modern psychology, though there are many others, some much longer than this.[10] I have included the facial expressions that are the human mark of affect and convey significant information to someone looking at a face. These affects were first described in detail by Charles Darwin. They were first observed and noted on the faces of primates. I reproduce them here to show just how physical and in the body affect is, emotion, for both humans and other animals. Every one of these affects may be observed in very young babies because they are innate. They are primal and precede cognitive learning, yet they come into play to a greater or lesser degree with virtually every stimulus. Such emotions described below are part of the essential biological equipment of the human animal; and thus emotions facilitate our management of language information, and therefore our management of Literature.

The Innate Affects

Positive

1. Interest — Excitement
   Eyebrows down, track, look, listen
2. Enjoyment — Joy
   Smile, lips widened and out

Neutral

3. Surprise — Startle
   Eyebrows up, eyes blink

Negative

4. Fear — Terror
   Frozen stare, face pale, cold, sweaty, hair erect
5. Distress — Anguish
   Cry, rhythmic sobbing, arched eyebrows, mouth down
6. Anger — Rage
   Frown, clenched jaw, red face
7. Distaste (Dismal)
   Upper lip raised, head pulled back
8. Disgust
   Lower lip lowered and protruded, head forward and down
9. Shame — Humiliation
   Eyes down, head down and averted, blush

Wordsworth goes to some lengths to point out that it is the *feelings that give importance to the action and events of his writing*, not the other way around. This is a profound and useful reminder to all writers and readers, certainly of poetry and fiction. Why does this matter? Human motivation, behaviour, and social organization are primarily energized by feelings, that is knowledge of emotion. The avoidance of pain, shame, loss, neglect, fear; the quest for pleasure; the experience of empathy, family love, safety, group acceptance, calm, excitement etc. — these are the driving forces shaping how we live and moving us to action. Reading is valuable when it helps us order, understand, organize, recognize and fine-tune our emotions. Literature is a tool that assists us in learning to *turn our emotions into information.*

Wordsworth sees Literature as an antidote to entertainment that brutalizes and desensitizes the "reader" rather than refining his or her "sensibilities." Wordsworth was very conscious of his purpose in writing poems. In fact, he was exceptional in his pointed purposefulness, his deliberate intention to teach readers and raise their awareness in very specific ways. He treats poetry as education, emotional medicine, psychotherapy and explicitly explains that he is doing so. He wants to enlarge the capability of the human mind, out of respect for "its beauty and dignity." "For the human mind is capable of excitement without the application of gross and violent stimulants...." Wordsworth does not spell out what these stimulants might be, but we can guess the sort of thing he means: bare-fisted boxing, Punch and Judy, freak shows at the Fair, dog fights, cock fights, gin palaces and bawdy houses. He goes on to explain that this task of the writer, the service to the human mind is "excellent at all times," but "especially so at the present day."

> For a multitude of causes unknown to former times are now acting with a combined force to blunt the discriminating powers of the mind, and unfitting it for all voluntary exertion to reduce it to a state of almost savage torpor.

What would Wordsworth say to our world, two hundred years later, with its moment-by-moment global transmissions of violence, cruelty, and an endless stream of bits of false, distorted and useless information that bombard whole populations into mental numbness and despair? Our gross and violent stimulants would include violent video games and movies, staged "professional" wrestling, "shock" TV, "reality" TV, rodeos, news of wars and murder embellished with video illustration, widespread pornography of every conceivable type. Such "gross and violent" stimulants presumably arouse excitement, and the fear, anger and vicarious emotion, along with the recognizable body changes that accompany such arousal. But these stimulants are unmediated by language and so do not enlist thought or the integration of experience into the language or story record. The responses are transitory and addictive. Indeed, they are the more addictive because they are self-contained and fleeting, not thought changing, and must therefore be frequently repeated to provide once more the direct emotional stimulus. They deliberately violate the thought/emotion cycle. Someone raised and trained on such stimuli and equipped with only minimal reading skill will be rendered correspondingly "thought less" and poorly individuated, with a craving for more such excitement, and dependent on ever more violent spectacles to experience arousal.

Moreover, continuous exposure to such entertainment will increase detachment from thought and decrease awareness of empathy, sympathy, compassion and feeling. Just as trauma blocks connection between emotion and language/thought, so violent amusement detached from language and the need for thought will increase the separation of the feelings/emotion aroused, and the language that would integrate that emotion, via feelings, into the construction of identity. The increasing violence of hockey, for instance, the uncontrolled violence of soccer crowds, along with the spontaneous violence of urban riots that appear poorly motivated and puzzle civic authorities, may all be understood in terms of biological conditioning by "gross and violent" stimulants.

Using Wordsworth's arguments, the case for Literature and for reading intensifies every day. We desperately need catharsis, not cathode rays. Wordsworth offers a number of ideas central to our purpose here. He never actually wrote the book he points to in the Preface to the *Lyrical Ballads*, a book, he hints, which would have determined the degree to which public taste in England was "healthy or depraved"; a book that would have embarked on a full discussion of how "language and the human mind act and react on each other"; a book tracing the "revolutions not of literature alone but likewise of society itself." But these pointers, along with his theory of the interactions of emotion and thought, reveal Wordsworth as a pioneer of neuroscience, perhaps the first such explorer. He was certainly the first who studied, with the close observation of the good scientist and a great poet, the relation of language and Literature to human biology. For a poet in the first half of the nineteenth century to have even conceived of such a book, one that would address the relationship of language, the human brain, and the social morality, was to be hundreds of years ahead of his time.

How Wordsworth arrived at his conclusions was extraordinary. He treated himself as a case study and made a detailed examination of his own creative process, beginning with sensory stimuli, the objects of nature that he grew up with, loved and revered, and then by noting how emotions became thoughts and finally poetry, and at last how poetry re-awoke the feelings by which thought had originated. Through self-analysis Wordsworth came to the conclusion that the "child is father of the man." How we are raised, what we learn as children, what our environment and influences are, will determine how we think as adults. So he came to the conviction that the stage was set in childhood development for the entire process of adult thinking and feeling.[11]

What struck Wordsworth most forcibly, and to which he refers again and again, is that the particular arrangement of words that can evoke powerful but ordered feelings derive their effectiveness by producing pleasure. The experience of pleasure in the reader is the overriding characteristic of good writing. He wants Literature to excite the mind. In this state of excitation, achieved through the medium of language chosen with extreme care, feelings and ideas become "associated." So important is this "fact" for him, that he believes and asserts that writers must create their work with the deliberate purpose of evoking this result. Nor is this pleasure principle a result limited to being its own reward. This associative pleasure has profound moral and social significance. By refining their own responses through reading, humans improve their empathy for others, their sense of human fellowship, and their understanding of their own nature, both as individuals and as members of a species. But Wordsworth goes beyond morality and suggests that human health itself is improved by reading, that poets are not only healers but must set out to be healers: "the power of the human imagination is sufficient to produce such changes even in our physical nature as might almost appear miraculous." Our "affections" can be "ameliorated" by poetry, or by prose as carefully, thoughtfully constructed as is poetry.

The ancient Greek philosopher Aristotle gave some thought to this in his commentary on the effects of tragedy upon the viewing audience. He believed that toxic, repressed negative thought and emotion could be purged, exorcised, by viewing a drama which echoed or paralleled such emotion that pre-existed in the viewer. A kind of recognition of self is forced upon the audience so as to produce relief and resolution. Ever since Aristotle, this process by which emotion, evoked in language, and used to purge thought and feeling toxicity suppressed in the viewer, a process often accompanied by tears, sobbing and relief, has been called catharsis (Greek *Katharsis*), whether in psychology or Literature. In this process, with its convulsive central nervous system reactions (recognized by the reader/audience as uncontrollable, visceral and overwhelming), the experience of pain and pleasure are inextricably associated. We shall explore this and other powerful responses to literature in Chapter 6, where we examine further the surprising truth that words, rightly arranged, can promote physical and mental health.

Emotion and thought are then necessarily inseparable and part of an entire response system that must be understood to come into play through the agency of language. For the reader, this language is acquired by decoding speech or text and then absorbed as "knowing" in the central nervous system. If different processes and functions of our biological storehouse are all part of one intricate and awesomely complex adaptive coping device, how did they become separated in our thinking? The history of science, politics and religion is a collection of stories. These stories were all designed to explain the mysteries of the world, including human behaviour. They were based on the information available. Sometimes they were cynically manipulated to further the power or economic interests of the story designers. Sexism, racism, colonialism, religious superiority, medical theory, have taken shape from stories that have been believed as "truth," as irrefutable accounts of the nature of things "as they are," rather than as we have chosen to see them. And this shaping of reality has meant preferring one thing to another, leaving some things out of the story and privileging others. The consequences of this fragmenting of experience is a large part of the history of humankind. Splitting the human mind into the rational god-like Prospero versus the savage, bestial emotional, barely human Caliban of Shakespeare's *The Tempest*, has led to slavery and genocide.

If our human future is to be more creative, more humane, more healthy and healing, we must change our story to more accurately reflect the wondrous involvement of all parts of the system. We need more self-awareness and more humility. We must come to Literature as learners. If we pay real attention to our own responses, to human experience, to the feelings of ourselves and others, and less to the mantras and dogmas of ideologies, then perhaps we will sense the harmony and enlightenment that Buddha saw in the lowly lotus. Literature is the manifest record of holistic experience. The more we read, the richer our knowledge of that experience becomes.

Some have believed that the greatest blessing wealth can convey is the leisure to read and study. Perhaps it is now time to start pulling ourselves together.

NOTES TO CHAPTER 4
THAT INWARD EYE: THE EMOTIONAL READER

1. Plato is an important player on the side of the literal in the history of the war between the literal and the metaphorical, though he himself depends on metaphor in his writing. Consider for instance his image of the cave — unless of course he meant that all humans actually live in a cave, literally.
2. Except in the case of severe trauma. Some emotional experiences are strong enough to block thought and the language that would formulate and organize such thought. This becomes a handicap that follows the traumatic experience and requires therapeutic treatment.
3. See Damasio 1994, 1999, and LeDoux, 1996 and their bibliographies.
4. I recently had occasion to ponder the converse of this. A patient told me that as a child she was about to read *Catcher in the Rye* as a school text, when her mother saw her with the book and went berserk, called the school and forbade the child ever to read it. Forty years later she still has not read it. So how did the mother's censorship help this girl? In fact, the mother deprived the child of important information about the world, and about her own isolation, information she desperately needed at that time. It probably contributed to an aversion to reading, since it made Literature dangerous.
5. *The Englishman's Boy* by Guy Vanderhaeghe. This is an historical "Cowboys & Indians" story that achieves beauty, importance and profundity. Of all the remarkable works in the twentieth-century flowering of Canadian literature, this must surely be one of the most satisfying. I am quoting pages 116-117.
6. It is interesting to me that humans behaving with exceptional cruelty or lack of empathy are described in non-human terms — bestial, brutal, wild, savage, animal and so on. Yet only the bipedal hominid has wrought the barely imaginable horrors our history and news reveal. We need an integrated development of identity in which thought and feeling are balanced and fully operational. Emotion without thought, and thought (ideology) without emotion produce deadly results. The problem seems to me to derive from our being partially rather than fully human.

   Being fully human requires that we recognize ourselves as animals. The human atrocities we commit come not from our animal nature but from believing we are gods. This particular form of human madness enables members and groups to persuade themselves *out of* compassion and connection to other people, to animals and to the natural world. The human record of world destruction is possible only to a species playing at being god while having the limited intelligence of being human. Neither animals nor gods would do the mad things we do to ourselves. Since we cannot be gods we had better be what we are, animals who make stories. The story that we are gods dooms us.

7. Preface to the *Lyrical Ballads*, 1850. Wordsworth's first version of this was published about 50 years earlier.
8. Of course, this is not much of a claim, since there may in fact be no other writing squarely focused on Literature and its biological function besides Wordsworth's Preface and the book you are reading here. Writing by Jane Healy, the American educator, and by Louise Rosenblatt, the reader-centred critic, point in the right direction, but in the one case Literature is not central, and in the other neurobiology is not central. Most other writing on the processing of Literature by readers skirts the issues that are being raised here.
9. Among the many neurochemicals and hormones that affect mood and emotion, one has been identified as particular to the pleasure associated with learning, or what I have called the "Aha" effect in this book. The pleasure mood results from one of the endogenous endorphins, Leu-enkephalin. Perhaps this is a clue that explains the pleasure of making connections, gaining insight, and making new language associations in the brain's left hemisphere that provide feelings of empowerment. The relationship between reading, pleasure and Leu-enkephalin could be confirmed by doing some very sophisticated blood work following the reading of poetry that gives intense satisfaction. See Rapson.
10. From Donald L. Nathanson, following Sylvan Tompkins, the pioneer of affect studies, to whom Nathanson dedicates his book, p. 136.
11. The importance of Wordsworth as a pioneer of psychology has not been sufficiently recognized. Most psychologists don't study poetry, being more engrossed in the behaviour of rats than of poets. Englishists (English professors) have had no interest in brains. "Critics" always place Wordsworth inside a literary tradition, called Romantic, whereas, like the mathematician he was, and like his friend Coleridge, he is best understood in a multidisciplinary framework of pioneering thought about the role of Literature in the formation of identity and the seed days of modern psychology, especially neuropsychology.

Chapter Five

Dualism vs Holism: A Cosmic Intermission

It is time to take a break from reading and from Literature, but not from story. For humans there is no break from story. We are the story creatures, members of the story species. The world we inhabit is the product of story. But we don't all inhabit the same, static world. At one time it is flat, at another it is round. For some the world is a village, for others it is an island. Some stories have gods in the sky and some in the earth. Some stories have people born over and over again and in others people are born only once. Some stories have us following a preordained destiny, an inexorable fate, and others have us living by accident moment to unpredictable moment. Some stories say that certain people should be killed and others say that nobody should be killed. Stories may be in conflict. Stories can compete and some can wipe out others. There is no shortage of stories, but which of them is "true"?

The true story is the one we believe in. Stories shape our lives. Stories determine our behaviour. So quintessential to the human brain is story that we must believe that the story gene or the story circuitry co-evolved with language. We construct all incoming data into story. Like the sequential nature of grammar itself, story is the sequential organizing principle of thought itself. Until we get a grip on this principle we are in trouble. We have choices about stories and this ability to choose is the source of our mental freedom. Sometimes stories have to be repaired, or even changed. Once we adopt an unchangeable story our freedom is lost. The very nature of story function must be its adaptability. Since print has now fixed stories in a way that oral transmission did not, we must have lots of them. The most important guiding principles for examining stories is, "does it help me be healthy, help me manage my life, contribute to making my own story whole?"

Let's look at a contemporary example. One story suggests that our economic and social behaviour is causing global warming, widespread pollution and environmental destruction and we must change our ways. The opposing story argues that the above is not "true" and we need to keep doing what we are doing to maintain our current standard of living. In the conflict between these stories, the storymakers on the opposing sides examine the evidence. Evidence is what is used in legal trials to assist judging between stories. But evidence is often interpreted differently to fit the needs of different story makers. So which story should we adopt? Surely it must be the one that is good for us, the one that we think helps us survive, stay healthy and ensures the health of our descendants. We won't do this if we don't embrace the overarching principle that *stories are within our control;* events may not be, of course, but stories are.

This knowledge that our human brains shape the world we live in by the stories we apply to it is our principle defence against deception. Some people will adopt and live by stories that deny their own personal experience. People are robbed, raped, defrauded, abused in innumerable ways every day by believing stories designed to deceive them. This is called *denial,* and is a persistent feature of an unshakable attachment to a story that experience must not violate. Stories exist in layers, and some can predispose us to believe those that are bad for us. We have stories like "we must find love to cure all our ills" or "we must be rich to be happy" or "we must find a saviour to lead us to security," or "we are one big, happy, successful family." We would do well to examine critically the stories that guide our behaviour and shape our quests.

Stories exist in hierarchies like inverted pyramids. Those that put the greatest weight on the tiny individual at the bottom are culturally determining, spreading pressure downwards through nations, communities and families to paralyze the individual "I" at the bottom. We cannot escape this burden until we see how we can be trapped by one story and freed by another.

So the first story we must learn to adopt is the one about the power of story itself. An example of this power lies in the genius of the Passover story of Jewish tradition. Here we find that the story of moving from slavery to freedom is an idea that is contained and transmitted, through the agency of the story itself, annually repeated and embroidered with and for children in every observant Jewish home around the world. This story had profound effects, not only on Jews, but on the black liberation movement in the United States, where Methodist Christianity took strong root.

If stories are powerful enough to shape our behaviour, how we live and what we think, then they must also affect our health. So before we can move on to the chapter on reading and health, we need to examine the context in which Literature has become necessary.

Oral stories preceded writing and these stories were the bonds that held together the people who shared them and passed them from generation to generation. The stories told people of their origins, explained their practices and customs, reinforced social rules and taboos, and taught people how to see and think about the world around them. The stories were the religion and the philosophy that gave order and meaning to the world experience of those who learned and heard the stories. Because they were not written down and passed on in "hard copy" as we now say, they could and did change. They were adaptable to the changes that occurred in nature and in the history and vicissitudes of the people. Floods, storms, wonders and catastrophes were incorporated and woven into the stories, much as they are into our historical record, or as they were in the pre-biblical stories until the Bible became a text fixed in time.

Humans have developed two contrasting stories about the nature of the world, the nature of nature itself and the nature of human relations to the non-human world. The Western or Eurocentric world view may be called "dualism"; the contrasting view characteristic of Chinese, Zen, or Taoist thinking I am going to call "holism." (This latter view also bears strong resemblances to indigenous North American thought as evidenced in the religions, folklore and rituals of numerous peoples.[1]) Dualism and holism are stories. How do they affect us? How are they good or bad for us? What can we learn about them that can be adapted to our individual and social needs?

Each story might be regarded as a Logos, that is, a world view or framework that contains the believer. From the inside, everything that is seen or known or thought is shaped by the Logos through which the believer perceives, like looking at everything through the tinted and shaped porthole of the ship that we live on. I want to compare two stories about the nature of the universe, or the nature of nature: the Western or Eurocentric story of nature and the Universe, and the Chinese or Taoist view. Let's look, then, at some fundamental similarities and differences between these two views. What we do know is that if we grow up in a Eurocentric culture, and especially if we are Christian, we will "inherit" and find hard to escape, the duality view of the world we inhabit, so that it becomes a Logos, a world view or story that will shape our thinking, our beliefs and behaviours.

Since the time writing became widespread in Western culture, the dominating story about the nature of the world we inhabit and about our own nature as creatures has been characterized by dualism. This means everything exists in contrary pairings, their opposites always in conflict.[2] In the preceding chapter we considered a similar kind of conflict: the separation of emotion and thought. This same kind of split is found everywhere in our Western thinking. Male and female are separated, a male is all male and a female all female. We have come to regard such divisions as "truths." God and the Devil, night and day, good and evil, these are all irreconcilable opposites and each pair is in conflict.

This kind of dual thinking is so deeply entrenched in our perspective that we have come to regard duality as "out there," everywhere inherent in nature in the actual organization of the world as given or truth — independent of our view of it. We have forgotten, perhaps for some people conveniently, that duality is a story of our own making. This is not the place to speculate on whose interests are served by duality, but it does not take much imagination to see how the story might be applied. For a slave owner like Plato, for instance, who is one of the great dualists of history, a world ordained to have masters and slaves as a condition of nature would be very convenient. Socially and politically we have been bedeviled by a long battle between the individual and the group. This duality has been at the root of conflict between Left and Right and has been used by each to confuse the reality that both individuals, and the groups in which they belong, are symbiotically entwined. The construction of integrated, well-balanced identities helps bring order and peace to communities.

Dualism has produced several significant problems for those who use it as a foundation for understanding our cosmos. For one thing, genuine dualism invites us to take sides. If the parts of the pair are irreconcilably opposite, we have to choose. God is good and the Devil is bad. Does any of us want to be bad? This problem Milton wrestled with in *Paradise Lost* with only moderate success. Satan has always been a sympathetic hero for countless readers, even if they do subscribe to the tortured theology that drives Milton to the edge. Free will is only free under certain conditions that are not free. In such a dualism God can hardly avoid being a tyrant. But what if this dichotomy is false? What if Milton is torturing himself unnecessarily? Why should Calvin have a monopoly on this story? The same problem occurs in sexism, a natural child of dualism. If I am male, must I root for maleness at the expense of my opposite? Yes, if I am a dualist. Another problem that attends upon the conflicts generated by dualism is its endless prompting of rationalization and denial. Dualism separates man and woman, adult and child, success and failure, black person and white, not on the basis of some knowledge scale or continuum, or on the basis of culture and biology, but on the basis of power. Sexism and racism are rationalized by stories devised to justify a power imbalance, and even research, the sacred cow of Western objectivism, is enlisted to sustain the status quo. Yet all of this vast paraphernalia of self-delusion is founded on a human story. We shall see by the end of this chapter how such problems are profoundly implicated in the Literature imperative.

The Taoist view of the world also contains what might at first glance appear to be a duality at its centre. We must not be deceived by this first impression. The Yin-Yang binary brings us face to face with the concept of paradox, for it is in paradox, so beloved of Gilbert and Sullivan, that the difference between East and West is revealed. A paradox describes a belief or proposition that requires two *ostensibly* contrary elements to be held in mind or accepted at the same time, and so represents a kind of conundrum. But a paradox exists in the human mind only, and is not a description of anything "out there." Rather, it shows how the mind holding it *thinks about* what is "out there." Moreover, a paradox is peculiar to Western minds, but not to Chinese, Zen or Taoist thinking. Paradox reveals that some minds confronting it cannot reconcile two elements which appear to be contradictory, but these elements are not necessarily opposed in other minds. Paradox appears to be absurd, untenable or impossible, but is not.

Paradox is the exposure of a false dichotomy and with enough thought and imagination, with freedom from imprisoning Logos, paradoxes become resolved. A couple of examples will serve.

A "blind Seer" is a paradox for a reader who fails to recognize that wisdom and knowledge are a form of sight, insight, as in the case of Seer Tiresias of *Oedipus Rex*. The second, Milton's famous description of Hell as "Darkness visible" seems a baffling paradox, but is in fact a masterful description and vivid representation of evil and weakness posing as understanding and power. Now that we have Milton's phrase it is possible to be aware of "Darkness visible" in many parts of our world.

Paradox is not congenial to Western thought and tends to irritate people or at least puzzle them to distraction. Taoists on the other hand have no problem seeing unity in dichotomy; but Western thought, since it is persuaded of the separateness of parts that *become* contrary, has difficulty creating unity out of apparently disparate entities, and therefore dismisses the juxtapositing parts as a logical trick, a *paradox*.[3]

A notable problem characteristic of dualism is its relentless simplification of experience. We see this in all aspects of our lives and the consequences are disastrous, in our environmental management for instance, in our personal and family relationships and in Western medicine. Simplification affects our attitudes to education and even to our selves and our bodies and minds.[4] Simplification also has profound implications for the Literature imperative as we shall see. From inside the duality Logos, only one view makes any sense. Indeed, there cannot be another view to account for everything. This is false, of course, for those outside of the Dualist Logos.

The Taoist view assumes that all apparent dual oppositions — male-female, hot-cold, dark-light, etc. — can be expressed as a unity. Such unity can be, and needs to be, applied to any and all apparent dichotomies.

Yin-Yang Sign

The Yin-Yang sign above or the "Supreme Ultimate," as it is called, signifies interdependent duality composing a unity, and resolves, metaphorically, four paradoxes which are its essential characteristics; the sign itself is, of course, a metaphor of a concept.

1. Nothing is totally Yin or totally Yang. Everything contains the seed of its opposite. The opposition of Yin and Yang are relative, changing, con-

stantly moving and rebalancing, adjusting. They are conceptual aspects of energy, the forces of everything. They are never fixed or absolute. All states are relative. Yin and Yang exist as a process and this process is a dynamic, unceasing balancing act. There is no such thing as a static state. The male contains the female and vice versa; they are therefore not at war.

2. Yin and Yang are different but mutually dependent. They are relative aspects of the same thing — one cannot exist without the other. They are mutually exclusive but necessarily compatible. They contain each other.

3. Yin and Yang are in a state of dynamic changing balance but are never equal enough at any moment to produce stasis. You must imagine two children of identical weight on a see-saw following a rule that they must seek balance but never become static by being perfectly still and balanced in space. They must, therefore, exert force against the ground to move up and down, passing each other as one or the other becomes higher or lower, in the ascendance (stronger) or in the lower (weaker) position.

In nature, and in humans, who are part of nature and governed by the same rules, there are two sets of conditions governing this shift of relative strength. One is internal. The body is hot (Yang) so it is driven to be cool (Yin), or the reverse. The other is external. There is a shortage of food (Yin), so aggressive hunting (Yang) is required. An electrical storm comes up (Yang), so inactivity and shelter are necessary as one submits to the threat of danger and we crouch quickly in a cave (Yin).

4. Yin and Yang transform into each other. In other words, the same force or energy transforms into its opposite. Passive food-fuel turns into active organic energy. Males can nurture while females hunt (or go to the office).[5] One would expect that a Taoist view would have a profound effect on the degree to which people compete or cooperate.

The Chinese view of the nature of things has one great advantage — it has provided a unifying, manageable and imaginable story that everyone can grasp and use. So basic is the principle of Yin and Yang to Chinese thought that this story is taught and learned by everyone in China. It has been incorporated into Buddhism, Confucianism, and Communism. It erases compartmentalized thinking and assists people to regulate their health. Remember, we are not speaking of the cosmic truth here but of stories, versions of nature, for managing the human experience of the world. In the West we do not have such a unifying story. Instead, we have competing theories and competing expertise that operate without the umbrella of a metaphor that can contain them all. Since we have no story that can encapsulate and reconcile all of nature into our minds, we live in a mental world of conflict. We are buffeted by endlessly opposing forces. The result is we are rendered passive and unknowing in the face of competing interests. We have no overarching grasp of ourselves and our intimate relationship to the world we inhabit.

There is no supreme ultimate symbol, nothing equivalent to the Yin-Yang sign, available for Western thought. To illustrate the contrast I am describing I need to invent one. Here is my idea of such a sign of traditional but current Western thought.

These two semi-circles represent separateness. They are absolutes and are static. They are irreconcilable. They might be thought of as repelling magnets, kept apart by their force fields. They cannot be whole and complete because each half-unity is aware that it cannot defeat or contain its opposite. Men are from Mars, women are from Venus. Good and evil are separate and opposed. Summer begins on June 21; winter is left behind and returns mysteriously complete on December 21. It is possible

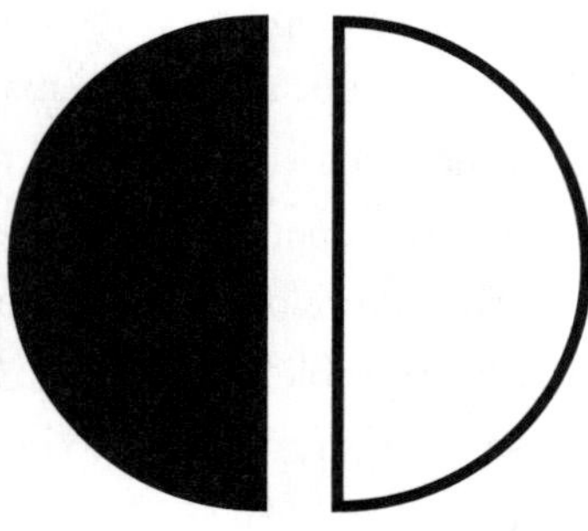

Dualism Sign

to think that winter never really disappeared, it only lost its ascendancy, but because dualist minds divide the world, we have forced ourselves to live within the divisions. Homosexuals are considered aberrations because we do not recognize the male or female as present together in all of us, on a scale of more or less ascendancy. Throughout Western history, it is true, there have been valiant efforts to alter such views. These attempts have aimed to engender tolerance, or holism, or have taken political shape as quests for equality, conservation, co-operation, animal rights. Yet such endeavours always fail, or fight a depressingly uphill battle, as the absolutist view persists. Well-meaning people always end up with labels like "tree-huggers" or "fags" or "feminists," outsiders excluded from the mainstream of power. The consequence, remember, of a *dominant story*, an absolutist vision, is infected by the content it espouses and so intolerant of any alternatives.

Before we can leave our interlude and return to Literature and how it works to assist our health, we must look again at the brain. The human brain is the latest object to come under the intensive scrutiny of dualism. Do we have two brains or one? The brain is an organ that looks a bit like a walnut half, with two sides or wings called hemispheres. This is not quite accurate since the two sides together do not actually make up a sphere. The left hemisphere is over the left eye, and the right over the right eye. The two are joined by a thick cable of nerve fibres called the corpus callosum. Through this bond of neural pathways the hemispheres communicate and send information back and forth, from one visual field to the other and from one aural field to the next. The left hemisphere of the vast majority of people has evolved a specialty for language and for sequential thinking; while the right hemisphere is better at spatial recognition, map reading, facial recognition, geographical orientation, music. Literature then, seems to come under the domination of the left, while painting, sculpture, music and dance require right hemispheric priority.

The brain operates by gathering data from sensory fields and submits this data for naming, categorizing, organizing, judging and storing. There can hardly be any doubt that this process of "conversation" between parts of the brain, along with all the referential input from emotion centres, memory, beliefs and autonomic inputs represents a complexity beyond our current knowledge and understanding. Given all the speculation on the whereabouts of consciousness itself, perhaps not even our imaginations can meet the challenge of an explanation.

However, the study of the human brain is subjected to the simplifications of dualism. For instance, much discussion of hemispheric function has taken place since neurosurgeons in the U.S. performed a number of operations on epileptic patients to cure their illness. The surgery took one brain and made it into two by severing the corpus callosum, thus rendering the hemispheres incommunicado. How far can dualism go? Steven Pinker seems convinced that to all intents and purposes we have two brains and nothing much was lost by severing the hemispheres. "After surgery the patients live completely normal lives, except for a subtlety.... The left half of their world has been disconnected from their language center."[6] Do I hear any volunteers out there clamouring for the completely normal existence described as "life after the operation?" I have never read any detailed accounts by split brain patients about their "normal lives" following surgery. I imagine they have their work cut out for them though, just trying to get their "normal" lives together — or worse, trying to apply language to an essay about their new-found split world.

According to Dr. Pinker, in searching for the language centres of the brain: "We can narrow down our search at the outset by throwing away half the brain." If this is a joke, I find it bewildering because the author of this statement is one of America's leading neurolinguists. What can we make of this? I think the confusion comes out of dualistic thinking. What kind of language would we have if it were not language-about-something? And what could it be about if not the material supplied by the right hemisphere. The left describes and organizes what the right supplies. The right provides the real-world spatial imagery of what the left describes. This cycle is continuous, interactive and mutually dependent. The most obvious illustration is instantly available to you through reading. Go back to the passage from *The Englishman's Boy* and watch as your left brain decodes the words and sentences and the right brain supplies the three-dimensional images, smells, emotions and ambient textures of the scene. The two halves of the brain are mutually enabling. Remember that the human brain has done three-fourths of its forming in the world of postnatal experience. Along with language it also learned all the applications and referents for that language. To speak about any intactness of language without its connection to the world is like saying that a fly with its wings removed is as perfectly self-contained an insect as it was before the clipping. The only problem is, it is no longer a fly. Someone with half a brain is not fully human. Language and space are like veins and blood. There is no point or function or health if they don't work together. Like the partners in a long, loving marriage, the two sides of the brain were made for each other.

I want to refer you back to the diagrams on pages 108 and 110. I want you to imagine that the Yin-Yang sign and the dualism sign are diagrams of the brain. The former is a description of the human brain by a person who sees it as a whole. Oddly enough, it would be hard to imagine a model more useful for indicating the actual working of a well-functioning brain, except that you have to imagine it in three dimensions. In this Yin-Yang model, the two sides are mutually dependent, integrally united, complementary in function, and always in balance when in a state of health. Their ascendancy fluctuates depending on the demands of the environment, the circumstances and the brain's history. We should note that the sign is founded on the concept that the organizing principle of the universe is *energy*, and the model describes energy, poles, or fields. The Yin-Yang sign can then be thought of as a description of the brain in terms of its *function*.

In the case of the dualism sign, we see clearly the view of the split-brain culture. Here the sign is based on the concept of *matter*, and the model suggests the structure or architectonics of brain arrangement. The two sides are independent, contrary, at war for ascendancy and mutually impatient. Some researchers report their own distress at watching split-brain patients arguing with themselves over the correct interpretation of data given them.[7] I suspect that guilt as well as identification might have something to do with their discomfort.

We must now return to Literature armed with a vital piece of information. It is not customary to discuss Literature in terms of its *function.* In asking what Literature does, how it serves our biological needs, we are virtually opening a new field. Well, not entirely new as I point out in my Appendix III, since attempts to advocate poetry on the basis of its utility are as old as Aristotle and Horace. Nevertheless in recent times, since vernacular Literature became an academic field, there has been little concerted effort to examine the function of Literature as a biological human behaviour. Regarded from the point of view of function, Literature takes on new dimensions as an aid to brain processes. I contend that from a biological approach, the human brain is disposed to connect and unify data. The goal of brain division of labour is to unite all incoming information into a meaningful model of the world, that is then carried in our neurons as a guide to position us in time and space.

In fact, the drive to connect, unify and make coherence is the overriding commitment of human brains. All experience is referenced for screening information as to its value, quality and placement in the record. Some parts the central nervous system experience and collect data and other parts process the data and organize it. The principle means of storing it is by a device known as narrative. Narrative, or more familiarly, story, is to brain what the Library of Congress catalogue system is to libraries, though story is infinitely more complex since it must arrange everything with reference to all its characteristics. The catalogue organizes books, the story organizes experience. This means not only examining the general content character of data, family related or work related and so on, but its relevance to our own security, tastes, personal history, sexual orientation — in other words, to all the features of our unique identity.

As I have said, the goal of all this gathering, sifting and filing of information is to unify, connect, coalesce the data into a meaningful story for managing the personal world. Now it just so happens that the novels and stories and poems that people compose, tell or write, and those that are heard or read by others, all have as their principal characteristic the compulsion to unity. Novels satisfy, and only satisfy, because they are organized wholes. The feeling of submitting to story control of information, following and discovering connections, and moving to resolution, is biologically congenial to human brains. In reading Literature, not only does our brain welcome language used to organize virtual life experience similar to the record of our own personal lives, it feeds upon models that assist it to create the life story it writes moment to moment. Literature becomes a kind of story nutrition. We read for our story strength the way Popeye ate spinach. Now we can see how this Literature imperative operates in a dualistic culture. We need help to stay balanced and whole in a world dedicated to fragmenting and simplifying. In the twenty-first century our need to read becomes more, not less urgent.

Before we examine the case for reading complex Literature in a culture that erodes story, we need to look more closely at the role of reading in maintaining personal health. We must help ourselves before we can correct cultural mistakes. As you will see in the next chapter, if we don't work successfully to connect and unify our story of our world and our relation to it, we can get very sick and become dysfunctional. Dysfunction is spreading precisely because we are starving our left hemispheres. Without sufficient language, and without the stories that our language constructs, we are helpless in the face of ideologies competing for control of our brains.

Notes to Chapter 5: Dualism vs Holism: A Cosmic Intermission

1. See D.M. Dooling and Paul Jordan-Smith, 1989.
2. The peculiarly Christian version of this Duality Principle is called Manichean. Its origins trace to the 3rd-5th centuries AD, and have at its core a cosmic conflict between God and Satan, a story still alive, well, and influential as evidenced by *Star Wars.*
3. The West cannot really understand how communism and capitalism can coexist in the same system of economic practice, but the Chinese have no problem with such an idea, however it may turn out in history, and have committed themselves to such a two-in-one view as an official policy.
4. Paradoxically the struggle to simplify (dualism), and justify simplification leads to enormously complicated arguments and procedures. The acceptance of complexity on the other hand leads to much simpler relations with the world. As always this is not a paradox when explained in relation to the larger world view model. When the system is very complex, nothing but confusion and destruction can result from distorting it into the simple.
5. *The Foundations of Chinese Medicine*, 1989.
6. Steven Pinker, 1994.
7. See Corballis and his index on split brains.

CHAPTER SIX

Reading and Healing: Balancing Over the Falls

For there is nothing, either good or bad, but thinking makes it so.

— **Hamlet**

Oh wad some Power the giftie gie us
To see oursels as ithers see us!
It wad frae monie a blunder free us,
An' foolish notion.

— **Robert Burns**

ON JUNE 30, 1859, ON THE EVE OF THE AMERICAN CIVIL WAR, Jean François Gravelet, known as the Great Blondin, walked across Niagara Falls on a manila rope stretched between two countries. He was the first person to do so. Carrying a balancing pole thirty or forty feet long and weighing forty or more pounds, he walked across, he walked back. And on subsequent walks he pushed a wheelbarrow across; he went across blindfolded; he stood on his head; he pushed out a stove and cooked an egg in the middle of the crossing; and finally he went across carrying a man, his agent, on his back.[1] In doing all this he earned world renown and was watched in his life by millions of people. When I read about this I asked myself two questions: How did he do it? And what was it about this tightrope performance that drew huge crowds to see Blondin whenever his stunts were advertised? In other words, what were the spectators' brains looking for?

My own answers to these questions will become clear as we talk about health. I am starting with Blondin because his feats of balancing over the deadly Niagara Falls provide the perfect metaphor for how we must negotiate our way through the perils of life. One of his biographers writes:

> In the center of the rope was a section of about forty feet that was totally unsupported by guy ropes. It was man against gravity here and Blondin could expect no help from any outside force. Only his ability to maintain his balance could get him across this stretch alive.[2]

Balance is the key to our well-being and to our survival, both individually and as a species. As English biologist Steven Rose puts it: "Healthy organisms are, energetically speaking, in balance."[3] I am going to argue in this chapter that Literature can be the balancing pole that helps us pick our safe path through, or over, the perils of the challenges to our life story.

Being balanced means being functional, being efficient. To be functional requires the expenditure of energy. Everything is always giving off energy in an effort to maintain its equilibrium, its status quo. This in turn requires an organism to take in "fuel" that is in a ratio balanced to the energy it expends. Our body organs are always at work, trying to correct imbalances, responding to too much sugar, too much salt, too little water. For each organism there is a maximal functioning balance, and this changes in response to environment and to aging. But humans also have a vastly complex and sensitive neural system that attempts to balance emotional and cognitive information. To be fully functional, humans also require knowledge, motor control, intention, motivation and planning. Being balanced requires mental and physical co-ordination and harmony. All mental effort requires the expenditure of energy, and all energy expenditure must be achieved in the most economical and efficient way to produce health.

Balance is a useful metaphor for other functions of human life relevant to our health. People can become lopsided by working too hard and not playing enough; by being too factual and not imaginative; by eating an insufficient variety of food; by sitting too much or being immobilized; by thinking, obsessing about one or two things. Most of these disorders derive from lack of information about self-care or self-function or from misinformation that is believed and therefore leads to self-harm. Beliefs and information, it may surprise some people to know, affect the functioning of body organs, blood circulation, body movement and posture, and sensory perception.

The concept of balance is well-known to Western medicine and is often called homeostasis, meaning stable, constantly the same. Homeostasis is best exemplified by the household thermostat which is a good model of self-regulation. The thermostat is sensitive to temperature and according to how it is set, will call for more heat (by being connected to a heat supply), when temperatures drop below a pre-set level (cool), and shut down heat supply when the temperature rises to another, higher pre-set level (warm). The goal of the thermostat is to maintain temperature within a constant limited range between C and W. The body, too, has a thermostat. We put on a sweater or have a hot drink when we feel cold, and take off clothing or have a cold drink when we feel hot. Such ordinary self-correcting behaviours that we seem to do without thought are easy to observe once our attention is drawn to them as balancing acts. Our physical self-regulation goes on all the time. We reach for the milk of magnesia when we have acid pains; we eat when hungry; we nap when tired; we stretch when cramped. These are all forms of adjustment necessary to balance. Normally we hardly notice any of this. It is even more difficult to notice or understand our cognitive balancing process, the times when our thinking and feeling must be adjusted to return us to narrative equilibrium. Since thinking occurs at the cortical level and is under our control and is not automatic, we may not make the effort to reflect and correct. The problem of balancing our views of events and experiences is complicated by our desire to avoid painful thoughts or feelings. This produces repression and denial of the discomfort brought about by bad news or change, making it more difficult to adapt our thinking and so regain our balance.

There are two things about this continuous self-regulation that we need to understand if we are to grasp the role of reading in health maintenance. For one, we are so highly evolved and complex as organisms that the thermostat analogy can be misleading. We are regulating hundreds of intricate systems and microsystems in a continuously variable environment with which we continuously interact. Second, we are not very good, at least nowadays and at least in Western culture, at achieving balance. We have a vast number of human health problems in an environment that is moment by moment being poisoned and made unpredictable. We are continually creating contexts that are a challenge to being balanced, so that unprecedented amounts of human energy are being expended, merely to decipher what is necessary to being balanced, before we can even make the adjustments. Bandura reminds us that managing our lives requires our conscious attention: "Like any other endeavour, effective self-regulation of health behaviour requires certain skills. Thus, motivation facilitates self-directed change when people are taught skills for self-influence, but motivation without the requisite subskills produces little change"[4] motivation and skills. The former must be based on self-interest in our health and control, and the latter can be greatly enhanced by reading Literature. Belief in the usefulness of reading precedes the knowledge acquired by reading. As we read we must know that we are constructing sets of information in our brains as tools for life management and planning.

The problem of self-regulation becomes immediately obvious and instantly illustrated when we contemplate the complexity of human biology. The more we discover about the workings of the human mind and body and their unity, the more we become aware of the inadequacy of our language, our terminology, to describe these workings. For instance, the term homeostasis may serve for a simple thermostat but it hardly covers the response-to-the-environment system of a living organism, any organism, let alone a human being. Steven Rose suggests the term "homeodynamics" for the very good reason that it is not really fair or accurate to speak of stasis in human adaptation.

> Lifelines are ... inherently homeodynamic. The present instant of our, or any organism's life, is simply inexplicable biologically if considered as a frozen moment of time, the mere sum, at that moment, of the differential expression of a hundred thousand genes. Each of our presents is shaped by and can only be understood by our pasts, our personal, unique, developmental history as an organism.[5]

There is constant change, movement, development, growth, aging and alteration in the organism itself, so that it cannot, must not, stay the same. We cannot achieve balance by striving to stay the same in the face of inevitable changes, internal and external, that we cannot control. On the contrary, all our complex efforts to avoid changing in the face of change throws us off balance and we are certain to fall and suffer hurt. The very energy we use to avoid adaptation becomes directed against ourselves, damaging our health.

Moment by moment the organism must maintain balance in *the service of the act of changing, and while achieving change.* The human organism must make continuous re-adjustment to maintain equilibrium and devise effective, functional coping behaviours while changing. The term homeostasis derives from a machine model and a mechanistic culture where the body is thought of as a machine, and cause and effect are linear and simple. But the human organism is not a machine and its systemic change and adaptation contain thousands of simultaneous adjustments and rearrangements, from thought patterns to metabolic heart rate to digestive processes. We are required to imagine an organism that is somehow homeostatic (constantly the same) while being homeodynamic (constantly changing) *at the same time.* In other words, we need a more multi-dimensional, complex concept to convey the notion that we seek to achieve the ability to regulate a reliable, constant, *process* of effective adaptation to change. We do not want the changes (of organism, environment and the interaction of both) to throw the organism-regulating process off balance.

Let's use an analogy. The downhill skier brings his experiences, training, intelligence and physical fitness to bear as he descends the hill in a competitive race. He reads the terrain, adapts to changes in snow conditions, to sudden disruption of the track, temperature and wind change, to the condition of his own body, and he uses all his knowledge and experience to adjust to all of this. But anything could interfere with the efficiency of his adaptive skill, the process — an argument with his girlfriend just before the start, indigestion from an unwise lunch, a sudden snow squall halfway down; a hole in the ground where it shouldn't be or losing his lucky charm on the way to the hill. The test of the skier's *homeoadaptiveness* is his ability to maintain his skills and concentration no matter what changes he encounters or what stressors he experiences. His success will depend on maintaining his balance, psychically and physically and this in turn depends on the stability of his adaptive process. Homeoadaptation (process adjustment) might convey more accurately the goal for a healthy organism than other terms I have come across, though it is quite a mouthful.

To get close to the heart of the problem of achieving this homeoadaptation, and therefore achieving balance, and to understand why we are so incompetent at it, we need a bit of cultural analysis. Only a bit is possible, for proper commentary on this would take volumes, and much more time and space than is available to me. We can start, however, by reducing the causes of disease (or the disruption of homeoadaptive stability), to four challenges to wellness. They may be listed as injury, malnutrition, poison, and stress. An accident like a motor vehicle or industrial mishap causes wounds to bone or soft tissue, which in turn causes pain and limitation of body function. Such accidents are never experienced without psychic injury also, to varying degrees depending on the individual, so that biochemical stressors are produced in the brain and cause toxic results, including an increase in the pain response. The patient feels depressed, wounded, helpless, victimized, in short, off balance in life management, social function, body image and physical and mental control.

Another source of disease is malnutrition. This can arise from poverty, famine, ideology or mental, emotional disturbance. The result is poor physical and mental functioning and a loss of physiological balance between functions, and loss of the motivation required and necessary to drive the function of brain, muscle and organ harmony. The third cause of illness or disharmony is poison. This involves ingesting or breathing toxic material that interferes with the normal functioning of the organ systems, brain, lungs, liver, spleen, pancreas and kidneys. An article from the *Toronto Star*, May 18, 2000, illustrates the point. The article is headed "Smog Killing 1,000 Annually in Toronto, Study Shows." It contains the following information: "The two pollutants identified by the study as the main culprits behind premature deaths were nitrogen dioxide (38 percent) and carbon monoxide (33 percent)." No study, of course, can isolate the cumulative effects of such pollutants from hundreds of others in water and food, a hazardous mix we have to combat. Nor can they show how a critical mass of toxic assault on the human organism is achieved when such substances as these are added to psychosocial stress, which is, of course, our fourth cause of disease. Stress might be experienced as the result of job loss, grief, divorce, relocating, toxic parenting, conflict, crime, abuse, noise, bad news, fear, indeed any of the insults that result in the organism being unable to remain in balance, and function efficiently, while enduring the experience of these challenges to the system.

The best way to understand the organism's response to these assaults on stability is to think of the human system as a very complex information processor. All of the causes of illness can be thought of as information that is received and processed by the receiving organism. Remembering that the body and mind cannot operate separately, all events that affect us have immediate and sometimes long-lasting consequences for both. It is easy for us to imagine "things" affecting us — bugs, toxins, bad air and smells, contaminated food. It is much harder to put pure information or news, whether read or heard, into a story in which our bodies change or react to the meaning of what we learn. News of job loss, or winning a lottery are items that the brain registers as requiring immediate life story adjustment, with attendant surges of neurochemicals like cortisol-producing depression, feelings of helplessness or fear, or maybe feelings of euphoria from a rush of serotonin.

Similarly, a sound without language can create a shock. Yesterday a logging truck roared by me so close in an illegal passing maneuver that it smashed my outside rear-view mirror. I heard the sound of a thud first. I registered shock, surprise, fear, and anger. I was certainly thrown off balance by near miss with injury or death. I regard such events as mini-traumas. The recovery from such traumas requires a number of actions and thoughts: telling the story to my wife; reporting to and conversing with the police; talking to my insurance agent; all the while my body is taking real time to recover from the biochemical reaction. Balance is recovered by neural adaptation, and language plays a primary role in fitting this event into the continuous review and construction of my life story.

This scary incident reminds me of my mortality, the way a moment can alter or end my life, or the lives of those I love. I am helped to overcome this fear, strangely enough, by reading. This event happened at precisely the time I finished learning about the death-defying feats of Blondin. He models balance for me and restores my focus to the present moment, away from paranoid fantasy about what might have been or what might be to come. Blondin says to me: “Concentrate, Joe, and balance, taking one step at a time.”

Information, news, is not the event itself, it is the interpretation of the event in our brains that affects our behaviour. So we can see how human bodies are thrown off balance by alteration, however received, and can become a disruption to our assumptions, and to the story we live based upon them. But we cannot bypass or ignore these disruptions and violations to the story we must continually create. We need to be actively assisting ourselves in the adjustment process. The role of reading other stories in helping us maintain balance becomes clearer as we learn to create our own story with awareness.

Health, equilibrium, balance, efficient functioning require continual adjustment, re-calibration, adaptation. Nothing around us or in us stays the same, and if we are unable to change we will not cope well. We might compare this change process to altering our clothes to fit changes in our weight or girth or height, or in response to fashion changes, making our costumes larger or smaller, our skirts longer or shorter. To make these alterations we must remove the clothing to work on it. How do we know we need or want to do this? By looking in the mirror, or having someone tell us how we look and what needs to be altered. The mirror, or someone else's view, removes us temporarily from our own assumptions so that we can make the necessary changes to our appearance before resuming some new assumption about ourselves, namely that we now look "all right" and can carry on unselfconsciously. We have, we hope, comfortably adjusted. Well, Literature is our *information mirror.*

This whole process is about perspective, point of view, angle of vision, alternative perception and new information. What is true about the "out-sight" of clothing, the knowledge that you can see how it needs a tuck in there, a letting out here, is also true of the "insight" about our beliefs, ideas, thoughts and attitudes. In other words, we have to be able to get outside of our "I" structure for however brief a time to see what needs changing. What will be our mirror, our perspective, the scenic lookout from where we can look at ourselves? And who is out there doing the looking if we are still here being looked at?

As someone who has a fair amount of experience at acting and directing, I have never believed it possible to direct and act in the same play. You can do it, of course, but you won't do it well; something will suffer. The same is true of the sports coach; only the coach can see the whole picture, design the team strategy and watch and alter the patterns and designs of play, see who is not doing what or fitting in where. You can't do this if you are one of the players, someone inside the design being observed. We are like weavers of a tapestry constructing a story as we sit at our loom.

We can never stop weaving, but unlike the Lady of Shallot, we must weave our stories even as we join the passing stream of life. Is this dilemma irresolvable? What can help us see ourselves as others see us? How are we to get outside of ourselves to see ourselves? Well, the coach could show us a video of the game and discuss it. We could then see ourselves in action and see what we are doing that needs changing. We can look at family photos and see how we are behaving, what they reflect back about how we felt or what we looked like, and we can admire or be horrified at ourselves. But how can we do this with thoughts and ideas, with our world view, the very stuff of our identity systems, our story? Who will help us edit that?

Edit and change, review and revise our stories we certainly must, there can be no doubt about that, if we are to make the shift to healthy functioning when the story gets stuck. You are the story you weave and create, so if the story falters, confusion and even sickness results. The ability to step outside the story you are in, long enough to decide what you want to change in it, is the highest level of consciousness available to us. This movement or shift (we can call it "mind shift"), from being a character in a story, to being critic or editor of the same story, is the quintessential hallmark of successful therapeutic process. All true self-knowledge, self-efficacy and self-volition depend on the ability to practice mind shift. The tricky part of imagining this is that the critic/editor of the self story is outside the story and inside *at the same time.* The wonderful thing about Literature is that it enables us to go through this mind shifting safely. We do not have to be at physical or relational risk to gain increased knowledge of ourselves. At the same time, we cannot live entirely in books because we need enough experience to make sense of what we read about experience.

I have said that videos and pictures can be useful in showing us to ourselves in action. I have done a lot of useful work with patients using photos of their childhood selves and their families of origin. There are four limitations to pictures, however. The first is they are always about the past, which is fine if you need to examine the past. It is necessary to talk about these pictures in relation to the present story we need to change. You wait six days for the prints to come ("some day my prints will come"), and your life has moved on, so what you have now are pictures of last summer's holiday, that is if you remembered to take them to the drugstore before the film faded. The second is that pictures are about surfaces and tell you very little about what is really going on. Language is required for explanation. If pictures are not "candid" they cannot be trusted, and if they are candid they don't tell you what is in the mind, motive or emotion of the image. Third, as a tool to help you get outside the story, the picture only works if it is a picture of you or a familiar character in your story. Otherwise, the image of the stranger is part of another story whose images exclude you. Unless they are therapists, people are not really interested in other people's pictures, no matter what polite noises our friends make. You cannot replace the image of the other with the image or idea of yourself on your mental screen because it is already occupied by the image physically in front of you. The final limitation is the limitations of the visual. Because a picture is not lexical, not in words, its range of reference is extremely limited. A picture of "mother" is not about mothers in general, the way the word "mother" is; it is your mother unmistakably and there is no other mother like her. Pictures of London being bombed are about London to a Londoner unless some photographer mounts an exhibit and calls them, "Pictures of War," using language to tell you how to see them.

This brings us to one powerful conclusion: the best device for removing you from your story long enough to see it differently, and so see what must be changed, is Literature. Changing the language is to change the story, and changing the story is to change our reality. It is for this reason that language remains the primary means of clinical therapy, no matter what other auxiliary techniques are enlisted. And of all forms of language, metaphors, adjectives, rhymes, proverbs, the most useful is sustained narrative. Remember we must be outside the story and in it at the same time — so how does reading make this possible when nothing else will? Because Literature endows us with symbolic representation of worlds we can occupy and live in while not leaving our real selves. While reading, we enter worlds composed entirely of language; the pictures and feelings associated with them are supplied by us from our life experience.

Literature provides numerous illustrations of this mind shift process. I recently suggested to a patient that she had been living in the wrong story, one her parents had created about her and which she had grown to believe as "true." After some time in therapy she started to question this version of herself as false, different from how she felt or saw herself. Her response to my remark was, "Like Alice; *she* fell into the wrong story." I regarded this as a powerful personal and literary insight. She said this was one book she remembered from school and discussions with her friends. Now it returned to "normalize" her experience and reinforce what I was saying. There was a book to help her understand through metaphor how one can drop into a story.[6]

Many people have to form their identity in worlds where they feel alienated and foreign. Many writers have treated this experience. Dorothy in *The Wizard of Oz* is one such illustration. So is Anne Shirley of Green Gables. So is the hero of *One Flew Over the Cuckoo's Nest.* So is Oedipus Rex. Hans Andersen's best known tale, "The Ugly Duckling," is perhaps the world's most famous story of a character who is in the wrong story and finally joins the right one, one in which he feels comfortable. The huge appeal of this story may derive from the sense many children have of being unwanted, misfits because they live *unrecognized* for so long in their families. The writers of Literature know what they intend, and it is up to us to apply what they teach, consciously, to ourselves. We must take these symbolic representations and gain distance from our own stories in order to see these stories from slightly different perspectives. In this way we can return to our own stories with new "writing" skills. For if it is true you cannot alter a story you cannot get outside of, then it is also true you must return to your own story if you are going to effectively run your own life.

A patient, call her Francine, is a bilingual, forty-year-old survivor of sexual assault, physical abuse and a fear-filled upbringing by a tyrannous, alcoholic father and a mother who was too afraid to adequately protect her children. Francine does not like to read fiction. She can't see the point of it. She reads and tries to memorize the textbooks for the course she is taking, but otherwise stays locked in her own fragmented story, handicapped by fear and self-loathing. One of the remedial paths I decide to follow is persuading Francine to read fiction. My reasoning behind what will turn out to be an uphill battle is fairly simple and can be explained as follows. The patient has social phobia. She mostly communes with herself. She does some journal keeping but it tends to go over the same ground. She seems to be trapped inside her story. She is finding it difficult to think about this story without disabling emotion, the result of trauma. Her thinking goes round and round, like a mouse on a treadmill. She cannot change her perspective, she cannot get "outside" her prior experience, or in terms of regressive therapy, she cannot enlist her adult person to review her child experiences. She is locked into the actual child fears and angers whenever she tries to work on her past. Communing with herself looks like this:

Francine Diagram A

She seems unable to break this circle. I believe that if I can get her to read a story that engages her attention she will be able to import the virtual experience as a new perspective on her own story. I want to change her thinking *process* however slightly. At the same time I believe that reading will alter and enlarge her language ability, and it is in the language part of her brain that she will reorganize, recognize, tame and control her emotional experience, the emotions that trap her into the circle of thinking,

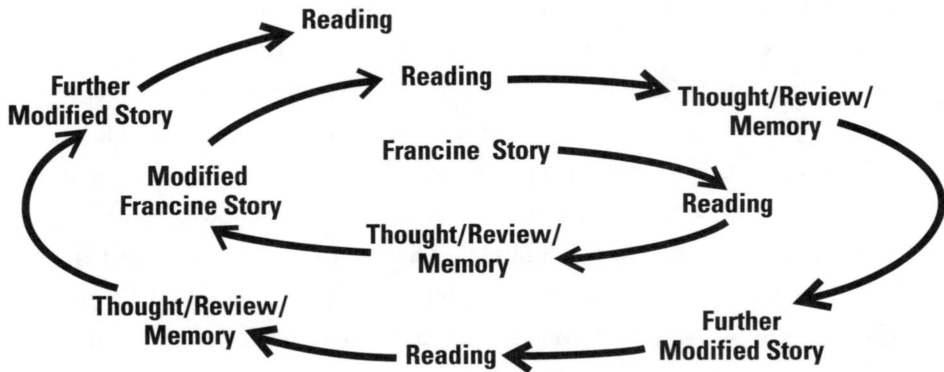

Francine Diagram B – Hoped for Result. As the circle widens, spirals out, freedom from the original "fixed" story becomes possible. The read stories are now part of the Thought/Review/Memory process.

habit, outworn clichés that limit her as described above. The circle, for the duration of the reading should then look like Diagram B.

To think about herself through the medium of the book-words will take her outside herself, and help her construct a workable identity by allowing her to see her story in a wider context. She needs to grow her world larger. To interpret, understand and make sense of the reading, she must enlist her own experience, not as a self trapped in a recurrent cycle of repeated unpleasantness, but as altered. The alteration will come through applying her personal experience to the interpretation of a virtual or simulated experience (the book), and this new reading experience will be *grafted onto* her own narrative construction of her own life story. We may call this the "grafting function" of Literature. She must pass through the book to get back to herself, but only if she will read a book, a story. She must filter her experience, via language, through the language of the text. In doing so, parts of the rational/emotional experience of the text adhere to her own brain and are grafted into her own experience and so become part of it.

Since the new version of experience she will have acquired by reading is acquired by means of language, it is necessarily under the control of her language neocortex, and so becomes conscious and manageable as a thought process. And she must use her adult ego and its language to do this. At some point in this process she comes to say of her personal life experience, "I rely on it." I take this to mean that she accepts her painful past as material she can work on, as a story she has a right to, and as a touchstone to her reality, as opposed to accepting other versions of her past. On the other hand, she has begun to move outside of the story that trapped her. She is learning to consciously control and use her past experience for growing up and getting beyond childhood entrapment.

En route to this stage we make several false starts with the English classics. She finally agrees to try an historical romance by Anne Perry. I have myself been reading Perry's novels and have referred several women to them. Why do I suggest this to her? These novels are well researched and convey very skillfully some of the social horrors of Victorian England, the class system, the gap between rich and poor, the abuse of women and the courage and principled behaviour of the heroine Hester who reappears in several of Perry's novels. Hester is a woman, and this is important to the identification process I seek for my patient. Hester is a social activist; Francine has strong views on social justice. Moreover, the hero Hester must overcome various challenges and hardships in pursuit of her goals. My patient's background seems to me quite like that of many poor women in Victorian England. The reading proves fruitful; at least she accomplishes one novel. We are finally able to discuss a fiction we have both read. We are able to talk about Francine's background, values, beliefs, feelings in relation to the reading experience. We are now able to talk about Francine's feelings from somewhere outside her trapped self-narrative. To do this we have needed another narrative. We can make a comparison to her own life. We have broken open the cage and the bird can leave and look at its former captivity from the outside. At least a little, at least sometimes. Small changes play a huge role in achieving health. Overcoming systemic childhood sexual trauma is a long ordeal.

Albert Bandura tells us there are four sources of information used in the construction of self-efficacy beliefs: 1. "Performance attainments," or the results of actions actually performed by the doer which feedback the knowledge, "look at me, I can do it;" 2. "Vicarious experience," seeing or visualizing others doing things that the viewer can then imagine herself doing, which in turn leads to increased ambition, or learning how to do something from watching others, or learning what not to attempt and so avoiding failure; 3. "Verbal persuasion" that encourages and motivates people to try to do things or affirming their potential to do things, "that's it Francine, you can do it;" 4. "Physiological state" information, that is knowledge of one's own body state that says, "I have the strength or power to do this" or "I don't feel up to it, I am not strong or skilled enough." Of these four sources, it seems that two of them, fifty percent, can come from reading. It could of course come from other sources as well, as in watching sports and athletics, or listening to a lecture. But for various reasons I have touched on previously, they come most effectively from reading.

Decoding a written text so it can be internalized as somatosensory (that is, known in the body), requires combining or uniting, composing into one story the vicarious, the verbal, and the physiological experiences that Bandura described as separate kinds of experience. The reader makes pictures or images of what is read, producing in the brain an action movie. This is internally generated from a combination of the reader's prior experience, the language by which the experience is accessed, and the activating, adjusting and reorganizing of this language store for the purposes of understanding the text being read. This combined mental activity, the reader's former experience, the language for describing the experience, the adjustment to the text being read and the physical registry of emotion are mutually reinforcing. These mental operations give particular energy and memorability to models for self-efficacy found in reading. And these models consist not only of people, characters, heroes, but also incidents, problems, places, thinking processes, and situations.

There is even some question as to whether reading with attention and emotional engagement is in fact just vicarious, only a second-hand experience, a simulated or virtual echo experience of the "real thing." As many readers testify, the thoughts and emotions experienced in reading feel very like the real thing, a new thing itself crossing from second-hand to first-hand experience. I talked to a woman about her reading of a rape scene in Peter Straub's *The Hellfire Club.* She said she did not feel as if she was being raped, but she did feel a flood of emotion, principally fear and anger, and these feelings were quite real, not vicarious. Indeed, people who are well-read often become confused about whether their recollections are based on their own life events or on something they have read. What people read can become so woven into their knowledge, their wisdom, their residue of self-efficacy apparatus that they cannot distinguish it from other personal experience. The two have become one.

I gave a patient, "Linda," who grew up with an alcoholic father, a book called *The Invisible Enemy.*[7] From it she read the story "The Navigator" by Susan Minot, or tried to. She was so overcome with emotional pain and discomfort that she was unwilling to read the rest of the stories. Was my patient's emotion vicarious? Obviously not. As she read about the children on a picnic, filled with hopes of a pleasant, "normal" family experience and hearing the pop of a beer can being opened by their father, the reader experienced the full surge of anger and disappointment recorded in her brain from many years before. The story itself does not describe the emotions and disappointment of the fictional children. In fact, the story ends merely with the "pop" of the beer can, shattering the peace and harmony of the setting. It was the reader who supplied all the unstated emotion in the text. She "knew" what *they* felt. Was that vicarious experience? It was first-hand experience stimulated and re-experienced *in conjunction* with the verbal text, so that now the story and Linda's own emotional memory combined to focus on a type, a typical moment emotionally and exactly related to her original emotions, and painful feelings, which occurred in many quite other circumstances than a picnic.

We are thrown off balance by physical ailments, serious digestive tract problems, an ulcer, a bowel disorder, a heart arrhythmia, chronic back pain. Yet all of these can be induced by psycho-social stress. Our work and family life is affected. We become dysfunctional, we are tilted — not on an even keel — and so we say we are sick. The same kind of imbalance can result from "undigested" information. This means we are carrying around a piece of news or information about ourselves, our world or experience that has not been integrated and accommodated into our story. Such a piece of "news" might be: "My father did not love me"; "I am a girl, but I should have been a boy"; "I must be a bad person or I would not have been treated this way"; or "They are all right, I am crazy." Such views are constructions of experience held as "truths" in the life story. Such "facts" are so disturbing and deeply troubling they must be put aside, repressed, while we get on with life. To dwell on them would be disabling, and indeed sometimes is disabling. But putting them aside while we marry and have children and go to work does not mean they are not there and known in our minds, and does not mean they are not throwing us off balance.

A very good example of "wrong story" construction can be found in eating disorders. Eating disorders can be quite complex, but they often have one central characteristic: the patient is deriving significant reward from either the refusal to eat, or the insistence on notable and dangerous weight gains. It is easier to understand this if you consider the hunger striker refusing to eat. Her refusal is a protest. When it seems to us that all power has been removed, we can at least refuse to eat. The eating problem patient is a character in a story and believes that the story message is: "We don't love you; you don't matter; you shouldn't be here; you have no power." Not eating or excessive eating becomes an embodied physical metaphor for the family story and requires the therapist to read the story. *Characters completely inside stories they cannot read are not conscious of being characters or of the parts they are playing.*[8]

Many patients wish they could have bad thoughts or painful memories surgically removed. Indeed, many psychotropic drugs are a form of neural surgery and produce numbing and thought blocking functions, but at a cost. The two problems with repressed negative story structures such as those I have illustrated above are that they operate all the time to distort, unbalance all the required normal functions of one's relations with the world. And second, the effort to repress them requires enormous expenditure of energy, which also throws the metabolic processes off balance, and often leads to disease. The most effective treatment for such disorders of thinking and feeling is to change the disabling story and bring it more in line with real family history, with the actual probability of what led to the formation of the story, and to integrate the story into a functional life account. We need a story that enables, not disables us to cope, adapt, and achieve, and it must be a story we believe. Now, if this were simple to do, we would have no need of therapists. The problem is that living inside a fixed Logos or world view about oneself precludes an examination of that Logos from the outside; so change becomes impossible. The "reframing" or editorial work of the therapist is part of the treatment, but Literature is the most natural and available resource for lifting the reader out of the narrow and distorting Logos through which she views herself.

What did the Minot story add to Linda's treatment of her wounded development and poor self-efficiency? Though she could not recall such an incident (the picnic, the silence, the one symbolic beer can), from her own life, she has now adopted this fictional incident as useful, and the best way to explain her own past, or part of it. She has been given a vehicle for discussing the attendant emotions. She has been supplied with a catalytic image. She has been aided in moving the emotional and debilitating, frightening emotions stored from experience. And she is not alone and uniquely afflicted because of what she had previously seen as her own failure. She is more educated about how such distortions of self estimation can occur. Her problem is "normal." The story and its language form enables her to shift memory into a different process, from a region of the brain called the diencephalon, into the neocortical language areas of her brain, where she can apply linguistic order, where she can achieve and offer review, comment, editorial refinement, and so achieve more self-awareness. By doing this she feels more in control of material from the past rather than feeling helplessly controlled by it. Fundamental to this shift in relations to the past is the feeling of moving from passivity to activity, from being helpless, victimized, to being effective and functional.

In some basic respects, and in accord with Bandura's classic work on self-efficacy, we might say that health accompanies the feeling of self-as-control. Certainly in the case of painful or traumatic memory, sickness is proportionate to the degree of feeling helpless and out of control. The corollary of this for psychotherapy is that good healing practice is proportionate to the effectiveness of the therapeutic process in assisting a patient to move from helplessness, to empowerment. All of the discussion about self-esteem, assertiveness, self-image, confidence and so on that has filled countless self-help books in recent years, can find their root usefulness in the restated formula: *good therapy is assisting the patient to self-efficacy through empowerment by means of language control.* We can call this thought, reason, awareness etc., but it all boils down to language cortex efficiency.

The goal of using fiction as therapy is to move the reader's brain into language/narrative action. Reading fiction is practice for reading one's own life and "reading" is used here to signify a self management, an active and creative thought process achieved in the medium of language. The tool that was the fiction or poetry, becomes incorporated into the reader's — the patient's — brain as a self-regulating processor, now spliced into her experience store of tools, information and language repertoire. The narrative language is the key: the fact that the experience was acquired by means of language, and the fact that the experience can be reassembled and possibly modified by means of language, makes neural change, brain change, identity change possible. Such change is synonymous with rebalancing and health.

Complex language *changes brains* and can provide the means for managing, enhancing, expanding and ordering life experience. Nowhere is this clearer than in the management of trauma experience. Complex language is perceived, acquired, and enhanced by reading. Reading fiction may in fact be difficult for those suffering from post-traumatic stress disorder, but it is crucial that language activity in the patient be activated and enlisted in relation to the trauma events. Why? Because the trauma events, especially if they occur over a period of time rather than on a single and brief occasion, have the effect of blocking a language response or interpretation of the event itself as it is happening. While the emotional record may be intact, albeit as a disconnected, event-related set of responses, the events have not been incorporated into the life narrative that is formed by language. Indeed, many patients testify to a memory blank in relation to trauma, a blank that sometimes spans years. In fact, there is now a growing body of evidence that shows a deactivation of language areas of the brain, even when the emotional "recall" of the trauma event is happening in the experimental setting.[9] In other words, it is easy enough to trigger the patient's emotional response to clues that recall the frightening experience, but it is clear that at the same time, language association is again deactivated, as it was at the time of the original trauma experience.[10]

This is quite contrary to normal recall or stimulation. Seeing scenes or pictures or hearing sounds or smelling odours that recall past places or events normally brings up language explanations in the mind. This is not the place to get technical, but we all know the silencing effects of fright. During times of extreme fear the body freezes, the breath is shortened or held, the eyes open wide and a kind of paralysis takes over. The goal seems to be to achieve a kind of invisibility. Access to commentary, verbal response or thought seems to be denied. This is of course further exaggerated in the case of a child suffering trauma, where the paucity of pre-existing language makes it more likely that terrifying events will lead to silence. This silence can be, and has been frequently misinterpreted by adults. It appears that this blockage to linguistic process is achieved biochemically. Various chemical neurotransmitters come into play during intense fright situations that effectively short circuit access to the language centres of the brain. A case will illustrate this most clearly.

Mary was sexually assaulted at knife point while walking back to a friend's house in a strange town she was visiting. In treatment, she could talk about this event in some detail, though she did so with extreme reluctance. Her therapy revealed that this event, late at night in a deserted parking lot, was in fact a re-traumatization. At a very young age she had been sexually assaulted in her home by a babysitter. About this earlier experience she could recall very little, and in fact, drew a blank on most of her early childhood experience. As far as language memory goes, she had effectively shut down for years. She only knew about the earlier experience, as I learned in therapy, because a great family furor erupted when, upon a genital examination by her mother, because of the child's severe local discomfort, clear signs of an assault were evident. We are not dealing here with memory "loss," but a failure of memory *formation*, the kind of memory of which life-story is made.

Reading Literature will not initially assist a patient to overcome the panic consequences and other symptoms of trauma. There are many benefits, however, that do result over time from such reading. For one thing, the language centres of the brain which are crucial for story formation are activated and trained. For another, the introspection necessary for construction of identity can be very difficult or impossible for trauma patients who turn away from the painful memory and knowledge of the self as shameful or damaged. Reading literature permits an indirect knowledge of the self. The reader can obtain new perspectives by taking a temporary and partial leave of absence from the "I" story. But since the "I" is doing the reading, it is still affected by the reading experience. So the reading is a form of experiment that facilitates self-knowledge and change of perspective without self and memory confrontation.

Persistent presence of fright chemicals in the bloodstream alter the victim's whole life. The denial of ready access to language centres and life-story formations diminishes the individual's control, free will and self-efficacy. The health of the patient depends on the acquisition of language skills and habits of narrative formation so that therapy must focus on motivating and cultivating the language skills, story reconstruction and distancing of the past to some memoried storage position where it can be managed and deposited; where the past is not dominant and continually re-enacted.

There are several reasons why those with poorly developed self-narrative skills cannot, or are reluctant to read fiction. Such people are often from backgrounds where language skill is poorly developed or where speech and storytelling don't flourish.[11] They have no practice and few tools for narrative and cannot relate to or identify with the process of sustained and complex narrative. They live moment to moment and need to be distracted by action or visual event or simple dialogue. They have few words, so reading is too daunting, too much work to attempt. They have a poorly developed and discontinuous sense of personal identity so they cannot be very interested in the stories of others. They are too anxious and nervous (hyper alert) and need to be constantly monitoring their surroundings for danger, so that getting lost in a fictional narrative is not comfortable, would make them feel not "on guard." Reading fiction requires some degree of confidence and security about the continuity of the reader's life story, about leaving one's immediate surroundings, so putting the life story aside to enter another story is not a threat to an identity or security that is tenuously held.

There was nothing tenuous about The Great Blondin. I asked two questions at the start of this chapter and I hope you have seen the answers in this chapter, but I will spell them out because they are important insights to health and the healing role of reading.

I have said that health is balance and I need a perfect image of balance. Blondin was the greatest tightrope walker ever. In fact, it is said that his feats and stunts at Niagara were not even his greatest achievements. At the Great Exhibition at Crystal Palace, to which he was invited by Prince Albert, Blondin did his stunts on a rope one hundred and seventy feet above the heads of a hundred thousand people. Women fainted, men turned away in fear, some were sick with excitement. How did he do it? He was balanced. Lest you regard this as absurdly obvious, let me explain:

Blondin was, obviously balanced on the rope, but he was also personally balanced before he mounted the rope. Blondin was gifted with balance, apparently from birth. He was superbly trained from childhood. He knew himself, and what he could do. He worked incredibly hard and kept himself in perfect physical condition. He was totally focused and never took his performances for granted. Over a span of six decades he never fell. Using Bandura's criteria, Blondin was the supreme example of someone demonstrating self-efficacy. He stayed entirely in the present and did not allow fantasy or anxiety to interfere with his concentration. He never became paralyzed on the rope. He managed to keep giving faultless performances into his seventies. The point I am trying to make is, we can learn from Blondin and transpose his balance archetype modelling into the maintainance of *a healthy, creative life.*

What of the millions who watched and were awed by his astonishing feats of balance, what were they seeking? He was not competing with anyone, he was not racing against time or opponents, he was not wealthy, he was not a movie star; he was giving solo, non-competitive performances. My guess is that Blondin fascinated and compelled his contemporaries for the same reasons that the idea of what he did affects me today. I am drawn to the model of his balance. We want and need balance and we bow in awe of Blondin defying all distraction, all gravitational threat, all the comfort of solid ground. He defied danger, but more to the point, he celebrated balance. He demonstrated control. He showed us some possibility in ourselves that we yearn for, and he touched a deep chord of truth in us — we could and can and must learn to balance, and learn to esteem balance. Every Qi Gong master would recognize instantly the greatness and the appeal of Blondin. Balance is health. Balance is attainable. Psychological and mental balance controls the physical. Literature is the mental balancing pole. When Blondin walked in the sky without his pole, as he sometimes did, and as the deadly waves and chaos of turbulence roared beneath him, *he had internalized the pole — it was part of his brain. Literature can be part of ours.*

Notes to Chapter 6

Reading and Healing: Balancing over The Falls

1. See *Niagara—River of Fame*, p. 311-315, and *Blondin*, by Dean M. Shapiro.
2. Shapiro, p. 26.
3. Rose, 1997, p. 162.
4. Bandura, 1997, p. 303.
5. Rose, p. 157.
6. Alice falling down the rabbit hole would undoubtedly be described by a Freudian psychologist as Alice being born. If so, she is born into a crazy world where she has to make sense of very puzzling experiences. Do most children feel like this, I wonder, or was it mainly Victorian children?
7. Eds. Dow and Regan, 1989.
8. A good therapist can join with the family story and help edit the "script" without making his "reading" of the story explicit.
9. See, for instance, Van der Kolk, 1996, esp. chap 12. The evidence stems from, of course, an experimental setting.
10. See Rauch et al., 1996.
11. O'Sullivan and Howe, 1999.

Part Three

Opposition

CHAPTER SEVEN

Lits and Bits: Surviving the Mind Fields

Things are seldom what they seem,
Skim milk masquerades as cream;
Highlows pass as patent leathers;
Jackdaws strut in peacock's feathers.

—W.S. Gilbert

Every single wrong will have to be corrected.

— Wu Cheng'en

The truth is that in 1917 there was nothing that a thinking and sensitive person could do, except to remain human if possible.... But, after all, the war of 1914-18 was only a heightened moment in an almost continuous crisis. At this date it hardly even needs a war to bring home to us the disintegration of our society and the increasing helplessness of all decent people.

— George Orwell

And don't tell me she was one of God's good creatures, generous and kind to small animals — because humanism was always a dubious concept, one which fortunately is dying day by day.

— William Goldman

LITERATURE CAN ONLY EXERCISE ITS CREATIVE AND HEALING POWERS for human beings if they can and will read. Literature is nothing without an audience. At this point in our evolution Literature cannot be taken for granted because its audience is being eroded by a sea of relentless forces undermining our attachment to reading. This chapter will examine some of these threats to our connection to Literature in detail. Before we begin, we must be clear about the nature of the contest, the consequences if Literature loses, and the complexity of the struggle.

The first thing we must come to terms with is that the contest is about our minds. The question is, who or what will control our thinking, our feeling, our values and beliefs? The outcome of the battle will determine whether we will emerge as fragmented or whole beings. If we are not whole in ourselves, if we are divided as individuals and are not bonded as communities of beings, consciously recognizing and acting out of our common humanity, then someone or something other than ourselves, will control our thoughts and behaviour. If we do not think and feel for ourselves, some other force will think and feel for us. I am going to call these two warring principles “Lits and Bits,” for simplicity and brevity. Lits refers to the holistic tendency of Literature and the human experience it represents and embodies; Bits is borrowed from computer language and represents the fragments of information that characterize our age and break up the mind’s constructs, which are stories that make sense of the world we internalize. I am taking the position that we are story creatures and we are biologically adapted to an holistic representation of ourselves in conjunction with the world. Lits is our primary helper for doing this, but requires our conscious use of it.

To return for a moment to my use of Blondin as metaphor: let us think of Blondin as the reader, just like you or me. He must balance his way across the deafening chaos of the river, but he is not alone. He has his pole, Literature, to keep him balanced. What is the rope? The rope is his own story, all the data that he reads and feels and senses as he walks his life path, suspended against the backdrop of death, nothingness. This one woven, continuous rope of information is a whole. But what if it were not? What if it were cut into a thousand short pieces, not connected, “short cuts” or Bits of information that could not be made whole? I have read there were those who wanted to see Blondin fall because they were jealous or wanted to win bets. On one occasion, one of his guy ropes was severed and he almost toppled; on another, a saboteur with a knife was chased away just before he could complete his plan. As readers dependent on reliable, whole stories, we are in a similar situation in a world of perils and shortcuts to knowledge that has been simplified to the point where we are unable to walk our difficult path.

The idea of humankind being fought over by opposing powers is ancient, and lies at the heart of some Christian stories. This chapter may be seen as one more version of it. I have changed the warring parties to Lits and Bits but the nature of the struggle remains the same: the fight to liberate or enslave the human mind. Milton's *Paradise Lost* may be the most famous of such works. Humankind is the prize to be won in a battle between God and Satan, Good and Evil, forces of Light and Darkness. The major moral theme of Henry James's works is a battle between two kinds of people who fight like good and evil angels over a third person; the evil angel seeks to own and possess, the good to liberate and support independence. I think we need to see ourselves as individuals and communities engaged in our own twenty-first-century version of this awesome struggle. There is nothing mysterious, magical or other worldly about it. The issues are: who will wield power over human minds; how can we exercise the freedom to be autonomous, rather than be cloned in or out of the laboratory; and how can we maintain the right to exercise and control our human mind rather than be programmed by others?[1]

Lits Versus Bits

Novels, poems, plays and short stories are language structures that describe human experience, real or imagined, in a shaped, holistic form. They aim for some form of resolution or completeness. They require decoding by a reader who uses a combination of language skill, memory, emotion, sensory recall, imagination, and thought to reconstruct in the reader-mind the mental representation or inner experience of the writer's language. The reward of the reconstruction takes real time and real neural engagement. The reader must be interested. The reader is invited to think about the relations between what he has made out of the reading and his own life, as assembled to that point. Lits are made by individuals from an autonomous authentic "I" perspective and are fitted into a tradition of existing Lits that are inescapably enlisted in the writing, because new writing must come from old writing and must lead to more new writing. The reader is drawn into the tradition. The writer requires the reader's time and thought and expects these. The reader expects the writing to enhance the "I's" resources in its quest to structure the world in language in the mind. Lits is *open*. It does not tell the reader what to think about the writer's constructs (hence the existence of lit crit.), and leaves a degree of freedom for the reader's personal life involvement. The writer and the reader have an implicit contract to enrich and expand the whole account of the human-world nexus that makes for a sense of meaning and control. Lits are bound by biological laws and commandments to connect: they connect the lives of reader and writer; connect fragments of language into coherent structures; connect events and experiences into imaginable stories; connect one story to another; connect past to present, and to future; connect people across space; and Lits connect ideas, thoughts and images into wholes. *Connection* is the primary and necessary characteristic of Literature.

Bits refers to the entire production of fragments of information and the technologies that make the fragments available to hundreds of millions of people at one time. Such disconnected Bits of language and image came to be characteristic of what has become mass media. Bits are used mainly in the service of advertising and propaganda. What began as the street cries of vendors selling their wares, "Lovely Apples, come buy some lovely apples," quickly followed into print the expansion of literacy. First the cries became signs, and then print in newspapers. They entered radio and then television and most recently computers. There is, no doubt, an economic constraint on Bits, since brevity is economy, but there is also a neural goal to short-circuit thought and consideration, the weighing of evidence or the consultation by the reader of her own feelings. This brevity of Bits saves time and money. It closes off debate and thought and demands belief and action instead, so it may be regarded as *closed* communication. Bits most commonly take the form of commands, "Just do it!"; announcements, "A new frontier in safety"; instructions, "You will never need to floss again", and warnings, "If you shop elsewhere you paid too much." Most significantly, Bits relies heavily on the visual, which greatly increases its closed quality. Bits are designed by teams of people paid to design words and pictures to manipulate the minds of targeted consumers. The writers of ads are not to consult their own life experience or their authentic feelings. Bits require countless repetitions to increase their memorability. They require little or no decoding, and along with their visual emphasis require little or no language skill or practice. They do not add to the language store of the reader/viewer. Bits can take the form of slogans, labels, jingles, names (the "Eatmore" candy bar for instance), "photo ops," flashing signs, logos. Moreover, when Bits take on story form, as in "infomercials," they use story for purposes of making one closed point only. The idea is to strip everything down to the barest and most impactful message. These are the differences between Bits and Lits. The consequences on human brains of world domination by Bits is of the greatest significance for our future as a species.

Bits

This is no joke: If Lits are going to be displaced by Bits it will be because our brains will have been altered. Bits can take bites out of consciousness. Bits are mind altering. It is possible to lose our minds without surgical lobotomy or the kind of operation that the Borg perform in *Star Trek.* We don't need Big Brother; we don't need thought police; we don't need censorship. All we need to lose mind control, the control of our own minds, is more Bits, or at least a failure to protect ourselves against Bits by means of Lits.

What happens to our brains and our thought processes if we become unwarily inundated by Bits, in ways I have described above? Bits can displace identity, which is formed by careful story construction as we live moment to moment and use language to organize experience. The loss of personal identity, carefully and necessarily built by story, thought and processed feelings, will be replaced by synthetic and virtual identities supplied from elsewhere: "Other People's Lives," or pseudo biographies, manufactured by the bit industry. Slogans and logos not only break down story but fail to teach the story-making skills which are acquired by reading other stories. Bits destroy sustained narrative. Processing thousands of Bits takes time which is lost to reading and thinking about connected narratives, our own lives or the big picture of our relations to our world. Bits are fragments of mostly useless and unconnected "information" and so teach us disconnection, which is the opposite kind of response to what we need for health and stability. Bits discourage thought and make thought more difficult. Bits reduce attention span and condition us to be impatient with sustained narrative, internal reflection and thought. Bits create a hunger and need for more Bits, because the vacuum that has been created by the associated loss of connection and story must be filled.

The world created in our minds by Bits is incredibly simplified. The nature of Bits is to simplify; and this is happening even as the world grows more complex. The result of this dichotomy is increased loss of control over the complexity we create and discover. We are thus in the business of engineering our own destruction. Complex problems such as global warming, mass unemployment, destruction of our habitat, breakdown of viable political systems, and genetic engineering, require complex solutions. We need thought and debate, informed discussion, time, seriousness, reality-based contact, awareness of systemic connections, language of sufficient complexity for descriptions of problems, awareness of past experience, trust in human thought and feeling, honesty, authentic and believable human speech, a value system that includes our healthy survival, and a knowledge of human biology and what we are doing to ourselves. Instead, we are producing the opposite of all these: deception at every level of public life; globalization without community values; trivialization of thought and feeling; brutalization of human response and the celebration of sensation and violence; breakdown of time and information into disconnected, meaningless fragments; the creation of addictions and phony identities; and manufacturing consent.[2]

Whose Medium is being Massaged?[3]

The disintegration of information is now widespread. The Bits phenomenon may be regarded as related to the biological story behaviour of human brains but manifests itself as a corrupt mutation. It is like an extra deformed limb that results from genetic misbehaviour and parodies the normal presence of two healthy limbs, functioning in balance. It is a mistake to regard Bits as progress or a natural successor to print and story. It is a diseased offshoot and must be seen in context and weighed in terms of human health. Is Bits good for us? Bits arises from human technological intelligence and is amoral. The fact that it could be done meant it was done, but it grew without any context of moral, political or health debate, much as genetic engineering or genetic alteration of foods is now taking place. I am not suggesting that Bits arose from any kind of world conspiracy. But it is a product of human ingenuity gone out of control. The use and application of Bits is another story.

Behind the Bits industry there is an alliance or union of interests that we may call the Media/Commerce/Political Axis (MCPA). These coalitions of power and money now form the world's elites and together they find that the deformed qualities of Bits can be used to control the minds and behaviour of most of the world's people. The mass media serve commercial interests almost exclusively, except for token gestures of public service. In doing so they become generators of wealth for a few people. The same is true for the political powers who have essentially become servants of commerce and in turn have also become wealthy. The powers of commerce are interested in money only and want to generate wealth for a few who in turn must control the media and political powers in order to keep the system going. The media and politics do not struggle very hard for freedom from these controls, having already subscribed to the idea that money rewards represent the highest good. What concerns us here is this axis has discovered that Bits is the primary means by which control of the mass of minds makes possible the capture of the world's wealth. For the purpose of my argument here we can put aside the economics of this shaping of the world. The problem is that without *necessarily* intending to enslave, say ninety-seven percent of the world's people, the axis and its Bits are altering our minds. The situation is a bit like the captain of a pirate ship who has stolen a large treasure trove from the natives and needs to get it home and to the bank. His crew is grumpy and a bit rebellious so he gives them rum or happy drugs to cheer them up and render them compliant. He does not intend to turn them into alcoholics or addicts, not that he knows or cares about them as persons, but they become permanently disabled anyway. It is not a question of means justifying ends. It is a matter of means without considering their incalculable and possibly devastating costs. Part of this axis indifference must be attributed to Denial, a divorce from reality so profound and cynical that it represents madness. The captain has lost his mind and the crew will become winos and the social outcome will be a hellish nightmare. Any goal, be it wealth, power, love, anything that becomes so obsessive that it blinds us on our journey to it, renders us amoral, guilty of indifference.

The Bits system of "communication," if it can be called that, displaces human story with fragments of signals by the tens of thousands. Robbed of their stories and eventually the story-making power of the brain, people come to resemble zombies. We can see the effects of story theft and destruction in the condition of indigenous peoples who lose identity, self-efficacy, independence, motivation, pride and connection. The same fate exactly awaits everybody who fails to become aware that they are in the process of being disintegrated by Bits. The MCPA is characterized by a number of operational and mental styles that find Bits most congenial to its goals of material world domination. The common denominator for all members of MCPA is advertising. Bits is primarily a system of advertising that has spilled into everything. Let us just review quickly the ways Bits operates and consider its effects so we can see how it is used to manage our minds. Bits produces:

a. Speed and brevity, not necessarily grammatical, not in sentences. The idea is to condition the receiver without demanding much brain work. Brain work is a turnoff and might start a thinking process. Bits seeks a belief/action response, not thought.

b. Disconnection. Connection takes brain action, thought and complexity. The idea is that a Bits message must be isolated, focused on as limited an object and goal as possible

c. Messages not disturbing and not provocative, mostly pleasant and never leaving a negative or unanswered question demanding a real response. Because Bits divorce us from reality and personal experience, it encourages the practice of denial.

d. Arousal only for those emotions that serve the purposes of the Bit. Guilt, for instance, in selling foster parenting, or fear about driving a car not as safe as the one on offer.

e. Language only to reinforce visuals, as language is critical to the human thought system and thought must be minimized. When Bits replaces Lits, language is lost. When language is lost, story is lost.

f. Closed messages. They work to avoid dialogue, debate, query, doubt and research.

g. An outcome that dehumanizes.

h. Descriptions of the world that simplify and so distort the complex.

i. Homogenizing and hegemonizing results. Variety is disappearing as you can see in your supermarket, and the same dogmas, e.g., "market forces," dominate thinking and belief.

It is becoming almost impossible to escape from advertising. In every medium, on every channel, on every surface, in every entertainment, on clothing, on placemats, in the sky, on bus, train, and plane, on the road, we are submerged by a flood of messages urging us to acquire something. Only in the depths of an unpeopled forest, very hard to find, or in Literature, music, fine arts will we escape advertising. Of these refuges, only Literature engages in its fullest activity the brain's language centres and their associated neural networks of thought and emotion. The effect of advertising on such a scale as now blankets our world is causing mental censorship and resistance, and leading us to shut down our message receptors, to become numb to stimuli. This desensitization to information finds its only antidote in Lits. But what of those who don't read Literature? They will remain numbed to thought and language activity, turned off and immune to the subtleties and complexities of real language.

The system of Bits and its manifestation in advertising have infected politics and education. The new ethos of Bits suits the persuasive goals of those who seek office, and can find the money to advertise. The anti-thought culture permits those who are uneducated, otherwise ignorant, ill-informed, barely literate, inarticulate, or free of compassion, conviction, and imagination, to seek and attain public office. Computers may have a role in schools but not in providing a full range of response, debate, dialogue, exchange of ideas, human voice stimulation, enthusiasm, concern and emotion. Computers have down days but not especially good days, inspired hours, joyous or excited responses; they do not express disappointment, genuine encouragement, original spur-of-the-moment insight, smiles and tears, compassion and empathy. In other words, they do not replace teachers, even when they take the place of teachers. This is one more example of the dehumanizing at the centre of the culture.

Advertising and pseudo education are well served by Bits. So also is the spread of misinformation and dogma. Mass media used in the service of politics and religion have led to an increase in the presence of religious fanaticism, totalitarianism, and the erosion of true democracy. Some of these features of contemporary life are the result of a backlash against dehumanization and loss of connectedness, to ourselves, our fellow humans and nature. Some of this is an attempt to turn back to past certainties. Most of our current problems arise from despair and lack of grounding in the reality of experience, the disappearance of thought and the sense of a pattern or story to guide us. The goals of MCPA are short-term, blind to consequences, and indifferent to human needs. We are losing, not gaining self-awareness in spite of more knowledge of the brain and human evolution, the complexity of nature, physics and biology. We are encouraged to turn away from complexity. We seek simple solutions. We cannot reconcile greed, materialism, consumerism with our need to be fully human. So to better understand the effects of Bits, let's look how they are manifested in and through brainwashing, spin, dumbing down and the erosion of time for being human.

Brainwashing

Brainwashing is also called "coercive persuasion" and is designed to alter the thought processes and the belief structures of the target population. The goals of Brain Washing (BW) are precisely opposed to those of cultivating individual, creative and independent thought. BW aims to standardize, manipulate, subdue and design individual and group thoughts and beliefs by means of some kind of central control. This control centre may be religious, military, ideological or commercial. In Nazi Germany, the control was ideological/military. In other words, the military was enlisted to enforce the ideological. To a large degree, commercial interests were part of the coalition of interests in Nazi Germany, as they always are, ready to serve any master that increases their short-term profit. In our own North American milieu, the control is primarily commercial and is enabled by a political structure that has lost its independence from the commercial. The politics of deregulation, "market forces," and laissez-faire capitalism, have supplied the ideology and its supporting propaganda to empower ruthless commercial interests.[4] Proof that commercial interests, are unrestrained, rapacious and irresponsible can be found in the rapid destruction of the environment and habitat of all human, animal and plant life on Earth.

The *Encyclopedia Britannica* explains brainwashing this way:

> The term brainwashing is most appropriately used in reference to a program of political or religious indoctrination or ideological remolding. The techniques of brainwashing typically involve *isolation from former associates and sources of information; an exacting regimen requiring absolute obedience and humility; strong social pressures and rewards for cooperation; physical and psychological punishments for non-cooperation ranging from social ostracism and criticism, deprivation of food, sleep, and social contacts, to bondage and torture; and continual reinforcement.* [my italics]

Various electronic entertainments serve to mesmerize and pacify, to brainwash in much the same way. In fact, tranquilizing brain functions helps make good consumers. People are shown to be much more susceptible to suggested ideas following extensive periods of television watching.

Television watching for prolonged periods alters alpha waves of brain activity; induces passivity; renders independence of thought very difficult; trivializes and simplifies complex information; fosters allegiance to consumerism and promotes desire for commercial products; encourages sexual desire as an adjunct of acquisitiveness, to the point of addiction; standardizes beliefs; isolates individuals from family and community and moves their connectedness to virtual families and groups; reduces interactive language and personal expression; significantly diminishes language skills and interferes with cortical language area development; stimulates emotion without thought; adversely affects sleep patterns and substitutes prepackaged simulated experience for real life experience. "*The depth and permanence of changes in attitude and point of view*" furthers Britannica, "*depend on the personality of the individual, degree of motivation to be reformed, and the degree to which the environment supports the new frame of reference.*"

The antidote to brainwashing by means of television seems to consist of several crucial parts. It requires:

1. Awareness that brainwashing is taking place.
2. An individual rejection of the process.
3. Limiting or eliminating television viewing.
4. Acquiring a variety of information from a variety of sources and by a variety of means.
5. Sharing, testing and validating experience by means of information exchange and feedback.
6. Deliberate cultivation of personal identity and individualized narrative.
7. Creating diversity by means of small, highly interactive communities not subject to Central Control.
8. Commitment to reading literature one or more hours every day.[5]

Spinning Webs of Deception

The idea of interpreting data to suit someone's political goal of persuasion and coercion is hardly new. Politicians have distorted the truth, made false promises and slanted their language to deceive voters, followers, soldiers and citizens throughout history. We can hardly believe that speeches made by Roman emperors and popes to assembled multitudes were not designed to persuade and influence minds. There are, however, several things about "spin" that are new. One is the term itself. What used to be known as spinning a tale, a story, a yarn, has become a professional technique to twist the truth practiced by specialists who advise politicians and heads of corporations. What was once a normal bias or shading of reality to fit the convictions of the tale teller, the persuader, has now become *the thing itself*. Spin has replaced truth, convictions, beliefs and sincerity. Spin has *become* politics. Moreover, we are now at the threshold of a passivity, a helplessness so profound that we risk accepting spin as normal and unquestioned political practice, a substitute for good and caring governance. This situation has now spilled over from advertising so that advertising *values* have entered our thinking as *the natural order of things*. Paradoxically, the power of spin is a testimonial to the power of language itself. Every psychological discovery, every piece of neuroscience research is available to those who want to control the minds of whole populations. Spin management has become a major political force, and public funds in huge amounts are spent by political power structures to enslave and confuse the minds of those who pay for their own deception. There are large teams of spin doctors on the public payroll who specialize in distorting messages in the service of their employers. *There are no rules against doing this!* Spin has taken over the political process and represents a bloodless *coup d'état* that topples reason, sincerity, discourse and mental freedom. Spin is the verbal equivalent of "image," and has supplanted policy with advertising.[6]

One example of the extremes to which spin can go I encountered recently in Ontario, Canada. The plan was to sell the idea that it was environmentally friendly to haul, by rail, twenty million tons of urban garbage from Toronto 600 kilometres through lake and resort country, and dump it into a Northern open pit mine filled with water that sits at the top of a gigantic watershed. It was recognized that telling the truth, namely that some people stood to make millions of dollars in quick profits at the expense of all those who lived downstream and could be affected, would hardly be a persuasive and compelling argument for gaining public support. Instead, the proponents used spin. I was shown a glossy brochure that advertised "garbage tourism." I exaggerate not! The idea that thousands would flock to the Northern woods and lakes on tour buses to see the depositing of mountains of city garbage was not regarded as an unsaleable, unbelievable, unattractive idea. Where campers used to watch bears feed at garbage dumps, it was now proposed that people would gather to *watch the garbage itself*. I try to make myself feel better by trusting this could not happen, but that some believed they could sell this idea in support of the plan is depressing enough. The further thought that people could have so surrendered their minds to passivity that they could be entertained by watching garbage pile up must boggle the mind of anyone who still has one.

Such was their faith in spin, that the persuaders believed they could overcome the real life experience of the population, the experience of smells, disease, vermin, toxins, gulls, traffic and on and on, characteristics of garbage dumps well-known and well-documented in a thousand other sites. Have we reached the point where it is really possible that by means of persistent brainwashing, endless television mind bending, passivity and despair, people are now so divorced from their sensory experience and their thought processes that they will believe any fantasy posing as truth? I think at this point we need to remind ourselves that spin is not Literature because it deliberately seeks to persuade and confuse by encouraging consumers to deny their experience.

Fiction is based on two great pillars that remain immovable: first, it always admits to being fiction. Even when Literature pretends to be history it invites the reader to see that it is not. It uses the language of story, not the language of a business plan or of a political diatribe. Second, fiction and poetry is always firmly grounded in the experience of the writer. The "I" of the writer's voice is present, not disguised as detached committee report or scientific paper. Propaganda is based on what can be done to influence the receiver, where the writer puts his own life aside. Making propaganda is a professional task and requires as little emotion as possible, much as a surgeon works on the patient's tissue. We want our surgeons cool, calculating and largely impersonal. Spin is founded on the belief that deception is the legitimate means if used in the service of acquiring wealth, which is the new, paramount, and only value. Could it be that we are actually nearing a time when you can, in reality, deceive all the people all the time? Answer: Yes, but *only if they stop reading Literature in an uncensored and literate society.*

Dumbing Down

My point all along has been to explain how reading requires and fosters intelligence, produces stores of brain information, constructs identity and promotes neural activity and ability. The motive of the seller and the motive of the buyer are quite different from that of the writer and the reader. When I was a graduate student in Madison, Wisconsin, I tried to support myself by selling sports cars on commission. One of the cars we sold was the English Morgan 4, a pretty two-seater toy of a car along classic lines with a wooden floor, shiny wheels and a convertible top. The sort of car a brainless P.G. Wodehouse hero called Bertie might drive. The company I worked for placed TV and newspaper ads that emphasized glamour, lifestyle and pizzazz. I did occasionally sell a car, but I remember one occasion when a family man with no money to spare came in, followed by his despairing wife. He wanted a Morgan and ignored his wife's pleading to give up the crazy idea of buying such a car, which would have been useless to the family. It was too much for me. I took the man aside and spent an hour, out of my employer's hearing, persuading this poor fellow to give up this idea. I lost a possible commission, but I have never regretted this anti-sales pitch. I also had no idea at the time that I was doing family therapy. How could a supposedly rational, barely coping human being with a wife and children, have come to the point of desperately wanting to own an almost totally useless, expensive piece of machinery?

The easy answer is that in his commercial context he would escape his economic, almost impoverished hopelessness by means of an illusion. He would possess a symbol of glamour and freedom, a symbol carefully created by advertising, he would taste the style of wealth, power, and show and "feel" better about his lot. To get to this state he would have had to virtually abandon thought. He would need to be free of analysis, self-knowledge, long-term planning, family compassion and responsibility, and have leaped instead into a fantasy, with himself at the wheel of a dream car, hurtling towards "freedom" from his problems.

Today's popular fantasy delusions are almost exclusively made up of aspirations to the acquisition of more money and the powers that money accesses. Advertising links money to sexual power, and social status by means of owning things. In our world that more and more resembles a

Disney *Fantasia*, these rewards — the company and intimacy of beautiful young women or men, and the power over them and others, the acquiring of surroundings and settings of luxury, access to the finest cuisine etc. — these are all available by means of delusional magic, by the wave of a wand. In the contemporary illusion, no work, no thought, no years of grinding study or labour are necessary to acquiring the payoff. You merely have to purchase the right car, the right insurance plan, or serve the right pre-cooked recipe to get love, security, popularity and a $500,000 home in suburban Peoria.

The latest set of delusional offers to wealth, sex, power and therefore, supposedly, happiness is related to phones, computers and Internet access. More on this a bit later. Now in order to perpetrate this belief fraud on human beings equipped with a neocortical brain, you must first "dumb them down." This dumbing process has certain vital ingredients and an important sequence of stages. The primary foundation step is to get people watching many hours of television. It is best to start them young so that addiction to images and deprivation of language can be well-formed by the time they attain purchasing power and credit cards. By means of television, it is possible to train people to accept messages that are fleeting, minimal in information and simplified to early developmental levels of language.

To create dutiful consumers and obedient believers in the value of material rewards, you must create passivity and bypass dialogue, questions and debate. Messages must be extremely simplified, visually stimulating and associated with delusional outcomes, and these messages must be frequently repeated. By means of such persuasion the brains of viewers remain virtually thoughtless; the neocortex is largely inactive and static; neural networks are slowed down in change and growth. The viewer must drastically reduce time spent in alternative activities that have quite different and antidotal effects, activities like reading, talking, debating, listening. This passivity-inducing simplification of everything is "dumbing down." Once you have a "dumbed down" population, anything is possible and your audience can be persuaded to buy anything, believe anything and endorse anything;

and vote for anyone appropriately marketed. And of course, the more that mass media such as television becomes concentrated in fewer and fewer hands, the more the same messages in different disguises can be perpetrated. So we see the same pattern spread to politics, where delusion, passivity and absence of real debate is now pandemic. Naturally, where entertainment and advertising are the only commercial interests (and all other interests except the commercial have lost their power), we can expect to see news and social commentary merge with entertainment and then gradually dissolve away altogether. Such mergers are taking place now, as television and newspapers, or what is left of them, fall under the same ownership and the same boardroom control and values.

What constitutes happiness, human values, mental and spiritual satisfaction, meaning in human life, the value of the natural world, the solutions to healing a dying planet: none of these are allowed into the mainstream discourse, let alone encouraged. I venture to say that if you remove the last remnants of public broadcasting in Canada (and the United States), you can assume that all serious discussion of values, politics and moral and ethical conduct will have disappeared from public life. More and more time is eaten up by trivial pursuits so that fewer and fewer people can say on their deathbeds, "I lived a life that had meaning, value and purpose and I spent my time thoughtfully, ethically and morally." Unlike Edith Piaf, I am afraid that few of us will have the right to say with conviction, "Je ne regrette rien."

Time Pirates

It remains to be seen whether the Internet and our new connectedness to our computers will lead us back to human values and the primacy of literacy and Literature. The one sure thing that can be said on behalf of cyberspace is that it has reoriented us to language; it has broken the monopoly of television on user time; and it has made possible rapid access to like-minded people around the world. This is all very new, and we have yet to see whether this access will be limited by totalitarian interests; whether the gap between the "information rich and the information poor" will continue to grow; and whether commercial interests and motive will simply crowd off the screen everything but flashing banners and distracting messages, which already make the computer's use a bit of a struggle. In the meantime we live in hopes and promises.

Ah, the Internet, that great glowing highway into the future where happiness may lie. Meanwhile, the promise of time saving is proving just as illusory to our Web world as were all the other devices that were going to save us time. We spend more time than did our forebears fixing things, calling repairmen, researching and shopping for things, going to and from garages, sending and receiving trivial messages, paying bills, attending to recorded, dehumanized phone messages, waiting on "hold," answering phone calls from advertisers and creditors via minimum-wage call centres, looking up numbers, forgetting our passwords, searching for bargains, listening to voice mail, trying to contact human beings, and figuring out how things work. Even if we were to save any time, what would we do with it? If we are dumbed down we can't and won't read. We spend more time watching sex than enjoying the real thing.[7] We read about sickness instead of maintaining health. We eat bad tasting and often dangerous food to save time preparing dinner. The companies who would sell us more and more high-tech devices, to replace or modify the devices we already have and don't have time to fully use, manage to persuade us that in some vague and undefined way the new machines will make our lives better. Somehow the quantity of information will wash away any question of quality in our communities and in our communication.[8]

Much of the information on the Internet is inaccurate or misleading. It is hugely fragmented. There is virtually no editing or control of information on the "Net," few standards and fewer regulations. E-mail gives us almost instant communication, but who can read it all, let alone respond to it? My own e-mail is now more than fifty percent unsolicited advertising, and half of that is pornography while the other half is about making money. Every now and then I am offered products that guarantee to enlarge my breasts or lengthen my penis. If I opened any of this I would waste more time than I am forced to use now just erasing it. And any attachment I open might contain a virus that will eradicate years of accumulated manuscript that I created. Yes, I know, I can hear someone saying as I write, "You can buy some new software that will filter your mail...." I am sure I can buy anything and with every thing I buy I will have to buy something else.[9] And when we do respond to our personal mail we find in our haste that we have been misunderstood, we have created conflicts and finally we have to converse on the phone to straighten things out. We have yet to estimate the human costs, in health, stress, eye strain, lack of exercise, frustration, misinformation and family relations of the Internet. But we seem puzzled by the enormous accumulation of stress symptoms, disease, road and air rage, divorce, violence against women and children, murder in the workplace and widespread fatigue and sleep deprivation. Then again, we are probably more easily puzzled than we would be without all the electronic help we are getting.

Worst of all, the Internet threatens to eat up our lives with a vast, even limitless array of trivia and Bits and pieces of useless information, none of it coordinated and none of it relevant to the whole life, which will have to be constructed from other sources. It takes time to converse meaningfully. It takes time to argue, think, meditate, be quiet, debate, listen, learn and teach. But such time is less and less available.

Michael Ende wrote a novel called *Momo*, in which a homeless child leads a revolution to save human beings from the thieves of time. The author has to make his girl hero homeless and "free," because if she came from an established family home she would already be enslaved by the time thieves. She would be taking piano lessons, riding classes, skating lessons, playing five sports and having a part-time job when not trying to fit in homework. We certainly need such a revolution now, but where find one?

In this chapter I have examined the concept that we are in a struggle for the control of our minds. Mind control will be the key to human survival. At the moment the prospects do not look rosy. Throughout this book I have been arguing that the last significant bulwark against the takeover of individual minds is Literature. Indeed, if I am right that current commercial, political and social forces threaten individual identity, let me ask respectfully what alternatives to reading Literature are available to assist us in our self-defence. We cannot switch off the barrage of slogans and images, shut off the commercial world and the vast design of misinformation projected at us. So widespread is the tyranny and hegemony of materialism and advertising that I don't see how we can escape it. And if we leave Literature out of the equation, how can we be informed and educated? Having lost our oral culture and our community stories, and having embraced commercial media and its messages, where will we find alternative stories to help us construct our world? Our writers and publishers are our last hope for freedom. If the press, the visual and electronic media, and governments are owned and controlled by the same interests as the giant multinational, multi-merged, corporate powers, where will we find the wherewithal for alternative thought and freedom to think in and of alternatives, to form identity for ourselves? It appears, then, that it is not only a matter of reading for our lives, but doing so while we can and while books and writers are available. I have personally come to the conclusion that most of my gifts to family and friends will now be books. It may not be a revolutionary gesture but if several hundred million other people do the same, and all the recipients start reading the book gifts and stop wasting time on mindlessness, especially staying away from the Box, it might make a difference. At the least, I think such a quiet thinker's revolution would greatly influence our children. Such a Literature Revolution might be the best we can do at this time.

NOTES TO CHAPTER 7
LITS AND BITS: SURVIVING THE MIND FIELDS

1. The best versions of the dangers of thought control are of course found in Literature, where else? Try Madeleine L'Engle's, *A Wrinkle in Time.*
2. I borrow the term from Noam Chomsky's masterful political analysis of the same title. This should be compulsory material in schools, I think for everyone, but how can its omission from civics, history and politics courses be justified?
3. Marshall McLuhan left us two clichés: "The medium is the message"; and "The Global Village." Both are seriously misleading. Both are meant to be reassuring. The medium is not the message; mass media corporations and sponsors conspire together to produce brainwashing effects. Globalization as represented by the Internet or the secret and inaccessible and nonresponsive deal making of governments and multinational corporations bears no resemblance to village life. The new world order is impersonal, non-accountable, remote and indifferent to the views of most people.
4. George Orwell makes the following comment: "The novel is practically a Protestant form of art; it is a product of the free mind, of the autonomous individual." *Inside the Whale*, p. 518, op. cit.
5. The absence of political philosophy, of even the semblance of a raison d'être, let alone a "vision" among contemporary Western governments is astounding. The almost naked goal is to get power, keep it, and support projects that benefit the big money interests that helped put them in power. Any idea of governance dedicated to the social, mental and economic quality of life for the people has long disappeared.
6. Who would have thought that a weak-minded, poorly educated, second-rate actor could become President of the world's most powerful nation? One answer might be Jerzy Kozynski, in his novel *Being There.*
7. At some point we will have to confront the reality that we have more violence in our cities, more jails, more crime, more corruption in public life, more divorce, more family abuse, more children at risk, more addiction than at any point in our recorded history. We can argue forever about why this is so, but more keeps becoming more, which must lead us to the conclusion that whatever we are doing now is not working. When do we intend to address the root causes of social breakdown and human despair?

8. What began as a stream of disturbing social commentary and analysis, with works by David Reisman, Rachel Carson, Neil Postman, Noam Chomsky and others, has turned into a flood. A good beginning list of recent work can be found in the book list at the back of Naomi Klein's just published book, *NO LOGO.* As I have been trying to point out, the roots of this concern for our humanist survival are found in Shakespeare, Swift, Dickens, Thoreau, Hawthorne and James, to mention only a few. We can say very pointedly here, that none of this commentary will matter if reading is lost to all but a few intellectuals crying in the wilderness, or in the place to which Huxley's hero is exiled in *Brave New World.* Ah, there I go again with another literary reference!

9 There has always been a recognition by the Green Party in Europe, especially in Germany, that to achieve the full-scale change required to stop the destruction of the Earth, a ban on advertising would be required. Such a goal would seem to be unimaginable, but we have begun to see some controls on liquor and tobacco advertising, in Canada anyway. Political will is everything in such matters and there is nothing like people power to bend political will, but people who don't read won't have any power. Cf. *Green Politics*, 1986, and *Natural Capitalism*, 1999.

CHAPTER EIGHT

Media Madness: Other People's Lives (OPL)

During times of economic or other cultural upheavals, a society's values could become so distorted as to be certifiably insane.

— **James W. Pennebaker**

Everyone did what was right in his eyes. The strong oppressed the weak, the rich the poor, the great the little. There was no longer any public safety in the land; yet the chaotic spirits of the time thought their new republic very well organized. "Everything's in good order" they said. "Everything's going its way here just like everywhere else. The wolf is eating the lamb, the hawk the dove, the fox the cock." However, this ridiculous state of things could not last. After the first wave of what people had thought to be freedom had vanished and they had grown sober again, reason asserted its rights.

— **John Karl Augustus Musaus**

HUMANS BUILD AND DECORATE SHELTERS, houses, outside of us, to protect us from the storms. In our minds we build perceptual structures, world containers like Noah's ark with ourselves as captain, to carry us with security as we navigate ourselves through unchartered waters. Our craft is called "identity."

Health depends on balance, as I explained in an earlier chapter, with Blondin as my centrepiece. We humans need clear and continuous identity formation and stable mental constructs to feel secure. Such "I" formation consists of continuous and moment-by-moment reconstruction of a personal world order. This world construction in the mind is an active, continual process that relies on the stability of the constructing, executive "I," which checks and adjusts for homeoadaptation against incoming sensory signals all the time. The resulting mental constructs consist of categories of information that govern and design the beliefs, behaviours, geography and the connections of the self to the not-self. This body of organized information is continually re-calibrated to accommodate or reject new information. Let us remember that we are the story creatures of our little complex world, and one way or another we must have stories to live by and through. Our identities are stories. If we do not have individual stories, complex enough to see us through life, and cosmic stories to connect us to our world, then we will be vulnerable to whatever stories are forced upon us.

A great variety of stories give us choices and create thought. As things stand now, there are many forces at work to undermine our identity formation, some of which I discussed in the last chapter. Our great fear that computers and machines will come to run the world and displace us is less well-founded than the more appropriate fear that we ourselves are unwittingly becoming more like those very machines. The real threat in the present state of things is that we will continually reduce our thinking to what artificial intelligence can accomplish. As Wordsworth puts it:

> Getting and spending, we lay waste our powers;
> Little we see in nature that is ours;
> We have given our hearts away, a sordid boon![1]

Can we be robotized? My answer is yes, all too easily, *when our brains are not protected by a well-founded identity system.*

Let us look for a moment at how this system works. You will remember that the human brain completes three-fourths of its formation after birth, in the world. At the same time we must think of this brain as the world's most complex information processor. This marvel of data management took millions (billions?), of years to get here, with masses of trials and errors and tribulations and refinements along the way. Unlike any artificial information network, the brain is shaped by the information it receives and processes. Far from the medium being the message, or the message being the medium, the medium is shaped by and in turn shapes the messages it receives. This process is organic where brains are concerned. Now let's imagine a crude organic analogy to muscles and organs of the body. If during its development the child's body is deprived of appropriate nutrition and exercise, the body's immune system will be weakened. The body does not grow in balance and strength, and therefore becomes vulnerable to disease and virus without the means to muster necessary resistance. The underfed or poorly fed, the greatly stressed, suffer more disease, more premature death and disability than those who eat well and exercise and relax and so resist viruses and toxic change. The brain suffers likewise as a body organ, but beyond that the brain is fed by information for its development. If the brain grows without sufficient language, and is deprived of appropriate story formation, it is subject to the invasion of viral messages that leave it unprepared to cope with the continual flow of life information which will render it non-adaptive to change and stress-inducing data. Self-grown story is equal to good diet and exercise. We require story nutrition. Literature is a powerful antidote to toxic information, the takeover of minds by unprocessable data. Literature enhances immunity. With it we can inoculate ourselves against the assaults of bits and bites of information that erode our story-forming equipment. All life experience is turned by our brains into necessary fiction, which when it helps us function efficiently, works as the map to our lives. Literature has been called the House of Fiction. In today's electronic world of bits and bites and photo distortions, we are like a house assaulted by a plague of termites. We must become conscious of the need to immunize ourselves, to make our house termite-proof.

The value systems that constitute the poles of conflict in our time are to some degree reflected in earlier chapters. Certainly they have to do with duality versus unity, separation versus connection, greed versus compassion, hegemony versus variety and inclusion, tyranny versus democracy, lying versus authenticity, and virtual reality versus real experience. As I see it, the world we now watch unfolding in the news and events of our lives, represents a real and immediate threat to our health, our humanity and our very survival. The threat to Literature and to readers comes from the replacement of reading sustained works of fiction and poetry by fragments of news, images substituted for language, managed information for purposes of mind control, and entertainment requiring a sensation response without thought. Media, that is newspapers and magazines, television, the Internet and radio, have all become agents of advertisers. Their goal is mass manipulation. Underlying the control of the media by fewer and fewer owners is the central value of consumerism. Materialism and its practice in the form of consumption has become the unchallenged characteristic of human activity. So dominant is this idea of production, consumption and the acquisition of wealth, that it is beginning to seem inevitable, the natural order of things. So in the struggle for human brains, Literature has to contend with advertising, the consumerism that lies beneath the advertising tip of the iceberg, and the contempt for thought, language and truth that drives the world's power elites. It should also be borne in mind that as media control is vested in ever fewer corporate boardrooms, all with a single view and goal, novels and poems become the only source of alternative opinion and perspective.

I am arguing that if we do not have a well-developed sense of identity and therefore control over experience, supported by a sufficient degree of language, we are subject to a mental disorder that makes us vulnerable to being "possessed" by a virtual or false story divorced from our own reality. The more we permit ourselves to become affected by a Bits-imposed fragmented identity, the more vulnerable we become to Bits influence. Identities are formed to a significant degree by the messages they receive. If people are told often enough, for instance, that they are stupid, wicked, ugly, lazy, and so on, they will come to think of themselves accordingly and act out a self-fulfilling prophecy. Similarly if people are told they need this and that, will be happy or beautiful by means of this or that, or if they are poor its their own fault, then these will become life-shaping beliefs. Our ability to resist being defined by other people's messages or stories about us, depends on the strength and assurance of our own identity, our own story. Those with poorly developed or damaged identities are more subject to fantasy and delusional beliefs than others.

We have seen how people must have stories and they must have identities. If they do not have their own stories they are open to "possession" by stories not their own. If they were truly without identity they would be authentic zombies.[2] The many legends of people who are said to be taken over by an incubus or some spirit looking for a living human body lodging, or the story of Legion in the Gospels, all have their roots in observable experience, some of it clinical, where someone appears to become someone else and speaks in a different voice and exhibits different behaviour. That people can live other people's lives, and become totally identified with heroes, or obsessed with love objects, is well recognized. This sort of projected identification is often labeled psychotic. Is it possible that entire populations can be so deprived of personal identity that they are easy prey for those who would create for them fantasy heroes who become real? Let us look at an instructional example from the end of the last century: two women known to all the world and two stories that could not be more different. Together they constitute a contemporary psychodrama, and a sobering warning to us all.

A Tale of Two Women

On August 31, 1997, Lady Diana, Princess of Wales, died at the age of 36, in a gruesome auto crash in Paris while being pursued by the press. Killed along with her was her "boyfriend," Dodi Al Fayed. She died playing with and among the richest people in the world. Five days later, on September 5, 1997, Mother Theresa of Calcutta, as she was known to the world, died of heart failure at the age of 87. She died among the poorest of the poor with whom she had worked for fifty years, rescuing them from the streets of Calcutta and comforting them.

Lady Di, as she was affectionately and familiarly known, had undertaken various high profile "good works," it was widely believed. She was beautiful, glamorous, photogenic, wealthy and notorious for her "playgirl" lifestyle. Her death was greeted by an international outpouring of grief, much of it hysterical, and all of it very puzzling to observers and analysts not caught up in what we would term, clinically speaking, identification with the princess. Following her death, we were entertained with endless media coverage, pictures, stories, commentary, royal funeral services and processions. The British Prime Minister, Tony Blair, called her, with a nod to his Labour Party, the "People's Princess." This is somewhat difficult to relate to reality. Lady Di was connected to royalty, extremely wealthy, very glamorous, featured in the news as a media star almost daily, a favourite for magazine covers, a playgirl of the rich and idle who never, never have to work. And it is very doubtful that the princess did any actual work either. She was a product of media image makers, an icon of "photo ops." She was certainly a promoter of "good causes," by which means she took on the role of aristocratic social worker, without discomfort, fatigue, or hardship. Nothing that Lady Diana did seems to have cost her anything. Unless it was her life in the game of hide and go seek she played with the press on a regular basis. How did she become the symbolic princess of "the people?"

I am unaware that Tony Blair had any sobriquet for Mother Theresa. Her death went relatively unnoticed by media standards. It was a news item, but it was swamped, displaced by the unprecedented mass media coverage, the hype, colour, imagery, the tears and words lavished on the youthful and beautiful princess. The story of this comparison is a modern parable that illustrates more pointedly than anything I can think of, the nature of a media-dominated world. The point of making this comparison is not to pass judgment on the lives of these two women, or to attempt an estimate of the human service each attempted. This is a book about reading and therefore about perception and how readers, human information processing organisms, form their reality. We live in a world contracted, shrunk by media, a world not value driven but image driven. Our world is informed by media-created personas, and stories of the rich and famous designed to feed our fantasies. Such fantasies are part and parcel of the culture of consumerism.

The response to Lady Di's death surprised everyone, including those grieving. Strictly speaking, it should not have — had we been thinking about it. Diana Spencer came from an aristocratic family and led a privileged life, complete with private education, including the Swiss "finishing" school. Yet the media portrayed her as a simple commoner, a rags-to-riches Cinderella whose foot matched the glass slipper. She divorced the Prince of Wales after a few years of media attention focusing on her as an actual member of the British royal family, by which time she had already become the darling of journalists and photographers. Having secured a gigantic financial settlement to ease the pain of marital breakup, she more than ever became a celebrity, reveling in "photo ops" and "good works" publicity. One photo shows her holding a black baby. Another shows her shaking hands with the chief of a leper colony. She patronized the Red Cross, the Great Ormond Street Children's Hospital in London, the HIV support network, and she championed the abolition of land mines. At the same time, she was frequently photographed sunbathing on the deck of Mohammed Al Fayed's thirty-two-million-dollar yacht, or in party situations, as the companion of Mohammed's son, Dodi Al Fayed. Dodi died along with her in the Paris car crash hours after buying Di a piece of jewellery, that if I remember rightly cost about one-quarter of a million dollars. Though Diana would never be queen, she managed to become the hero of a fantasy in which she combined the acme of wealth and pleasure with the image of someone who cared about the poor and suffering. This entire story was achieved by means of photo journalism. She was the playgirl with a social conscience and the status that could lift her beyond the centrefold. This fantasy figure became irresistible to millions who secretly projected themselves into her identity and whose secret fantasy life was exposed when she died and they lived to face the drudgery of laundry, kids, nine-to-five work, paying bills, trying to lose weight, washing up, and going to bed with Bob, who was no Prince Charming.

The media love affair with Lady Di never ended and followed her into death. She left a legacy of imagery as the Golden Girl and she earned a reputation for "do-gooding" that outshone Mother Theresa's lifetime of selfless service and voluntary impoverishment. Diana Spencer became the princess of good works, and all of this was packaged into a "fairy tale" of glamour, riches, yachts, diamonds and dancing in palaces and playgrounds with the most privileged people on Earth. This was a story that, unlike real fairy tales which can be kept in their place, was offered and received as "real life." It was ended by the shocking violence of the real world impinging, and with the extraordinary aftermath of popular grief and mourning.

The death of Mother Theresa was a very different story, just as her life was very different. No fairy tale quality attached to any of that. This Albanian born, Yugoslavian nun died at age 87 having spent all her adult life among the poorest people she could find. In fact, Mother Theresa and her Sisters of Charity gathered more than 60,000 street people and fed and nursed them, and this was a deliberate hands-on choice for a way to live. When she was not holding, loving and washing the feet of the people who owned absolutely nothing but their own lives, she was travelling the globe seeking financial support for her mission. What Mother Theresa was attempting to model was one of the messages she took from her own hero, Jesus, her God. This concept of charity and service to the poor would define her story, represent her identity as a person whose beliefs, values and behaviour were of a piece. She took a story and made herself into a living embodiment of what she saw as an instruction. It was almost too simple to be interesting, and too challenging to appeal to many people. She appears to have been indifferent to image, indeed to everything except her mission. A reporter once watched her bathing the feet of a woman in her shelter and said, "I would not do that for a million dollars." "Neither would I," replied the nun. Mother Theresa became a legend and byword for charity, for service, for what she saw as Christian values and humanitarian acts at the most caring level of fellowship. So she came, I believe, to represent in her own person and by her work the antithesis of indifference, affluence and excessive acquisitiveness. But you could hardly say she was popular. She never became a figure the public wished to identify with, and in some ways her life was an embarrassment to the glamour-worshipping world of television watching and magazine covers and articles. She became an embarrassment to capitalist economic theory, and she exposed the hypocrisy of a story that said you could be Christian and excessively rich and indifferent to the poor at the same time. There was no entertainment value in Mother Theresa, and since she represented a prick to the conscience of an affluent society, and since she could not be associated with things you might want to buy, or have, or she did not represent how most people wanted to live, the media and their sponsors and advertisers were not rushing to display her unglamorous person or gruesome settings. She did not have a *body* to identify with. She only offered the unappealing work she did until she died.

Together, these two very different women's stories form a morality play. They are quintessentially contrasted, or at least I am contrasting them to illustrate something about the perception-forming forces at work in our world. While both women became icons for an era, they represented a profound conflict of values. The nun chose a long life, of sacrifice and service. Hers was governed by immersion in the reality of hardship and suffering, the extremes of poverty which she chose to share. The Princess lived in a media-dominated fantasy of self-gratification, sex, glamour, riches and play. The former passed into history with barely a media ripple. The latter died amid a tumult of press coverage, ceremony, and hysterical public grief.

If we try hard we can imagine a world where the responses to their passing would have been reversed. Such a world would have to be grounded in the reality of life experience, peopled by those with strong individual identities, thinking people socially connected to the humanity of others, and aware of the power of story to construct perception. To see how this failed to happen we must turn to an examination of the identity-forming world of clinical mental disorder created by media-managed fantasy.

Collective Delusion

The biological component is missing not only from the study and understanding of the role of Literature. It is also sadly absent from economic and political life. We are in serious trouble as a species because we have proceeded recklessly along a technically inventive path that affects our lives profoundly, without self-awareness or the reckoning of how we function as animal organisms.

I chose my title for this chapter quite deliberately. Various forms of severe mental disorder are characterized by a breakdown of identity, of "I" formation. Such states of mind reveal a problem in constructing a reality that conforms with the sensory data, the external evidence that is transported via nerve endings from the world of the "not-I" into the brain of the receiver. We are living lives in which our beliefs and behaviour are increasingly divorced from our actual experience.[3] This splitting of experience and belief can be called schizoid, and can operate without appearing to be psychotic or dysfunctional. It produces a story that is largely make-believe and leads to serious stresses in personal relations, at work and at home, but can go undetected, partly because it becomes normal in a schizoid society.[4] Where the split from sensory reality is extreme, it cannot be hidden and becomes completely dysfunctional. In true schizophrenia for example, objects take on properties that they don't have in material reality. Brooms turn into snakes, clocks turn into faces, voices are heard that no one else hears. If objects do this in fictional works, as in the Harry Potter books for instance, they can be imagined and enjoyed without being terrifying as actual experience. The reader's identity, if healthy, holds her in place as an underlying grounding. For the schizophrenic, such writing would not be amusing. For one so afflicted, the ordinary material world can be a frightening and confusing place. The sufferer tries to create an identity but in a world of unstable objects his story cannot function efficiently or effectively. This leads to a lack of control over the undependable data being received by the senses but subsequently distorted. The sensory world cannot be trusted, so people also cannot be trusted. The world of even ordinary and familiar objects and people becomes a source of disequilibrium.

In true paranoia the victim feels oppressed by a hostile and threatening conspiracy to his well-being when there is no external evidence to support this view. In dissociative identity disorder, formerly called multiple personality disorder, the patient has two, and usually more, observable identities that appear to take control and manage separate life stories that live alongside, but without much awareness of other internalized life stories. This leads to serious and complicated social problems and severely interferes with efficient life management. Time frames don't mesh. Places and events don't come together. I don't want to summarize here the entire *Diagnostic Manual of Psychiatry*, so suffice it to say that mental disorders can usefully be viewed as *problems of identity formation*, accompanied by absence of efficient social functioning, and diminished security and comfort levels, and having to do with a damaged sense of control, self-efficacy and personal life management.

To understand what happened to thousands, maybe millions of people when Lady Di died, is to enter a world of clinical mental disorder characterized by problems of identity formation. Fairy tale princesses that little girls identify with are not supposed to enter real life. They remain harmless and even useful, when they remain manageable as folklore in the process of identity formation in the minds of readers. Diana Spencer became the "virtual princess" that we discovered millions had believed in and thought of as real when they mourned her dreadful passing. The violence of her death, the mangled flesh and blood body that her worshipers had to confront, was a shocking wrench to the fantasies of those who woke to find their fairy tale turned into a horrifying betrayal. The Diana worshipers turned angrily on someone to blame for their ugly awakening. To turn on their dead hero for failing them would be like turning on themselves, which they lacked the self-awareness to do.

The enemy they chose were the paparazzi. And then they turned the life of the virtual princess into saintliness or, most amazingly, the iconography of modern feminism.[5] Diana was a fantasy creature, a hologram, created by media with her own participation. She was created out of pictures, images of her smile, her jewellery, off-the-shoulder gowns, the props to be later auctioned for huge sums of money. The role she played in the minds of millions of celebrity watchers was a product of the virtual era and could only have happened when people began giving up their own lives and started living vicarious lives as a substitute. This has not happened on a mass scale before in human history and was not possible before. It could not have happened, for instance, to any of Henry VIII's put-upon wives, to Lady Nelson or to Josephine of Napoleon fame. Diana's image-story is interesting as evidence of a new epidemic mental disorder, created by an identity vacuum waiting to be filled by images supplied by an image industry.

When you check out at the supermarket, you will notice by your side a display of tabloids designed to intrigue, entice and seduce you into a world of picture stories about the lives of celebrities. The world of mass media is the world of "Other People's Lives" (OPL). These lives have become a secondary entertainment industry that has proven to be much more effective for engaging public interest than any talent or performance that originally created the celebrity status itself. For instance, the lives of screen or television actors is more salable than any roles or professional performances the actor delivers. The same is true for the very wealthy, for royalty, and for colourful political figures. What Abraham Lincoln said was more important and more memorable than any details about his personal life. Not true of president Clinton, who hardly said a memorable thing, I can't remember anything worth quoting anyway, while what he did in private with Monica Lewinsky has become part of political legend and dominated the interest of millions of people for many months around the world. Clinton turned into entertainment. We are forced to wonder why sexual intercourse, fellatio or cunnilingus would be more interesting if it involved the President of the United States, than it is in the homes of media watchers, who would, we might reasonably assume, be more interested in their own such activities. Not so! Because OPLers are *not at home;* they are missing identity.[6]

Watching Is Not Being There

The power of OPL can only be found in a growing epidemic of identity disorder that constitutes a cultural mental health crisis. And this epidemic is spread by a kind of biological warfare conducted by mass media. I mean that brains can be controlled and even formed by deliberate selection of information supplied to them, and by the way in which it is supplied.

Television is not a stage in the evolution of language, as though it had outgrown and replaced Literature. It is a quite different and seductive path we are invited to wander at the expense of Literature, a competitive path. Television is a package, a container for transmitting something. There are two ways to make a container. We can construct it to fit the contents, or as in the case of the novel or poem, let it be shaped by the contents. Or we can design all our contents to fit one kind of container. Everything on television is *adapted for television.* If television is the medium to which McLuhan refers, then it has become a tool in the hands of advertisers.

Literature is symbolic. It is coded and decoded in the brain from multi-sensory input, but it lives in the brain by means of a grammar and semantic code. Television is mostly visual, which is why small children who can't read, and even monkeys, can watch and follow what is on television. Literature is not in any way shaped by the medium that conveys it. It can be rendered by print, by handwriting, by computer screens, by word of mouth, learned and transmitted by hearing and from memory, in which case it has no material substance at all, and by physical embossing as in Braille. In a real sense Literature is not a medium. It is a biological brain *function.* Television, the machine, is, on the other hand, a true medium and is visual or nothing. So as a medium it shapes, determines the nature and quality of its transmissions, for to induce people to watch it, it must be entertaining above all and intensely transient. The medium is not so much a message; *the medium is the package* to which all the contents must fit, no matter what they are. So all television messages are appropriately distorted and altered as necessary. But this is only because it has been hijacked to advertising. The medium is owned by those who are in league with those who supply the messages. Television is no more evil in itself than money. It is one more tool in the armoury of those who want to control our minds and steal our identity.

What we really need is a medium with a message worth hearing. There is nothing inherent in the nature of television to dictate that it must be used for the propaganda of advertising. But it does seem that if television were to give primacy to language and the important discourses of politics and social issues, it would have less to offer than radio, which does not require the static, trapped positioning of the viewer. In McLuhan's view, what is the message of radio? Presumably that sound is what is important. But there is a world of difference between an FM broadcast of a Bach concert and a commercial ad for "Guido's Pizza." Watching a concert on television hardly makes sense.

What is true for commercial television applies equally to commercial radio. Public radio, financed by taxes or fees, can be and is somewhere used for discussion, documentary, education, news analysis and social critique. That private radio stations have become owned and dominated by advertisers, profit interests and political propaganda in no way means that this is the nature of the medium. Similarly, television used as long-distance education, for lectures, science experiments, political analysis and documentary exploration proves that there is nothing inevitable about sound bites, selected visual imagery, obsessive entertainment and distracting trivia. Mother Theresa never became a "star" because she was politically undesirable and non-commercial, though these aspects of her life and work are of course intimately connected criteria.

The assault on our minds is taking many forms and our best defense is awareness and exposure. Ours is a world where a little paranoia can help immunize us. Our worst enemy can be our delusional selves. We are likely to join the other side if we are unaware that the other side is really there. We must become especially wary when those taking over our minds start being extremely caring and solicitous:

> You don't understand what a wonderful place we've come to. You see, on this planet everything is in perfect order because everybody has learned to relax, to give in, to submit. All you have to do is look quietly and steadily into the eyes of our good friend here, for he is our friend, dear sister, and he will take you in as he has taken me.[7]

If this gives you the creeps, you are still OK. Just do not forget the warning.

Wordsworth talked about a world we "half-create and half-perceive." What he meant was the world as experienced by human beings is half created by their imaginations, or in other words by their data-arranging brains. We are rapidly losing the "half-create" portion, so that our world is almost all "perceived." This means we live in only half a reality; we have replaced the other half with illusion. In a prepackaged world the room for the creative part of data assembly in the brain is seriously diminished. The imagination is short-circuited, made increasingly inactive and reluctant and becomes less used. What the human imagination would normally do is to assemble and connect images, words, representations of objects in the "not-I" world, colours, textures, ideas, all the data material of brain and sensory processing and mold them into some kind of composite story or picture. The consequence of losing this creative mental ability is a growing sense of alienation, of displacement, and of disempowerment, not merely at a political level, where it is obvious, but at a neural level where it is more profound and less obvious. Some brains are better at this creativity than others. But in a world where commercial propaganda messages are everywhere bombarding human brains, especially young forming brains, the room for imaginative activity is greatly reduced in everybody.

Learning to read, and reading increasingly complex material, would seem to be a lot more work than flipping through a glossy magazine, or watching a very simple show on TV. Yet the rewards must be very substantial indeed, from what readers report. Moreover, the rewards seem to increase exponentially with the amount of reading that you do, as the range of reference and the skills increase, just as exercise gets easier and more rewarding over time. From the point of view of identity formation, reading Literature supplies a most surprising biological reward. I have said that Literature is autonomous, and audible as a collection of unique voices, making and shaping language into countless worlds from which the reader can build her own, adding from the store to her own unique structure. Now it turns out that the practice of such reading, processing, activating characters and events through one's own reading mind, the very decoding of other identities in stories and language, develops the identity-making power of the reader's mind. It must be that the brain functions called into play to decode Literature into mental representations are the same functions used to create identity/story out of first-hand world experience. This is a bit like a concert pianist developing strong hands by playing the piano six hours every day. He did not do it to get strong hands. He did it to make music. The hands got stronger and more skilled incidentally and the music was made more easily because of the incidental benefit. The knowledge, pleasure and power we get from reading Literature, incidentally but inevitably, enhances our own identity.

If you could be persuaded that what I am saying here is the way things really are, that our minds and freedom are actually threatened, and that Literature is indeed the best protection for maintaining our health, our independence of thought, our control over our lives and the species' well-being then what course of social action would you advocate? Where would we direct our attention for this remedy and what kind of social, public and political program demands our resources? The answer lies, of course, in public education and in our schools.

NOTES TO CHAPTER 8
MEDIA MADNESS: OTHER PEOPLE'S LIVES (OPL)

1. From Wordsworth's sonnet, "The World Is Too Much With Us."
2. Zombies might be thought of as the walking dead. That is, they appear to be human more or less but have no consciousness or will of their own. Are they merely metaphoric or conceptual? Much philosophical and computer science debate has been generated over whether such a creature is possible. The Voodoo religion, originating in West Africa, and transported with the slave trade to the Caribbean, especially to Haiti, has been thought to generate Zombies. Some have claimed that the *bocor* or shaman could raise the dead. Others have claimed that ritual participants have been given a powerful drug that induces a coma or death-like state from which they are aroused by another drug. On return to animation the Zombies appear to have no will of their own and can be made to obey orders and serve another's will without question, maintaining a trance-like state. The reports of these claims are very sketchy, but the concept of Zombie is a useful one to us, and there is plenty of evidence from brain damage cases, and from a variety of tests that there are degrees of consciousness and huge variations in levels of free will and suggestibility.
3. Literature, rather than increasing the separation of our brains from our experience of the world, helps to reconnect us. We must read with this purpose in mind.
4. Compare this with comments by the grave digger in *Hamlet*, who observes that the prince is being sent to England where his madness will not be noticed because everybody there is similarly afflicted.
5. For a discussion of Diana as a feminist icon, another contribution to the continuation of fantasy about the princess, see *Inventing Herself*, by Elaine Showalter. The symptoms of grief evidenced by the response to Diana's death could be found among countless thousands of male mourners also. It is interesting to contrast this phenomenon with the widespread sorrow expressed by readers to the death of Little Nell in Dickens's *Old Curiosity Shop*. The latter was catharsis experienced by readers all too familiar with infant and child death. Diana was not a fictional character. Nor was she a real person in the minds of people who grieved her demise without personal knowledge or thought of her. She was something new in cultural history — *a virtual person* —something between a soap opera heroine and an actual live celebrity. Nothing in her personal life would of itself have made her famous or adored. Only her soap opera life with the Royals brought her world attention. From her exposed marital problems onwards, she became a media creation. It was this creation that occupied the big screen. There was no other Diana known to the millions who abreacted to her death.

6. "Knock, knock." "Who's there?" "Nobody." "Nobody who?" "Yeah, nobody who!" To some degree recent pop put-downs suggest not mere absence of intelligence but an awareness of a deeper absence as of consciousness itself. For instance: "The lights are on but nobody's home"; or "Get a life"; or "The space cadet"; all these may reflect a growing sense that more people are suffering attention deficit due to brain inactivity induced by the bites taken out of brains by bits.
7. Madeleine L'Engle, *A Wrinkle in Time*, p. 136.

Part Four

Action

CHAPTER NINE

Respecting Our Minds: Language, Reading and Public Education

My father liked to say that by multiplying the number of books in the world we multiply the number of readers. And with each new reader the ranks of the book-burners thin out a little more.

— **Thomas Wharton,** *Salamander*

Remember
First to possess his books; for without them
He's but a sot...

— **William Shakespeare,** *The Tempest*

THIS CHAPTER IS NOT PRIMARILY ABOUT WHAT EDUCATION IS, or is becoming. It is about what education needs to do and the central place language and reading must occupy in our schools. I believe that language, and the Literature that embodies it and embeds it in the culture, has a natural, a biological right to a core place at the heart of the curriculum. I have already given a number of reasons, grounded in human biology and culture, that explain why reading is important to human well-being. Let us remind ourselves of these.

a) Symbolic language woven into stories is the defining thought process of being human.[1] Most attempts to describe human thinking and learning are not radical enough, that is, they do not get to sources for the power and intelligence of human thinking, the sources from which language is now inseparable. For instance, here is what one textbook much used in universities says about the unique qualities of human culture:

> What is it that leads humans to develop cultures so different from those of any other species. Two basic human propensities seem crucial (Tomasello, 1995; Tomasello, Kruger, & Ratner, 1993). *One is the propensity to teach; the other is the ability to learn from such teaching*. People throughout the world teach to the young in their midst the traditions and discoveries that they and others in their group have made in the past. This enables the new generation to stand on the shoulders of their predecessors, rather than having to start anew. In contrast, apes in their natural habitats do not engage in even the rudimentary teaching that every two-year-old child does. They do not spontaneously point to objects to call others' attention to them. Nor do they hold up objects to show them to others, much less engage in the elaborate kinds of scaffolding activities of human teachers. [my italics] [2]

While the text goes on to mention human language, it fails to privilege language as underpinning everything claimed above for human teaching, though language dependency is clearly implied in the teaching activities described. Birds teach their young to sing. Cod teach their young to migrate. But humans teach their children how to make meaning. Since language is the primary skill that leads to most of the activities that make us human — that differentiates us from other mammals — we must put our best effort and our primary emphasis on teaching language and Literature.

b) Symbolic language models and describes the "world out there" and brings it "in here," to our bodies for storage, memory and retrieval. By means of language and its shaping into narrative, we can organize large impersonal worlds, and all the objects we encounter in those worlds, into manageable personal ones. We are able to share and exchange these worlds with others and so build a society. And we are able to cross the barriers of time, and our own time and space limitations, by reading the past and writing the future.

c) By means of language we create personal identity. Because of this "I" construction we can transcend the inherited self and mould our ways of seeing, thinking and believing to make each of us a unique contributor to the whole of which we are part. With language we can express, refine, grow and enhance our life management skills and form who we are. Identity is formed the way we assemble a jigsaw puzzle, except that it is never complete. The pieces of this identity jigsaw are never the same: they come at us from everywhere and must be rejigged to fit what we have so far assembled.

The Current Situation

So far so good. For all these reasons our education system must incorporate language, and the consciousness that we have good reason for teaching language at every point in the system. We need make no apologies for doing so. Whether the school system *will* ever do this is another question, but if it won't we must pursue our language acquisition for ourselves by reading, writing, listening and speaking, outside the system. Reading will be our primary means to this end.

In the first few years of our lives, the home is the place where language learning happens. Remember that the brain is being formed *at the same time language is being learned.* The other day I teasingly asked a friend's six-year-old if she could now talk. She threw her eyes up to the ceiling in contempt for such a silly question and said, "I've always been able to talk." I told her father about this. He laughed. I said that her response about speaking from birth was *natural* because her brain had been forming at the same time she learned language. Her father said, "No, it's because her mother never stops talking." The father of course was joking, but it seems we were both right in a way, since the mother that talks to her child and in front of her child a lot is doing the best job of preparing him to be facile with language.

Analog vs. Digital: Education for Life

I want to discuss the fate of public education by means of analog and digital, two ways in which information can be presented. The simplest way to explain how these two methods work and their effect on human thinking is by means of clocks. Clocks now come in two forms, analog with a face and hands, and digital with a number display only. The word analog comes from analogy or comparison. Let's look at this first. To do so we must briefly review the history of clocks.

My reason for looking at the historical origins of analog clocks is precisely because they were and are analogues for the actual human experience of the passage of time. I have described how phonetic writing was well established by the time agrarian societies were prevalent, about five or six thousand years ago. The same period provides evidence of the earliest clocks, and for the same reasons. An increase in the complexity and commerce of agrarian societies required better record keeping, better communication over distance and more efficient control over time management. If you are going to call meetings you must have a way of getting participants to arrive at more or less the same hour. We can also expect that the place of these developments would be the same, that is in the fertile river valleys, first of the Euphrates, where Sumer was established, and then of the Nile, where Egypt flourished. The fertile coastal plain of Israel was also the site of early agricultural settlement, and presumably of trade, both east and west, as it lay between Sumer and Egypt. Whatever was new in one of these places would not take long to reach the other two.

The earliest clocks were various forms of sundial and this is important for the point I am trying to make. The passage of time takes place in human brains, as they observe first the binary contrast between light and dark. In the apparent movement of the sun across the sky, time passing could be seen, tracked and so recorded, first on sundials of different sorts, the first of which appear to have been obelisks which cast a shadow on the marked ground. After that, day and night were divided into units of time measured on sand clocks, or on marked candles, or in water bowls with a hole in the bottom and so on. In every case there was never any loss of the connection between the human observer and the physical world where the sense of time passing was noted and determined. The relation between the natural world and the human observer was the basis for all time calculations, and still is. The only basis for time measurement that we have depends on the speed of Earth's rotation and the relation of that movement to the planetary system in which Earth is located.

When we get to the modern analog clock we are still in the realm of metaphoric representation of time. The earliest clocks all showed a model of the *passing* of time and conveyed a sense of continuum. When the sand runs from the top glass to the bottom glass it is still there to be seen as spent or lost time; it relates to how we *feel* in relation to time. Our modern clocks have a face and hands, as we do. They show all twelve hours and they have to be *read*, no easy task and not learned by some children until they are nine or ten. I think it is fair to say that the analog clock has a human face and reflects our feeling of participating in the passage of time, the sense of flow from minute to minute, the carousel-like quality of continuity. This is especially true of those clocks with sweeping second hands that never stop moving.

The real shift in consciousness about time comes when we move to the digital clock. Digital has to do with pointing, as in a digit or finger. What is pointed at is one unit or bit of information. Telling time by LED crystal readout is to recognize numbers as isolated units of data. The numbers show no quality of connection to hidden numbers that precede or are to follow, and reveal no connection to planetary movements, transitions or records of time passed. The numbers are *discrete* labels for an isolated point in time. The advantage of the digital display of the hour and minute is that it requires no *reading* or figuring out and very little associated feeling or sense of a whole day. It simplifies. The digital clock does not have a face or hands *because it is not human.*

I am using the clock story as a metaphor by which to discuss what is happening in education. The problem is this. The digital revolution, the binary computer evolution, has many technical advantages, including speed, accuracy, minimizing variables, simplifying interpretation. Is there a downside? Can this revolution affect human brains? Are we at risk for turning into digital, yes/no, on/off creatures? I say yes to all these questions. We are in danger of becoming dehumanized by the dominance of the digital, when we become so adapted to digital efficiency that we are willing to sacrifice human abilities to machine benefits. We can see that all our social trends are towards bits and fragments of discrete and unconnected information. We are browbeaten by mantras about efficiency. We are inundated with trivia. We are frantic about saving time, of which there seems to be less and less. We are reductionist. We just want the facts, like Sergeant Friday in *Dragnet*. In other words, we begin to look more and more and behave more and more like digital devices. But we are not digital machines. If we think and behave as though we were, we can expect to pay a very heavy price in our health and happiness and social management. What will happen to the human bits we don't use? I am arguing here that education in North America is on a fast track to simplifying information, dehumanizing students, and shrinking curriculum. We live in the age of reaction against *complexity*. Given the levels of complexity we have created and uncovered, this is a very dangerous trend indeed.

Digital communication led to the revolution in which computers have taken over much of the world of communication and information storage. This science is called cybernetics. There has always been a serious problem at the point of interface between the human and the computer, and much of the work in artificial intelligence has been directed to overcoming this problem. Many years ago the University of Waterloo, where I was teaching, bought me two computers and I gave up on both of them. Had it not been for Macintosh and their Apple machines I would not be typing on a computer now. What Apple did was invent a friendly interface, which simply meant that on the human side was a translation from computerese to the words and icons that humans use. I had seemed incapable or unwilling to invest my brain in learning a machine language, and never did learn it.

The effects of computers on human thought and on education have been profound, in spite of the steps to humanize computers. An analogy such as this might be considered. If you want to go jogging with a small child you will have to reduce your pace, alter your route, exercise way below your capacity or what you need for yourself in order to accommodate the needs of the child. In reality adults do not jog with small children for all these reasons, but they do go with computers, as it were. In dealing with computers, however, we continually modify our goals and our performance to adjust to what computers can do. This has had an effect on education and I can give you one example from my own experience.

A colleague of mine devised a scheme by which students could learn to do literary criticism by computer. For a given text, say Conrad's *Heart of Darkness*, a set of questions would be devised by which the student would be led to a pre-designed set of right answers. This would constitute the student's understanding of the text. Forget the fact that each student reads the text itself slightly differently. Forget also that the "right" answers are merely the programmer's opinions. Finally, forget that the student's own creativity in reading, in writing, in formulating difficult expressions of interaction with the author's words, is part of the purpose of reading in the first place. One of the most complex human behaviours had been reduced to what could be done by computer. Nothing else mattered. The same problems arise with all machine-administered and machine-scored tests. Some information can be tested by machines, say in learning the names of body parts in anatomy. But this is in itself mechanical and rote-learned information. When it comes to art, or human thinking or language at the level of the creative, the machine must be left behind to jog along at its own speed. So far, machines evidence no comprehension of any kind of human art or language and no quality of thought at a level beyond that of the simplest of viruses.

What Is a Horse?

The movement to the anti-metaphoric, anti-holistic and anti-human is not new of course. It is rooted in the reductionist "pragmatic" literalism of the worship of things commercial that dominated nineteenth-century education and which has returned with a vengeance today. Charles Dickens satirized this trend most tellingly as it affected education practice in his novel *Hard Times*. Sissy Jupe is a pupil who comes from a circus background. She knows horses first-hand, knows what they feel like, smell like, act like. She knows their variety of colour, shape, size and temperament. But she cannot define a horse in the manner of a dictionary. (A dictionary is a useful piece of book technology that functions like a digital computer.) In the education system described by Dickens, all the children have a number rather than a name. Sissy Jupe is girl number twenty.

> "Give me your definition of a horse." (Sissy Jupe thrown into the greatest alarm by this demand.)
>
> "Girl number twenty unable to define a horse!" said Mr. Gradgrind, for the general behoof of all the little pitchers. "Girl number twenty possessed of no facts, in reference to one of the commonest of animals! Some boy's definition of a horse. Bitzer, yours."
>
> "Quadruped. Graminivorous. Forty teeth, namely twenty-four grinders, four eye-teeth, and twelve incisive. Sheds coat in the spring; in marshy countries, sheds hoofs, too. Hoofs hard, but requiring to be shod with iron. Age known by marks in mouth."
>
> Thus (and much more) Bitzer.
>
> "Now girl number twenty," said Mr. Gradgrind. "You know what a horse is."

This would be funny if we could feel we had escaped the dangers revealed in this novel. True, the irony and satire here is hardly subtle, but what matters to me is my sense of the looming threat of a return to the training of mechanical "little pitchers" waiting to be filled with information designed by and useful to industry, no matter what the cost to the humanity of those being "programmed," like Sissy Jupe. The students' life experience is discounted and dismissed. Complexity is annihilated. Reality is reduced to the literal. Language is reduced to digital as much as possible. And learning is reduced to rote, mechanical repetition. A system of instruction founded on such goals leads to the creation of human robots.

What is going on here, in Dickens and in this chapter, is essentially a debate about language. There is of course nothing wrong with the attempt to make language "objective," factual, as in dictionaries. But what we have here is the goal of *eliminating* metaphoric language and any attempt to allow the language of subjective, personal experience to colour and affect the discourse. The two languages in conflict here represent two kinds of observation, one inwards and one outwards, and two kinds of value systems. The educational crime illustrated in the Dickens quotation is the willful limitation placed upon student learning. Students like Jupe and Bitzer need to have command of more language, not less. Though Bitzer gets approval he has learned nothing new in this class. Jupe has learned that school is irrelevant to her life experience, that she has nothing to contribute. She is a perfect drop-out candidate. Dropping out may be an act of rebellion that we should pay attention to, if it is the result of an increasingly dehumanized education system.

The more language learned earlier, the more learned later. The more language we have, the more sensory data we can internalize. The more words we have, the more things in the world we can "know" and manage. The more skills we have to arrange and relate words that point to the world, the more organization of the past and planning for the future we can accomplish. Literacy skills are critically pre-formed in the pre-school years.

At some point, say at six or seven years of age, the learning process shifts to school, where the child will now spend most of its waking hours. When the school takes over the teaching from parents does language teaching go on, consciously and deliberately? Public schools are supposed to be the great equalizers, supplementing the gaps left by the home. Do the schools fill the language gap sufficiently? — for they can only do it through language. In most cases I think not. Teachers are mostly not conscious of the paramount importance of language and not deliberate or careful enough and not sufficiently demanding in its transmission. They are too busy teaching "subjects," keeping records and filling out forms, and are not really aware (and have not themselves been taught) that these "subjects" are just a language of a specialized sort. Besides, they could not accomplish what I am suggesting here unless their students were willing and eager partners in the process. Teachers are fighting computer games, movies, television, and have few language allies. Moreover, classes are too large and there are not enough well-educated teachers to cope with all the demands. Furthermore, resources are being deliberately withheld in many jurisdictions. And worst, teachers seem to be at the mercy of governments that represent business interests, and these interests want public school systems to provide trained seals for their work force. So education is being replaced by training institutes without further debate — a debate that would expose the nature of this educational shift.

In the service of their full development and humanity, children must learn words and expressions, spend time reading, writing and talking, and they need to know why they are doing this. They need to know how their brains work, how they can be empowered by means of language. They need library training that is provided with at least the same level of energy and concern that is put into their toilet training. They need to be helped to be conscious, aware, so that they not only learn language incidentally but deliberately and with powerful motivation. Language is identity. Language is power. Indeed, public education originated in the need for literacy and for a population that was being democratized and given the vote. As you will read later, any move to privatize education is a move to steal away democracy and power from *the people.*

How is language to be taught in our schools? For one thing, an attempt to teach language without Literature will be doomed to failure.

Children do not learn grammar by repeating rules taught out of context. They learn it from speech patterns in their mother tongue. The best models of grammar, amongst other things, are found in Literature.

Let's consider what is gained by teaching Literature, for it has been far too long since the case for teaching Shakespeare and Thomas Hardy, for instance, has been examined, or re-examined, especially in the light of contemporary knowledge of brain processes. Such an examination becomes ever more urgent in the face of competition from other media for students' time. And without such an inquiry where will the motivation to teach Literature come from? We should remember through the entire discussion broached in this book that reading is difficult, demanding, and must be learned, and people, like water, will often choose the path of least resistance. We force ourselves to go to the gym only if the rewards are so enticing that we can overcome our natural inertia. We are no longer driven to hunt and gather by the need for food — we can now go to the store and get overweight with hardly any effort at all. We are no longer driven to read in order to be amused — or be put to sleep (people are dropping off like flies in front of TVs every night all over the world). We will have to understand then, that reading has a big payoff and it is well worth the effort. We have to know this before we are likely to insist that our children be taught to do it above all things.

Here then, are seven reasons for teaching literature.

1) Reading exercises and trains parts of the brain that seem to specialize in decoding language. This is a separate but connected area from speaking and listening. But the language parts of the brain, like other parts, do not work alone. They are crucially connected to areas of sensory input that require information being received from "out there" be represented in usable form "in here." They are also connected to many kinds of memory located in many parts of the brain.

2) Reading improves language knowledge by repetition of formal structures, by mental copying of sentences and by learning new words, willy-nilly, and by practice. The ability to form in the mind, to speak and

to write coherent grammatical sentences and put together sequences of thought is enhanced by reading.

3) Sentences and words have to mean something. Meaning is provided by calling on other parts of the brain to provide spatial and sensory information stored in memory. Many parts of the brain are thus activated by association. Pictures, sights, sounds, sensations and smells are needed to provide meaning. Reading activates memory and continually causes reorganization of past experience and future planning. It makes possible, indeed requires re-evaluation and reassessment of the past, and so actively creates a controlling consciousness, an identity.

4) Reading provides new data because writing has become the principal means of storing the species record. For the most part, if it is not written and preserved, it is lost. Information in books is new not only because it is original, but also because it combines in new ways old information. These new combinations are the source of ideas in human brains. And this continuous recombination is essential in the face of time and change which is itself continuous. Humans contribute hugely to the changes taking place on Earth at the very same time they appear to be abandoning their own brain power. We cannot maintain control over the forces we unleash which impact both us and our environment if we cannot control our own thinking and knowing processes. Reading is the best, fastest and cheapest means to improve our brains.[3]

5) Reading provides models of narrative, which are the essential organizing principles in memory and identity. Narrative has evolved as the human way of arranging time and experience. Narrative is the most effective means of teaching. Narrative is the primary means of exchanging crucial information from brain to brain.

6) Reading provides the most satisfying and self-contained form of entertainment available to humans.

7) The power of the human imagination appears to be virtually unlimited. With the combinations of information the brain can produce, we can think to do and experience almost anything. This power helps indi-

viduals organize, plan and enjoy their lives in many ways. Imagination is involved in personal relationships, cookery and clothing. It is the crucial factor for success in marketing, management, commerce, industry, inventing, and the evolution of software. Most actions we take, except for reflex reactions, are imagined before we perform them, in the short or in the long term. So what is the best way to educate and develop this imagination? You've got it, by reading Literature. This is because reading cultivates the *process* of imagination, not merely the content.

From a practical point of view, reading is also the most available, cost effective and most accessible means for training the abilities of mind outlined above. It gives real coded and usable knowledge of worlds much larger than the world we experience by direct sensory access alone. It gives us infinite combinations of language that we cannot get in any other way.

"I could be bounded in a nutshell and count myself King of infinite space..." wrote Shakespeare in *Hamlet*, and I would like to add, If only I could read and had access to libraries.

What Shall We Read?

Speaking of *Hamlet*, this is a good point in our discussion to raise the question of what material should be read in schools. What is the best body of Literature to use in our education systems? There are two goals at work here and we must meet both of them.

Reading, like all learning, is scaffolded, that is, one structure is built on another to permit continuous and higher climbing. We must take as a given that students need to build a mastery of literacy complexity, by starting with little hills and moving on up to the Alps. So we need to offer reading that is age appropriate, not too easy, not to hard, familiar but novel all at the same time. Moreover reading has to connect to the life students lead when they are not in school. Every child in a classroom has a number of life tasks to accomplish, and these are changing and developing all the time. No teacher can afford to be unaware of the child's life outside of school. Of course, this means classes cannot be too large or teachers too tired. And this in turn means providing the funds to adequately staff the enterprise.[4] It is difficult to understand the prevailing mantras of today: "we want the best for our children"; "we don't want to pay taxes"; *all at the same time.*

The child's life tasks include learning to cope with and adjust to family; learning how to cope with her changing body and feelings; forming identity; learning social values; pleasing parents; selecting friends; dealing with conflict; surviving sickness; coming to terms with mortality; encountering religion; managing money, and so on. So there is no point in assigning *Macbeth* for six months of minute analysis and expecting that this will produce a lifelong love of reading. A scholarly approach to the text, such as the teacher learned in university, will surely kill off the sense of the whole sweep of narrative for a less sophisticated or committed reader. Other texts relevant to the appropriate life stages are necessary *along with* Shakespeare. *The Great Gatsby* like *Macbeth*, is a study of ambition, but it is presented in terms of contemporary money worship, in a more readily accessible language and context. *Lady Oracle* explores female concerns with body image, the power of story, and the need to form identity, independence, and leaving home. *Catcher in the Rye* conveys the painful struggle of the adolescent to find a comfortable way to be human, social, and not a misfit.

Our two goals then become, first, to keep students interested and engaged. They must enjoy what they read so they want to read more. And this enjoyment will come from *seeing connections to themselves.* Second, they must grow to *use* reading, to enhance their own language skills and to understand their own culture better and more deeply. Culture is built on what went before. It too evolves in a scaffolded or building block process: learning, adapting and recombining what is known with the changes and demands made by the present and the future. Remember that the present and the future are different from the past *because of the past.* The past always lives in the present. This is the case for studying history. Our science and technology is different from, but exists because of, experiments and thoughts from hundreds, even thousands of years ago. Cars came from horses, so to speak, and from the invention of the steam engine. A stylus led to a quill and then to a keyboard, and so on. Our language and our culture are rooted in the documents of the past which inform the present — but only if we have documents.

Complex Language and the Meaning of Shakespeare

I think we should get away from "better" or "best" when speaking of Literature. Instead, we should describe texts in terms of complexity. If we are going to grow beyond the whims of taste and fashion, if we incline to the biological view of Literature and its uses, then we must look for a way to distinguish writings on the basis of the challenge and growth they offer readers. The Literature we require students to read will be of increasing complexity as their brains and experiences grow, as their hormones change, as they make more connections and as their language skills increase.[5] Remember, it is the home and school that will assist this increase, or it won't happen during the critical time children's brains are forming.

What makes for complexity in Literature? There are three ways complexity is managed in Literature. First, there is syntax. Students should be helped to unravel, decode sentences of increasing difficulty. Such sentences will be longer, have more modifiers, more dependent clauses and require more patience and memory retention than simple sentences. As a professor of Literature I was very conscious of the fact that my students — these are English Literature majors — did not for the most part like or understand Henry James's novels, especially his later ones. Among my efforts to help them was this: I *read* to them "The Beast in The Jungle." I am a good reader and I exaggerated all the punctuation, the pauses, the emphasis and vocal nuances required by the text. They were surprised and I think delighted to see the text unfold and reveal itself in a way they could understand. Here was a story that they could not unravel for themselves and which therefore frustrated them, a challenge they seemed unable to meet, a riddle that would defeat them. But "The Beast" is a story rich in human wisdom and conveys an insight, if you can find it, a profound and moving psychological insight about intimate relationship and grief. There is no point in my giving this story to patients who are not very sophisticated readers. But what a challenging and useful tool it could be in psychotherapy, in grief work, if patients could read it with understanding. This is an example of the sort of deprivation of knowledge, the loss of the wisdom of others, that follows the exclusion from language skills. We must shrink the ever widening distance between the oral and the written, so that both will not be lost.

What happened to my listening students? What had my reading aloud done? Because they could follow the syntax of my reading, they were able to pay attention to the meaning of the words and instantly use their own language and life experiences to relate the story to themselves, or to what they could imagine or construct, and so experience the pleasure of novelty, discovery, wisdom, and the activity of their own brains, along with the sense of relief and satisfaction in decoding what had become for them the Rosetta stone. All this was done on one reading, without commentary. These students, like everyone else in our society, had virtually no experience hearing a series of complex, connected sentences patiently and precisely formulated and read or spoken aloud.[6] Therefore they had no models and so no internal voices with which to decipher James's writing. For those who have grown up with television and film, the loss of aural skills is a serious deficit. Those of us who depended on radio for our entertainment were very fortunate. This was the same generation who were the most avid readers of the last hundred years. Hearing sophisticated language read by professionals must be the best training for bringing mental voices to text, to make it mean something and to make it come alive in our brains. The print, after all, originates in sound. So it is obviously important to supply spoken Literature to students if they are to make sense of texts.

Students who go to university today write and speak in simple sentences. Should this concern us? I have to answer with some questions that I hope will illustrate the problem. Can you build a modern computer with a hammer and nails? Can you measure pharmaceutical ingredients with a kitchen scale in order to fill a prescription? Can we fly to the moon on a glider? Human language is an instrumental brain tool evolved over millions of years. If we don't use it more we must use it less. I am convinced that there can be no stasis with language. It grows or declines. Like everything else, it is subject to the laws of entropy, in individuals and societies. I suppose the pages of James's novels can be used for toilet paper. You tell me if anything will be lost.

The second method by which complexity is achieved is by use of *metaphor*. Metaphors are an implied form of comparison. Since language is sequential, linear, each unit depending on what went before and what is to come, and since it has no materiality, it must invent devices, themselves linguistic, to add dimensionality and layers of meaning. So we may call metaphor the principal of these devices, or "layered meaning."[7] We might say of a writer that *she gave birth to a novel.* Have we added some meaning to the simpler, "she wrote a novel?" We could go further: "she laboured mightily and brought forth a mouse." Has the meaning been further layered? The answer to these questions is, of course, yes. We have affected the reader and revealed attitudes in the mind of the critic who slipped in a point of view without adding many, if any, words. Birth associations have been evoked in the reader to alter, colour and shape response, not to mention the twitching of our brain cells by the pun on "labour." *Pun* is another device for layering meaning to overcome linear limitations.

Metaphors are used in speech all the time, whether people know it or not. We say: *It's raining cats and dogs. Time flies. Stick with it. Feeling down and out. What's brewing? What's cooking? I'm dog tired. The market will crash, it's a bubble. Blind to the truth. Going straight. Riding out the storm. Playing it by ear,* or *Playing it by the seat of our pants. Getting stuck in a rut. Speaking garbage. Sailing too close to the wind.* And on and on. Indeed, it is hardly possible for humans to communicate without metaphor and there is some evidence that those who use more metaphor achieve better control of their lives.[8]

Metaphor is shorthand for compressing multiple references into simple utterances: it works like solid fuel or the energy in tiny batteries. Metaphor may in fact be potential energy, released when read or heard and activating higher levels of neural activity. The listener, in some lightning speed decoding, calls forth pictures, sounds, smells etc., to enhance the meaning and understand more fully what is being said. Metaphor makes language concrete and less abstract, less vague. More parts of the brain are used to decode metaphors than to decode sentences without them. But metaphors can lose their power with overuse and familiarity. At some point they don't require much decoding and just become stock phrases requiring only a flat and fixed response. If I say to you, "I'm dead beat" or "out on my feet," you don't picture me as one beaten up, dying of fatigue or standing punch drunk in a boxing ring. You merely instantly know I am very tired. To call forth your complex brain input from many sources I must invent a new metaphor that forces you to think and assemble material from your memory. If I say to you, "I'm sleep walking" or "I'm a rag doll," I might get a bit more empathy or understanding from you. Good writers have a talent for finding original metaphors to enliven their language. When people search for metaphors to explain themselves they are working hard to communicate; they are overcoming the *limitations of literal language.*

Now, the principle limitation of language is its dependence on sequence extended over real time. That is, you have to wait till the end of a sentence, or a series of sentences, keeping in mind words already spoken, before you know what it all means. To some degree this is overcome when the words are printed and stay in front of you. But the principle method invented by human brains is metaphor, which layers meaning and forestalls sequence and time lag. There is a lot more information in saying the speaker was "casting pearls before swine" than in saying the audience did not understand the speaker. The best way to learn metaphors and how to make them is to read professional writers whose stock in trade is the creation of metaphor. The more layered the writing, the more complex — and so more rewarding is the text. The goal is for readers to arrive at the most complex and satisfying of reading outcomes. At some point when this happens there is a sense of revelation, the discovery of the reader's own brain power and the sense of control and liberation that comes with insight into the nature of language and complexity itself. The height of metaphor making is found in the writing of Shakespeare:

> That time of year thou mayest in me behold
> When yellow leaves, or none, or few, do hang
> Upon those boughs which shake against the cold,
> Bare ruined choirs where late the sweet birds sang.

This is metaphor, timelessly effective, reaching so far beyond "I am getting old," that it creates webs of meaning and emotion by reference to the entire realm of natural loss: mankind facing mortality at a personal level, giving voice to everything that must die. To me this is as near to poignant as language can get. It is achieved by metaphor that evokes ranges of imagery and emotional experience in the brain. These are forced together from memory and emotion into a synthesis of meaning in the neocortex.[9] The meaning is the coalescence of all references necessary if the reader, or listener, is to experience personal recognition, or make sense of the code. To arrive at this requires and repays study.

By the time we reach the end of Shakespeare's *The Tempest*, *Cymbeline* and *A Winter's Tale*, we are encountering a writer whose work has achieved and revealed that language, poetry (metaphor) is the shaping force of human reality, reality shaped and created by the words we learn and create. Shakespeare comes to the realization that all his work has really been about language. Shakespeare's enduring power is his awareness that language and poetry transform all other sensory information into the *humanly knowable*. The plays themselves become metastory and metalanguage, stories and plays about the transforming power of the language in which they are written. This is the pinnacle of language achievement. It is this "breakthrough," this $E=mc^2$ of language, that gives Shakespeare's work the quality of inspired wisdom and penetration that readers have for centuries marvelled at. In truth, the achievement of Shakespeare is not that he had new insights or great philosophical breakthroughs. What he produced was a daring and audacity with words, a stretching of the language that expanded our capacity to grasp the sensory reality of the world and bring it into our brains.

It is a very unusual teacher indeed who can transfer his own enthusiasm for the awesome intelligence of Shakespeare's metaphors to students. But what if a teacher does not have that enthusiasm? What if it is the gym teacher who has to teach Literature? What if Shakespeare and Dickens are removed from the curriculum as irrelevant to business interests and work force training? What if more and more schools have to abandon art, music, and even physical education itself for lack of funding. Can Literature survive this onslaught? Schools would never be allowed to exclude computer courses, book keeping, whatever. "English" only hangs on by its fingernails because of some foothold in the rock face of "business" concerns, such as report or letter writing. What teachers lack, and what must somehow be provided, is an awareness that they are offering students the secret of metalanguage, *language writing about its own power.* Students must learn that they can derive *personal* benefit from reading Shakespeare. They read him now because he is a sentimental leftover from the past, like a once great fighter who is now allowed to hang around the gym because nobody has the heart to throw him out, even if he is a dreadful old bore. Teachers and students need to know that Shakespeare is to be read for his amazing achievement with language, and knowledge of this language can be a reusable treasure trove stored in the minds of readers. This is an investment that provides an "income" for life. You can help yourself to it whenever you need to and in doing so vastly enrich your own life skills, *but only if you have invested your brain.*

Shakespeare seems to have been entrusted by nature, historical confluence or destiny to explore the possibilities of the vernacular, that is, native English. His poetry is the culmination of the English language and the foundation for most writing in English that succeeded it. It is hard to find any subsequent writer not influenced by Shakespeare. Short of reinventing the wheel and beginning from scratch, we must understand some of Shakespeare's writing or be deprived and diminished. If teachers lose their nerve teaching Shakespeare it is because they have forgotten or never learned the point of the entire exercise. *Macbeth* is not "about" ambition; *Hamlet* is not "about" revenge; *King Lear* is not "about" vanity and power. These plays illuminate and create the language of ambition, revenge and power; they are metaphors, embodiments for these abstract states of being human. If you prefer, they are models of these abstractions in action. They represent versions of the psychological and social energy that humans expend in the struggle for power, control and love.

If we understand *why* we must read Shakespeare, namely so that we can be awakened to the possibilities of human language, we can also see the case for reading other "classics" of English composition, the works of Dickens, George Eliot, the Brontës, Blake and Wordsworth to name but a few. Of course, the rewards are not merely personal. We are members of a group, a culture, and the principle glue of the culture is its language and the ideas and images formed by that language. The common heritage is the common language. If you want to learn and understand or succeed in a French or Chinese culture you must read French or Chinese Literature. You must read Flaubert and Baudelaire; or *Journey to the West* if you want to know how the Chinese think. Just as Qui Gong and Tai Chi masters pass to their students the movements of the masters gone before, so teachers must pass on the inventions of the language masters who went before.

This brings us to the third hallmark of complex writing: complex structure. We start out with simple stories — nursery rhymes, *The Little Engine That Could, The Little Red Hen Bakes a Loaf* — but if we stay with simple stories we will stay with simple minds and simple thoughts. I am not making a moral or value judgment here. Those who believe that complexity is too much work will join a cult or watch TV or become members of some extreme right wing ideology and simplify and literalize everything. What I am describing here is a neurological, a brain condition. If we don't acquire complex language, we simply won't use and experience the consequences of our brain's potential power. If I buy a powerful computer, and only use it to keep track of birthdays and shopping lists, I am not really "using" it at all. I am extravagantly underusing it, like buying a Rolls Royce to use as a cocktail cabinet.

To make stories more complex, and so keep us entertained, challenged and also to reflect real life experience more accurately, writers play a number of tricks with narrative. They introduce subplots, secondary stories tangential to the primary; they multiply characters within subplots; they shift time sequences. They can start in the middle or at the end of a story and they can work backwards, forwards or outwards from the middle. They can run parallel narratives of equal importance that reflect on each other. They can create interior monologue or dialogue, never heard by others in the story. They can shift their story between locales remote from each other. They can disclose little or everything to the reader and choose when to do so. They can write stories within stories, like Russian nesting dolls. They can suspend plots while they make us wait. They can draw attention to their art or keep us immersed. They can write novels made up of correspondence, or novels in diary form or pretend autobiographies like *Robinson Crusoe.* Countless thousands of such stories, in most languages, have been written and published and read in just a few hundred years.

Story-making writers appear not to have much option about the writing process. They *must* create written narratives. Some compelling brain organization drives them to do it and only doing it gives them relief, temporary though it is. I believe that natural selection within groups is at work here. Just as strong, clever and adaptive individuals and their traits survive better than weak ones, so too, groups need and produce individuals genetically "entrusted" with special group-serving talents. The group is strengthened through writers by having its cultural history and wisdom (from experience) embedded in entertaining and memorable narrative records. By sharing stories, the group bonds together, a good thing as unity is less stressful than enmity. Having models of language constructed by specialists, groups can grow their reservoir of language skills and information for life management.

Traditionally, the skilled storyteller was among the most honoured members of a society. It is important for us to explain to students why this was so; to remind them and ourselves that the reasons for this have not disappeared in our time. We still *need* community, bonding and language skills. We will not lose these without paying a huge price. Print has given us the means whereby the language and thought of our storytellers can be heard over vast expanses of time and space. So writers have come to create a great pool of Literature that can be viewed as a kind of extrasomatic "gene" pool that can be accessed by those who can read. This store of information is a species resource, a sort of invented extra-brain module available to enhance our well-being. *Literature can be presented to students as part of their biological human inheritance to which they have rights and without which they are handicapped.*

There are other features to complex writing worth mentioning. One is symbolism. Another is allusion. Perception of these features requires training and the knowledge of a body of Literature. This can be learned in school and for most people only in school. Symbolism is like an energy cell of language and concentrates into itself a range of instantly understood associated meanings. Desdemona's handkerchief in *Othello*, a gift from her husband Othello, represents her fidelity; the theft and display of this gift leads to her murder. The word "heart" means love. *The Scarlet Letter* weaves an entire novel around one sign, the letter "A" for "Adultery," which Hester is forced to wear on her bosom. This "A" also stands for Adam in the Puritan primer: "In Adam's Fall we sinned, All," an added richness recognized only by the well-read. To Robinson Crusoe the single footprint in the sand means the presence of human beings where he expected none. It is one more puzzle for him and the reader to solve. Symbols are signs pointing to a network of paths of meaning.

In a mystery novel I have just been reading the author puts the following thought into the character's mind.

> The day was gently sunny but Verity found it oppressive. The sky was clear but she felt as if it would almost be a relief if bastions of cloud shouldered each other up from beyond the horizon. It occurred to her that writers like Ibsen and Dickens — unallied in any other respect — were right to make storms, snow, fog and fire the companions of human disorders. Shakespeare too, she thought. *We deprive ourselves esthetically when we forgo the advantages of symbolism.*[10] [my italics]

Dickens and Ibsen are of course closely allied in many respects, but she is right that symbolism is characteristic of Literature designed to overcome the gaps between the "I" and the natural world "other." And not only "esthetically." We forego the power to understand, arrange, organize, make sense of, feel in control of the environment surrounding us, if we do not have the linguistic tools to describe to ourselves what we are feeling. When our brains recognize the connection between our feelings and the storm as symbol, we feel less passive, helpless, alone and detached. We acquire this skill/knowledge by reading. We learn from skilled writers like Ibsen, Dickens, and Shakespeare how language makes the connection between the feeling *in here* and the environment *out there.* The connection is in our minds, and *only in our minds;* only anywhere, in truth, by means of language.

Allusion is another shortcut to a multiplicity of meanings and associations. It is achieved by making an implied reference to other Literature, but it will be undetectable to the reader unfamiliar with that literature which is in reference. The more Literature the reader knows the more the writer can employ allusion to enrich textual meaning. Allusion works as a cue to associative networks of cortex and memory. A writer like Dickens informs his entire corpus of work with allusions to Shakespeare. Later writers make frequent allusion to Dickens. A writer might refer to a character as Pickwickian, a teacher could be a veritable Gradgrind, but these allusions will be lost on a reader who can't picture Pickwick and all his attendant characteristics from *The Pickwick Papers*. Entire novels can be allusory, especially when a new work is based on an old one, as in, for instance, *Rosencrantz and Guildenstern are Dead.* These are but a few of the devices that complex writing employs to entertain and instruct us.

Summary

There are some who think that language began as recently as 32,000 years ago, signalled by the dating of cave drawings like those at Lascaux in France. These "depictions" are supposed to represent the earliest forms of communication, indicating the beginnings of speech. This is hardly likely. But these drawings of men and bison do seem to indicate the antiquity of recorded storytelling, long before writing. The problem is that without any lexicon to explain what we see, it is not possible to know what the drawings mean. With the invention of writing, meaning becomes primary and when humans write, they do so to convey and implant "meaning" into other brains: this is how I see the world; this is how I feel; this is what happened to me. These meanings are thus joined to the reader's "meaning." And through the numerous devices that have been added to written language, all meaning deepens and broadens.

We have discussed metaphor and how it multiplies and layers meaning so that recursively, meanings come to adhere and nest in a complex structure of references. We have looked at structure, whereby single stories turn into multiple stories woven together, so that they come to resemble the actual interweaving of the relations and roles we experience in life. We see that symbolism, the very nature of language, can be deliberately built into a story so that objects, signs, bits of evidence can be strategically placed in a story to represent people, places and incidents. These symbols can then be held in mind as portholes for viewing whole sections of meaning. We have seen how Literature is cumulative, and how one known story or character can be used to refer to other writings, so expanding the reader's range of reference. This device is called allusion. And we could extend this list showing how sentence structure itself conveys entire states of mind and society, as in Hemingway's masterpiece of understated violence, "The Killers."

I hope you will see by now that in our schools, if we don't teach language and teach it principally by means of reading Literature, doing so by a carefully constructed, scaffolded, age-appropriate architecture leading to the teaching of complex Literature, we will deprive our students of vital information and skills. We are wasting their precious time and an opportunity that will not come again, for when they have the time, maybe in retirement, they won't have the forming brains. Today more than ever we need reading in education, as television and computers eat up more and more of our childrens' time. Our fear of machines becoming too intelligent is rooted in our deep intuition that a machine that can think will be impossible to control. Why should this same fear not apply to ourselves in reverse? By not having enough language we will be rendered helpless and passive. We must have more language and brain power, not less, not just enough so that we can follow the instructions. Alexander Pope was precisely right: "A little learning is a dangerous thing." In fact, in the light of what is happening in our world, he could hardly have known how right he was.

For readers, writers, publishers, teachers and librarians, it is comforting to look at current numbers in book sales and think reading is alive and well and shows no signs of declining. These numbers, however, are highly deceptive and dangerous to the future of reading education. If we subtract from the sales figures all those titles on how to make a million dollars, books about computers, books on diet, cooking, travel, self help, course books, tax, gardening, hobby books, all those books that have very little to do with narrative, emotion, story and language, then the overall numbers drop alarmingly.

For the rest, fiction, poetry, classic reprints, philosophy, ideas, social commentary and analysis, children's books, well, I wish I could say I was optimistic. What worries me is that today's children, the people in our homes and schools from one year of age to eighteen, will fail to be the reading population that we have counted on in the past to keep language and story complexity alive. Book clubs, aside from being composed mostly of women (a traditional imbalance for readership, but the absence of males is not cheering), are skewed to members whose ages rarely dip beneath thirty plus.

Let's briefly list the reasons for concern about how our education system might fail us. Given the current political and economic milieu, the pressure on public education is to serve the interests of multinational corporations and the governments they control. The traditional goal of public education, "*mens sane in sane corpore*," a healthy mind in a healthy body, is being replaced by job training, computer skill acquisition, and service to *The Market*. Tax dollars are being used to supply the needs of business interests at tax payers' expense, not the human needs of children. This training implicitly creates people who are servants of machines. It cultivates passivity. It also breeds boredom, a worship of money and depression. Drug, tobacco and alcohol use among teenagers is epidemic as our youth find schooling more and more irrelevant to their mental and emotional needs, their brain needs, their developmental needs and their need for human-based social interaction. This is the current virus. It is *alienation*.

Funding of education at all levels is more and more directed to job market forces, with attendant shrinking of programs in language and Literature, music, art, drama, history and thought. These essentials are considered irrelevant to the job market by short-sighted people in business and government who only think from one quarter to the next, or from election to election and then apply this thinking to human development and species survival. In reality they don't of course "think" about such survival or the quality of human life at all.

Children turn more and more to computer games and television for entertainment, the effect of which consumes their brain growth time with learning how computers think and less and less with how they themselves think. As a result, people seem more and more willing to elect leaders who are high-school or university drop-outs who can barely speak or read or write themselves. So the downward spiral continues.

The trend to superstores, mergers, news monopolies, and trivialized entertainment means less variety, fewer thought-provoking texts, social criticism, challenging Literature and less unconventional art and imaginative, human-centred production. The information age, so called, is concentrating its time, energy and resources on the *means* of transmitting information and forsaking any consideration of the value of what is being communicated.

There are signs of hope. More and more people are becoming aware of their own impoverishment of mind and spirit. Individuality can be marginalized by lack of language and story, just as people's political influence can be marginalized by low income. Human brains will not accept this crazy limitation on their evolutionary achievements, any more than the Earth will tolerate the levels of abuse currently afflicted on it. We can affect the quality of human education by demanding that schools return to the development of the whole young person. The centre of this renewal must come from full and highly developed literacy. Nothing else can justify the expenditure of public funds on education. The failure to confront the social cost of dehumanizing our children, depriving them of their biological birthright to Literature, will be social disaster. Treating human minds, along with natural capital, as free, disposable raw material without any reckoning of the human, social and environmental cost resulting from its loss, has to stop. The message to writers, publishers, book sellers, readers, librarians and students is: don't count on Literature just being here forever. You will have to preserve it, and use it, or lose it.

What is required now is nothing less than a radical shift in thinking. Before we can restore sanity and the public good to public education, we will have to become believers. Making the reading connection will require a deliberate, a conscious decision to break the trend that now prevails toward passivity, toward acceptance of the status quo. We will have to speak out, to take up a mental fight against the neural inertia and ignorance that is spreading like a plague. To get back our mental energy we must cultivate a reading attitude. We must start early — and we must change our schools.

Notes to Chapter 9
Respecting Our Minds: Language, Reading and Public Education

1. Terrence Deacon's recent book, *The Symbolic Species*, is most admirable for its insistence on focusing our attention on the uniquely human symbol-making feature of our language. This is called "species specific." Contrast this with definitions that emphasize grammatical structure, syntax. I agree with Deacon's implication that grammar is only necessary because of symbol-making features of human language. Deacon does not, however, acknowledge the forms that symbol language takes, which is my emphasis here. For me, symbolic language is as co-evolved with story as symbolic language is with brains in Deacon's thesis.
2. Robert S. Siegler, *Children's Thinking* p. 19.
3. For one recent description of the problem see Thomas Homer-Dixon's *The Ingenuity Gap*. I find the concept of "ingenuity" vague. I think the loss of language, brain skills and the efficiency dependent upon them deserve detailed consideration not provided by Dr. Homer-Dixon's book. He speaks only of the need for better "communication." Homer-Dixon does have one important passage on metaphor and its transforming powers on page 395 of his book. It might be said that I am devoting this entire book to an elaboration of a thesis about language that he only touches upon. I mention this because I think both his book and mine reveal our deep anxieties about the future of humanity.
4. Basil Bernstein is one the most interesting thinkers on education writing today, or rather for the last thirty years. The problem is that he is almost unreadable. The following passage, however, points to my own interests and is worth explaining. Bernstein writes about "identities" formed in institutions of English education. He contrasts what he calls the market identity with the therapeutic identity. Here is one comment on the latter: "I call the identity 'therapeutic' because this identity is produced by complex theories of personal, cognitive, and social development, often labeled progressive.... This identity is orientated to autonomous, non-specialized, flexible thinking, and socially to team work as an active participant. It is very costly to produce and the output is not easily measured: the position projecting this identity is a very weak position in all contemporary arenas so the social group which sponsors it has little power." pp. 68-69

   I am afraid this is how sociologists write, but the meaning is important, so let me explain. The therapeutic identity is designed to serve the human life needs of the individual who has such an identity. It is highly individualized and not programmed to meet the needs of market robotization of workers and consumers. Any traces of such idealism for individual therapeutic holism, autonomy (independence), such as surfaced briefly in the sixties and seventies, seem to have been swept aside by the flood of right wing brainwashing in the last twenty years. Such goals as "non-specialized, flexible thinking" are not evident in the official educational practices of most "arenas" as Bernstein puts it. He goes on to explain that those in a "strong position," the power elites, are unwilling to dedicate resources to create the "therapeutic identity" in public education.

5. For one theory on the three brain structures most heavily implicated in language and what they do, see Damasio and Damasio, 1992.

6. See Neil Postman on the language differences in public speaking in the age of Lincoln, compared to today in *Amusing Ourselves to Death.* One of the things I learned from this classroom experience was that punctuation must be heard, that behind the signs are pauses, emphases, rhythms and inflections. These are learned by hearing a text read well while you silently follow.

7. The term "literal" has come to mean the opposite of the metaphorical. The Nicene Creed created by committee at the Council of Nicea, was an attempt to strip the Christian story of metaphor and to render it literal and therefore historical. I believe the entire history of Western civilization could be usefully understood as determined by the conflict between the literal and the metaphorical, though this book is not the place to pursue such an inquiry. For a discussion of the psychological implications of this struggle, see James Hillman, *Healing Fiction.*

8. See Christopher Allen Wynot, 1994.

9. The neocortex is the upper layer of the brain, much larger in humans than in other mammals, where meaning and story seem to be assembled from materials in memory, and from emotion, much of which is processed in deeper levels of the brain.

10. Ngaio Marsh, *Grave Mistake,* p. 115

CHAPTER TEN

Get An Attitude: The Fight of Your Reading Life

As no other medium before or since, the book promotes a sense of a coherent and usable past.

— Neil Postman

WE LIVE IN A WORLD THAT IS HOSTILE TO READING, at least to the reading of fiction. Not explicitly of course: you don't hear everybody around you saying reading is a waste of time; and there's still plenty of lip service to the virtue of reading *something*, though again not principally fiction. No, what I mean is there are social and economic forces at work which militate against reading, so an advocate for reading Literature as a biological imperative feels as though he is swimming against the tide.[1] Perhaps hostile is the wrong word. Indifferent or mildly contemptuous might more accurately reflect the current social attitude toward reading Literature, in the same way the young regard the old, or those with computers feel about those without. Readers are old fashioned, not "with it," out of the mainstream. There is a worship of the New, a trust in technology at the expense of self-reliance and personal resourcefulness. Less and less do we teach the tools for resourcefulness, among the best of which is Literature.

In previous chapters I addressed some of the current challenges to reading and publishing and the implications, both social and personal, of a possible decline in reading. Are more videos rented or viewed in a year in

North America than books borrowed or bought and read? I don't know. Should we be worried about such numbers? I don't know. But I certainly know we should be worried about raising generations of people who don't actually read Literature and what this will mean to them personally and to their society.

In *Amusing Ourselves to Death*, Neil Postman describes what it feels like to move from the world of print that some of us grew up in, to the electronic world. I quote at length because his imagery is so effective:

> Changes in the symbolic environment are like changes in the natural environment; they are both gradual and additive at first, and then, all at once, a critical mass is achieved.... A river that has slowly been polluted suddenly becomes toxic; most of the fish perish; swimming becomes a danger to health. But even then, the river may look the same and one may still take a boat ride on it. In other words, even when life has been taken from it, the river does not disappear, nor do all of its uses, but its value has been seriously diminished and its degraded condition will have harmful effects throughout the landscape.
>
> It is this way with our symbolic environment. We have reached... a critical mass in that electronic media have decisively and irreversibly changed the character of our symbolic environment. We are now a culture whose information, ideas and epistemology are given form by television, not by the printed word. To be sure, there are still readers and there are many books published, but the use of print and reading are not the same as they once were; not even in schools, the last institutions where print was thought to be invincible.[2]

Postman has managed to free himself of the scientistic pretensions to oracular objectivity of his teacher Marshall McLuhan, but he has substituted an aura of despair to his otherwise excellent social study. There is no reason to accept, and I for one cannot afford to accept as inevitable, the disappearance of print or of Literature. If we are persuaded that reading is good for us, even essential for human well-being, then we had better make sure the practice stays alive and strong.

The problem today is that passive visual entertainment is so pervasive that we are in danger of believing that *not* reading Literature will not deprive us in serious ways. My hope is that people can be persuaded that by not reading they will impoverish their cognitive and emotional lives. Millions of people who own cars, or travel by bus or train nevertheless visit gyms, walk or jog, play sports of every kind. Why don't they just give up moving unnecessarily altogether, avoid exercise and try to sit as much as possible? Either their bodies tell them, or they are otherwise persuaded that their health depends on physical activity. Perhaps we need a reading Olympics.

In the face of contemporary attitudes which dismiss reading as old hat, you will need conviction and motivation if you decide reading is important to you, mentally, emotionally, or as a source of pleasure or reliever of stress; you will need to be confident about this activity and feel validated and justified in devoting time to it, time not spent watching TV or being sociable. Otherwise, you can't resist the crowd anymore than an addict can resist the pressure to have a drink at a party. An avid reader who marries a non-reader (a common occurrence) encounters a serious obstacle to companionship — for the reader will certainly not give it up. People (but not texts) are altered by reading. They learn new roles and new ways of seeing. This constitutes a kind of mental, spiritual and emotional growth and if this is not shared, if growth is not mutual, both communication and bonding weaken and couples grow apart. It is not sexual intimacy but language that bonds human beings most lastingly together; or let's say that language can be a form of sexual intimacy. And Language bonds not only couples but groups as well.[3]

Attitudes are convictions or beliefs based on experience and knowledge, mental positions we take in response to all kinds of ideas and moral or social issues. It seems we have attitudes toward everything, and our attitudes are a powerful source of self-motivation and action. We are not going to read if we are not highly motivated by seeing its benefits. Reading is difficult, active, mentally demanding, and time consuming. It is very difficult to do anything else while reading. I find I am able to pay bills or file papers while watching a soccer game on TV. In any Portuguese bar in Toronto there is plenty of noise, conversation, eating and drinking going on while the inescapable soccer dominates two or three television screens. You won't see much reading in such a setting, it would be virtually impossible. We must believe, then, that reading Literature is so sufficiently rewarding, enlightening, amusing, that we become dedicated to it, and in the twenty-first century this will require considerable determination. The computer game, the Net, the TV, overwhelm our environment. We will have to be fiercely proactive about reading. We will have to model it for our children, believing it to be healthier for them than many other behaviours, some of which we model all too effectively.

While the act of reading a novel is private and isolating in the first instance, its consequences are quite different. Reading provides connection to bodies of information known to and shared by other people. Parents are the first and most powerful models for children in their first six years, so they should see us reading. Thereafter Literature itself can be the most reliable and inexhaustible source of behavioural modelling. In fact, reading fiction makes it possible *to share* the most stable psychosocial models available to us. The shared novel or poem is the convergent point for separated minds.

I can illustrate this point with a story told to me by a graduate student. Marion had been seeing a therapist in Toronto, a man she found wonderfully kind and patient, but to whom she could not speak at all. She would faithfully attend the sessions, but while there she just sat and cried, and her therapist waited, or tried to be encouraging. "This can't go on," she thought. Finally, out of frustration, she left a book in his office as though she had forgotten it. Fortunately the therapist had the sense to read it and in their next session Marion was able to speak to him about it. In discussing the book, she was, of course, speaking indirectly about herself, as represented by a model of experience written by someone else. This seemed safer, and so workable for her, that they were able to make a start. After this she regularly took him reading that explained herself without the need for direct disclosure.

Reading is also the best way for adolescents to obtain information. They need tons of it, and also have a way of finding it. Research I did a few years ago told me that adolescence is the time when people read most, read quite a lot in fact, or at least they used to.[4] This is true even for those who as adults read very little. Adolescents have to get ready to be wholly independent. Older adults often aren't much help. It also happens that children go through adolescence at a time when their parents are most involved in careers and mid-life issues. The enormous resource of reading is what comes to the rescue. I knew a boy who was a true male Cinderella. He was adopted. When his parents began to have children naturally, he felt more and more emotionally excluded until he believed he was an exploited stranger. He was extremely reluctant to admit these feelings, but he showed me who he was by sending me in the mail his three favourite books, the treasures of his own bookshelf. I read these books and they sent a powerful and clear message. I saw who he thought he was and what he was trying to tell me. One book was Jean C. George's *River Rats, Inc.*, a robust adventure about two boys striking out on their own. The second was Cynthia Voigt's *A Solitary Blue*. Here again a rejected, lonely boy tries to win his mother's love and attention, and fails. The boy in the story survives with his father's help and the friendship of an orphan from his school. The third was also about rejects, children who don't belong, who aren't wanted and who have to make it by themselves. How could my young patient possibly convey to me the complex and elegantly described situations created in these extended models? By sharing reading interests he was able to point me clearly toward how he felt and saw himself, in a language not available to him, by himself. He also had to reveal his feelings without condemning his adoptive parents, which he could not do because he was truly grateful to them, in spite of his negative emotions about his situation. These readings undoubtedly helped by showing him it was possible to survive his pain and loneliness. I don't believe he had the language or skill to explain himself to me. He greatly furthered his therapy by simply offering the books, books that were points of convergence for his mind and mine.

My gift to him was *I Am David* by Anne Holme, one of my favourites. David escapes from a terrible prison camp somewhere in southeastern Europe and sets out to find his Danish mother, whom he has never seen. It is a wonderful story of a boy's suffering and survival. Readers are often stirred by it and enabled to see their own plights in a different light, and with a more detached degree of pity, or compassion for their own earlier child self. They can take courage from David's example and hope from his survival. This kind of recognition of a character-who-is-oneself makes acceptance of one's own situation possible, and acceptance, in turn, makes change, action and planning all possible. The experience of the reading breaks down isolation.

When I gave my gift to Andy, several messages were transmitted. Without discussing the meaning of his books, without interpreting them or him, without exposing his private pain to discussion, I showed him that I understood and recognized how he felt by matching a similar book to the ones he gave me. Second, I showed respect both for his reading and for the *process* by which he was choosing to pursue his therapy. Third, I helped to normalize his experience of being lonely and rejected, because while he might have said to himself that his finding books "about him" was accidental, I was saying to him, no, what you experience is widespread and well-known.

What is going on in these examples above? We are looking at a form of show and tell. The best way to explain what is in one's head is to show it. A model of what one thinks and feels is sometimes found in writing by those who read. Putting "how we feel" inside, in our hidden silence, "out there," to be read in the form of a story by someone else, and ostensibly *about* someone else, makes what we need to convey accessible to others, without the risk or challenge of self-disclosure.

So reading makes feelings, conscious and unacknowledged emotional states and memories accessible for discussion and feedback. To this we can add that states of mind expressed in writing created to be read also acquire stability. Writing provides a kind of photo-fixative to thought. Text can be referred to, transferred, yet remain in its original form as a record of what we meant at that time.

Since the invention of printing and therefore of infinite testimonies to the power of reading, to which we all have access, why should it be necessary to make the case for reading now? Well, to add to Postman's observations above, in the electronic age, and in a world of global politics, there are forces at work that undermine positive attitudes to reading. These forces are reaching into our homes and into the public education system.

There have always been social, political and economic forces working against reading. We will examine them in a minute. Today the primary barriers to reading are the terrible demands made on our time and energy, and the distractions of consumer culture and the pursuit of wealth. Competition for the individuals' time and energy has become intense and seductive. You will have to be dedicated to reading if you want to withstand the easy seductions of passive amusements like TV, advertisements and commercials via the tube, the Internet, newspapers, billboards and the invasion of your home by telemarketers. And you have to resist getting brain-stunned by voice mail and e-mail, and collecting countless bits of unrelated information from magazines and talk radio.

Too many people are walking around in a semi-exhausted daze, mentally spinning with confusion, and losing personal integration. They are not grounded. They are not calm. They do not feel in control. The ills that beset us, in health, pollution, politics and our moral and ethical values, result in part from a widespread submission to commercial propaganda. One thing that reading sustained narratives does is alter the reader's brain by shifting attention from what is "out there" to the development of what is "in here," to the thought and emotion of the reader's own inner life. This is a shift from passivity, mere reception, to activity, from fragmentation to holism, from automatism to awareness. And it is in the growth of self-awareness, a consciousness of our own mental processes, where personal and social healing will be found. We need to read because reading in itself produces an organizational, mental "collective" of understanding. But we must go beyond this now to a reading activity informed by the knowledge and belief that we are doing what is good for us. *We must be aware of our own mental processes.* We must become active in forming our identity, beliefs and values. This is an imperative antidote to chaos and submission. If we abandon reading, we agree to accept our own powerlessness. We need the primary tool of Literature, not only to inform ourselves but to *form* ourselves. As we are formed, so we will form our societies. We must read for our whole lives, remembering that as we do we are communicating with our selves and improving our skills for communicating with others.

There are three main anti-reading attitudes we must overcome. They are not new, but still operate in full force. We will call one *The Frock Coat of Literature;* the second *A Waste of Time;* and the third *Criticizing Literature to Death.* One of these is disguised as a friend of Literature, another as a friend of reading. As we will see, we need to choose our friends carefully.

The Frock Coat of Literature

You will remember that Jacob made his favourite son Joseph a coat of many colours, a garment that was a mark of distinction. It made Joseph stand out and announced to the world that Joseph the dreamer was special. For a long time Literature and the knowledge of it was worn by an elite as their costume, their mark of distinction and it became socially a kind of mental frockcoat, the dress-up sign of a "gentleman." First, reading was the preserve of the clergy and the greatest source of their power. In the days when learning and reading were conducted in the classical languages, Greek and Latin, it was only the clergy who learned and taught from books, for Greek and Latin were secret languages. This allowed the Church to reserve all of its power to itself. Then the aristocracy became more powerful than the Church and it was the rich who became the custodians of reading. When the vernacular replaced Greek and Latin, "gentlemen" gradually substituted the classical coat of English Literature for the coat of the classics. And it was this coating that made them special. Even though everyone spoke the vernacular, reading it still retained its "dressing up" quality for those who went to Oxford and Cambridge, Harvard and Yale, Toronto and McGill. The study of Literature as a Frock Coat was known as *belles lettres*. This means fine writing and one who practiced writing or reading became a man of letters or a "lettered" man. Knowing how to read and write well gave a man distinction. (I use the term "man" advisedly of course, as women were excluded from this process.) A gentleman could quote, refer to famous books, and pepper his speeches in parliament or the drawing room with allusions.

With the advent of public education and the spread of "red brick" universities (as opposed to the "superior" "grey stone" ones), people from working-class backgrounds, people like myself, could attend university with state aid, and study Literature. Strangely enough, the Frock Coat attitude, even though it was completely inappropriate, continued, and maybe still does prevail, in universities where we teach our teachers who in turn teach our children. I offer an example from personal experience. When I was an undergraduate in the 50s in England, I studied "English," which consisted mostly of reading a lot and participating in what was called a tutorial. Education in English universities has traditionally taken place through the tutorial. This means that once a week a professor or lecturer, reader or fellow, gathered together in his office three or four students assigned to him for a one-hour discussion of some book or other everyone was supposed to have read. On one occasion our subject was *Tom Jones* by Henry Fielding and one of us had prepared an essay for delivery. My tutor, who was fairly young but prematurely aged, extremely bad tempered, crusty and pretentious, bustled in, full of pomp, circumstance and impatience. I don't remember what the essay of my peer was all about, but I do remember that when he finished reading it, I found myself conscious of the fact that both I and the novel remained untouched. What I mean is that my whole experience of *Tom Jones*, all his adventures, all the vast panorama of eighteenth-century England, with its multiplicity of tastes, sights and sounds, all the characters and erotic episodes, and the sense of depth, of allegory, of meanings hidden in textured layers — all of this was as nothing, unnoticed in the academic essay and the discussion that followed. This interaction between the text and my decoding and internalizing of it found no answering empathy, support, echo or connection in that group. What had happened to the text after it had become part of my consciousness remained a private, secret, unshared and therefore unvalidated, unexpressed, even unformed experience, for it is in the expressing that ideas get formed and organized. Perhaps similar educational experiences partially explain the popularity of today's book clubs that flourish all over North America.

My tutorial never hinted at being a book club. There was a set of rules that the tutor knew but I did not and they were not written down anywhere. I was not a gentleman, so I did not know that gentlemen assumed certain "truths" about reading. These assumptions included knowing that Literature was art, that it was to be read as art history and that reading great books was like getting fitted out in the right clothes. Also, the prescribed books were "Great" because professors said they were, and that was good enough for the likes of us. No further explanation was necessary. Now, this disconnection between my reading and the tutor's rules was of course a mystery to me, and I may say only one of many mysteries that class life offered this young "outsider" in England. I had naively believed that the University was the place where I would find out things, a place where the pursuit of knowledge would make the institution classless. Before my arrival there I had always been part of a working-, lower-middle class world. Most of my fellow students were from similar backgrounds, but the faculty had removed themselves to a higher sphere, at least in their minds. They were following "gentlemen's" rules. I did not know what was going on.

What I did know was that a novel was a chunk of writing set between two covers, a word sandwich. I knew it had a design, a plot, characters and so on. What I did not know was how it got from out there into here, into my brain and viscera. How could all those scratches on paper turn into a simulated life? How could I be emotionally aroused and intellectually enlightened by this arrangement of words? What happened to all that power when I closed the book and put it back on the shelf? Where did the characters go? I therefore asked a question that a gentleman would not ask: what exactly is a novel? The wrath of the professor came down on me like the pouring of a cement foundation. "If you don't know that, you should not be in university!" he thundered. I was shocked, humiliated and silenced, and I remember his response like it was yesterday.

To a dedicated, skilled and inquiring reader, the sorts of questions that were on my mind in the mid-50s would not be surprising or naive. The power of the pleasurable and exciting reading experience naturally makes one wonder what is happening — *what is the process by which this form of language alters me?* It is now possible to recognize that the questions I asked then led to this book. I have spent the last forty years scratching this itch, or to be more honest, validating my questions, perhaps fighting the hard-headedness and -heartedness of my tutor. It is also only fair to say that my questions were ahead of their time and that nobody knew the answers. So it was then I encountered the Frock Coat syndrome of Literature. Gentlemen understood; they "knew" even when they didn't; they read "classic" works of "English" and knew how to speak of them. I have figured out what my tutor meant when he said I should not be in a university: I did not deserve the privilege of a university education *if I did not know the rules governing the way we conducted our approach to Literature.*

No one in English studies could possibly have known the answers I sought would require some knowledge of neuroscience, since neuroscience did not exist as such until the middle 60s, long after I graduated. It is interesting, though, that my teacher was not even interested in finding out more about my questions or about me. He might at least have said, "What do you mean?"

I have always loved reading and books. I drank down Literature like a thirsty navvy at a free bar in July. But I had always been at play, wallowing in the delicious mind worlds of language and story. I had never been a "critic." My first real attachment to Literature as an independent reader came from English comic books, the kind full of stories, rather than strip cartoons. These comic books are immediately recognizable to people of my generation — *Wizard*, *Hotspur*, *Champion* and the like. What these comics did was take famous stories, either short stories or novels, and rewrite or adapt them in a serial form that we read, from week to week, almost like an adventure soap opera. I lived a lot of my preadolescent years waiting for the arrival of these comic books so I could get on with the real life they contained. I was lucky. I was not discouraged from this, because I had parents who loved to read though they had no high-school education at all. And my teachers had not been through the rigours of professional "English" training, so they could accept enthusiasm for Literature as a good thing in itself.

A Waste of Time

The Belles Lettres or Frock Coat fashion prevailed as long as class was based on birth, and red-brick proprietors were aping their grey-stone betters who had the jobs the red brickers couldn't get. The University of Birmingham could never, while I was there, overcome its shadow life of inferiority cast by that university "down the road," Oxford. As long as the value system was rooted in the favours bestowed by birth and money, attitudes to reading as "gentlemanly" education prevailed even though social reality had already transformed the class system.

Gradually, however, the world described so perfectly in England by John Galsworthy (*The Man of Property*) and Charles Dickens (*Dombey & Son*), and in America by W.D. Howells (*The Rise of Silas Lapham*) came to dominate. Wealth replaced birth as the mark of distinction and importance. So today we live in the full culmination, on the very crest of a wave set in motion by the Age of Industry. Greed, once a Deadly Sin, is not only permissible now, it is our main motivator, the driving force, our most widely approved virtue. We know who the "best" people in the world are by adding the numbers and finding out who has the most billions. These people now run the world so they must be the most important, the brightest and the best. Copying them and lusting for more money has replaced aping the manners and tastes of birth aristocrats. Where has this left *reading attitudes?*

The birth aristocrats were supposed to be innately superior, that is, they were born "better" than the rest of us. Even their blood was a different colour. They used to say of themselves that "blood tells." They were also supposed to inherit wealth and land, so they were known as the leisured class. Being "leisured" meant they could adorn their lives and amuse themselves with decorative and morally uplifting pursuits — like fox hunting. Actually the first among these pursuits was Belles Lettres. The pursuers of wealth, however, have no such leisure, they *do not want it* and *do not know what to do with it.* Their highest goal is the pursuit and acquisition of money and the power it brings. The pursuit is the goal in itself. Resting from it is a *waste of time.* "Time is money," and every minute wasted on reading Literature is time lost from acquiring wealth.

The acquisition of other less tangible benefits is of no consequence to these people. Since time is a commodity, information must be reduced to tiny coded fragments; politics, speech, conversation and personal relations are conducted in bits, bites and slogans. Reading takes real time, and reading well takes thought and feeling. People on the track to fortune can't afford to pause for thought, and do not want to be sidetracked by feelings. Feelings may get in the way of the *bottom line,* so whatever evokes feeling must be avoided. Fiction is regarded as fantasy, the role of imagination in human thinking not understood.

The rise of the novel in eighteenth-century England produced a literature thought to be trivial, suitable only for wealthy, idle women to amuse themselves with, but certainly not approved by men of taste, men of affairs or men of business.[5] These attitudes have become powerfully reinforced in our own day. Book clubs are mostly frequented by women. Women have always outnumbered men in English studies since I began teaching. Men cannot see the practical use or application of Literature. Oddly enough, the poor and the uneducated often share this view with the money pursuers, that reading Literature is a waste of time. As one acquaintance of mine puts it, "I've got no time for other people's fantasies." Such a view indicates the absence of an inner life, an absence of his own fantasies, desires, thoughts, dreams. This is a practical man who believes in tangible things. Trucks and tools, boats and motors, to him, the material world is "reality." So of course he has no knowledge or interest in Literature as a powerful educator, a powerful healer, and the most useful means of all for creating identity. This man, a decent fellow, just is himself and has no knowledge that he can change himself or anything else. This man has little or no formal education and has not seen the value and pleasure of reading Literature which is not "fact." He, like other low-income people, has worked hard all his life to survive and put bread on the table for his family.

So the poor don't have time for reading; the uneducated see no point in reading and don't really know how to do it; and the pursuers of wealth think reading Literature is a frivolous waste of time. So we can see that the marginalized join in their own disempowerment by subscribing to the values of those who exploit them. The rich and powerful impoverish their personal lives if they won't read, and they impose values and models of behaviour that impoverish others, both psychologically and economically.

In this model the haves teach the have-nots that wealth is the only goal worth pursuing; that the poor don't have it because they don't work hard enough or are not clever enough ("tough bananas, buddy"); and if you choose other goals like learning, love or conservation you will just be proving how stupid you really are and therefore don't deserve power, so stop whining. How often have we heard that gasp of admiration: "He is worth millions and he never went to school." Once upon a time people went to school for other reasons than to get rich.

Criticizing Literature to Death

We have seen then in this thumbnail history of the social fate of modern Literature, how first clerical, then aristocratic, and finally the middle commercial class used and abused Literature to reflect their values. Now we turn to recent academic uses of Literature, an interesting history in itself. Ever since the vernacular (English) replaced Greek and Latin in texts and documents as the material for study in universities, there has been a compulsion, a psychosocial need to justify the activity of reading by a professionalized analysis and judgment of Literature. Once the Frock Coat syndrome was no longer obvious, once middle-class and working-class children went "up" to study "English," there was a need for professors to justify their positions. Professors must represent professions. If they are unsure what it means to practice a "profession of English," they will have to "professionalize" the activity by putting an imaginary horse before the real cart that is already there. They will have to assume the priestly function of interpreting text, preaching sermons, or mystifying language. But the cost of these justifying devices has been the flight of countless students from reading. The problem, I think, is age old — how to do what you love to do most (i.e. read), and get paid from the public purse for doing it?

Thus it was that "schools" of criticism, originating in universities, evolved and succeeded each other and have inexorably trickled down their fads and fashions until they have flooded the school system in successive tidal waves. The first of these was the *moral imperative*. This grew out of the religious origins of literary study and was a natural successor to the decorative or belles lettres reason for reading. After all, if you have to justify any activity, the first argument you typically look for is that it will make you a morally better person, it will "do good" and "improve" behaviour.

This view held sway for a long time and was only washed aside by the Holocaust, which proved beyond a shadow of a doubt that lots of well-read people were racists, fascists and murderers, and of course still are. Though the moral imperative is a spent force, I don't think it is without merit, in the same way that hydrogen is not without merit, in spite of the bomb. But the moral imperative was not grounded in anything and it gained supremacy by an assertion, unaware, unexamined and unselfconscious. I think it will make a comeback in a different form once we have confessed what we are doing in our classrooms, examined and explained the case for teaching Literature and grounded this justification in human neurology and psychology, so that morality, decent and caring behaviour, will not be merely a nice, abstract idea. Literature is not the cause of morality, it is a tool for the moral person.

The moral imperative gave way to the *historical imperative.* This advocated that Literature was cumulative, each age depending on and reacting against a preceding age, so that in order to understand the "growth" or "development" of the whole you have to start at the beginning and work to the present. When I was an undergraduate we started with Anglo-Saxon, Beowulf etc., went on to Middle English and got about as far as Hardy and Houseman. There was considerable resistance to the study of contemporary literature (T.S. Eliot, Evelyn Waugh and others, who were, in truth, hardly contemporary), because students required "historical perspective," and if writers were too recent you could not tell if they "would last." In my undergraduate experience the Frock Coat was implicit, which was why I did not see it and got fouled up by it, but the chronological study of Literature was explicit. We studied Literature by century.

The historical imperative has been considerably weakened by other arrangements of Literature that are not chronological — genre studies in poetry, fiction and essay for instance, or gender-based literature, or even more splintered sub-genre specialties like science fiction or the fantasy novel. Yet the historical organization of Literature has been very persistent and underneath all the stencils and varnish you can still see original Edwardian paintwork shining through curricular redecoration.

In the continuing quest for validation, justification and exclusivity, professors had tried being priests. They had tried being historians. Now they would try being *anatomists of the text.* So they invented New Criticism, the prevailing orthodoxy of my graduate school years and the dogma to which most of my colleagues clung, first with a belief in its "truth," then with bulldog tenacity to its safe familiarity, and finally with the desperation borne of not knowing what else to do. The New Critical dogma asserted that texts could be analyzed and dissected outside of history, outside of historical and even social contexts, and only by trained specialists who would tell you what particular texts "mean." According to New Criticism, each text could stand and speak on its own, indeed only on its own, and only the anatomist-critic could dissect this speech, with all its metaphor, symbols and devices, lay them all out for the uninitiated to wonder at, and put it back together again in a seamless package that would show no scars. These critics would demystify Literature and bring objectivity to criticism. This was as near as criticism would come in attempting to be a science and so lay claim to revealing an impersonal "truth," somehow inhering, lying inside the very essence of the text itself, like the kernel inside the nut.

The critic/professor in this equation would lay claim to a kind of unassailable objectivity in winkling out the true meaning of the text's workings, and in so doing she would prove once and for all that vernacular studies could take a proud and justifiable place among the "disciplines." The fact that so many "objective" experts disagreed on what a text might mean seemed not to bother anyone very much.

As with all fashions, the anatomist approach foundered because it was a false representation of the symbiosis between text and reader. It took little or no account of the writer, the period, or the place, but much worse, it left out the non-academic reader entirely. The only discernible reader was, of course, the professor teaching or writing the critique. She steadfastly refused any form of self-examination or responsibility for her own biography, or even gender, class or ideology, as determinant of, or even relevant to, the interpretation she espoused. Partial truths are also falsehoods. I have played all these games. I know them well. The next game however, I refused to play.

Passive-Aggressive Criticism: The Post Modern

Now, historically, the search for professionalism and expertise took a crucial fork in the road. It seems to me that at this point there were two tracks available. One headed along a dangerous route ending at a barrier that stood in front of a misty swamp; posted on this barrier was a sign that read: "Danger! Road Ends, Quicksand Begins!" Criticism that suddenly became "theory" took this path, ignored the sign and careened right onto the shifting ground of linguistic philosophy, postmodernism.[6] The other path might have led to communication theory, rooted in biology, behaviour and functionalism. *The road not taken* at that crucial fork might have led to the reader as constructivist, and to the cognitive science of reading, to a new psychosocial understanding of Literature, to psychology and neuroscience in the service of language. The main convoy of criticism took the philosophic path. This was not the philosophy of abstract ideas (and so back to morality), but the philosophy of "postmodern" discourse. My theory about this extreme form of obscurantism is that its appeal to professors of English lay precisely in its extremity. It was an extreme form of despair, for if new criticism could not in fact excavate the one "truth" of Literary texts, then there must be no truth in them at all. Literature could not be trusted. We thus face the astounding professional mutiny of those teaching and advocating Literature: the baby sitter murdering the baby. To change metaphors, this must be the most glaring case of foot shooting in academic history.

You will remember that professors had before sought validation by inventing techniques and jargon by which to claim an expertise. In truth, professors had never recovered from the loss of Greek and Latin that had once distinguished and privileged them. With almost audible whoops of joy they rushed to embrace the mangled language of the postmodern. In their enthusiasm for creating a tangled brier patch of language only they could penetrate, they shared the motive of the Brer Rabbits in sociology. Sociologists were already notorious for obscurantist language, which they cultivated in order to make language a secret code and in the process "professionalize" and "scientize" their disciplines. But English profs had another motive they disguised even from themselves. Postmodern and deconstructionist theory was a revolution against the establishment of Literature and the domination of the classics. To perform this revolution explicitly, openly, would be to eliminate the jobs and salaries derived from departments of English. Moreover, to question the worship of the classic texts, to challenge the popular respect for the giants of Literature who founded the canon and were the very raison d'être of English studies, was unthinkable. The postmoderns could not be merely destructive so, like any hostile coward, they were passive-aggressive. They turned on language itself as a means of undermining the authority of the text. They revelled in the pure realms of intellect and deconstructed Literature to prove its distance from life and meaning. They sought to estrange the uninitiated reader from the pleasures and relevance of the text. All the time, in the fine frenzy of this text-shredding dance macabre, they seem not to have noticed that their intellectual orgy was taking place on the *Titanic.* Critics would stand and applaud their colleagues for speeches they had rightly failed to comprehend, even as the icy water was creeping over their ankles. Professors got promoted for being impossible to understand. Relevance became a bad word. Those like me, who thought Literature and life were inseparable, began donning our life jackets.

Postmodernism had the effect of disconnecting text from the daily life of the reader. It turned professional study of Literature into an anti-textual, scholastic pursuit of completely privatized discourse, all in a language abstracted and peculiar enough that it successfully excluded ordinary readers, those like you and me, those who loved to read precisely because we see that what we read relates to the lives we lead when not reading. Readers like us were shut out of academic discourse, where theory, and very bad theory at that, replaced *Literature* itself, which was, of course, the raison d'être for the English professoriate in the first place. This can be compared to earth scientists who have no interest in soil samples. The result was as if sports commentators enjoyed their own monologues so much they came to ignore the game itself, and were then surprised to discover that no one was listening any more and the hockey league had died. So powerful a force did this anti-textual influence exert, that some novelists began writing stories to fit critical theory. This is like designing a camel to fit the description of it by someone who has never seen one.

Naturally, such novels are afflicted with the same lack of readership and inaccessibility as the critical theory that shaped them. These novels of course delighted the critics, but excluded "normal" readers, thus striking one more blow against the usefulness of Literature and the benefits of reading fiction and poetry. Postmodernist critics/teachers have successfully specialized themselves at the expense of the enterprise itself. In doing so they have lost both the audience and the text and now seem set to lose the entire profession. We are reminded of Lady Bracknell's bon mot to Ernest: "To lose one parent is a tragedy. To lose two is sheer carelessness." As one student I knew put it when announcing her departure from English to Philosophy: "If I'm going to study philosophy anyway, I might as well go where there are experts to teach it."

Now there is a general falling-off of enrollments for Literature courses. Unless the profession and the professors can quickly retrace their way back to the fork in the road, departments of Literature, and the professors who staff them seem doomed to extinction.

Road Not Taken

In 1987 Mark Spilka, a professor of English and editor of the journal *The Novel,* hosted a conference at Brown University called "Why the Novel Matters." My invited contribution was "The Function of Fiction, A Biological Model."[7] At the conference itself I was among extremely distinguished, and as I was to find out, hostile company. Most of the critics were "postmoderns" and they hated my thesis: the novel matters because it speaks to the lives of readers, helps them organize and cope with life experience and is an evolved form of psychosocial tool making, a neural adjunct to human adaptive learning.

The novelists who were present liked this idea and were willing to consider it. For the rest, well, it caused a storm of controversy which was reported as puzzling by the local press. How, one journalist asked, could anyone object to such an obvious, benign, pro-literacy point of view? Those of us on the inside, the cognoscenti, knew very well what was happening. What I had written threatened an enormous, costly, painstakingly constructed yet fragile craft. This boat could not sink, argued my colleagues, the English professor designers of the leaky vessel we were all sailing on. They had invested heavily in the success of their enterprise. The postmodernists had bought non-refundable tickets for their passage, and they took refuge in denial of the ill wind sent from interdisciplinary and therefore unmapped regions. I threatened to blow their ship off course, doomed though it was. (The priceless cargo, let's remind ourselves, was Literature, and in my view it had been hijacked.) Too many reputations hung in the balance.[8]

Literature is a resource of such individual and social importance to our mental and communal well-being that it must neither be dismissed as peripheral or merely decorative, or captured and preserved for members of the club only.

Dysfunctional Literacy

The effect of all this territorial fighting over Literature is evidence of its power as information. The struggle resembles the history of Empire itself and the latest forays into the professional elitism of criticism is one more form of colonial tyranny. At this point we seem to have accepted functional literacy as good enough for the masses, but is it functional? Certainly to have no reading skill at all is to be truly handicapped and socially disempowered.

Can you believe someone wanting to kill himself because he could not read? I worked with a patient who felt like this and came close to suicide. To understand this you must imagine the following: Think of yourself as a pre-literacy, pre-print human in a world where no one can read or write, where there is no writing. One morning you are transported to a world where people communicate and receive information in written signs, silently. Everyone is reading, showing each other documents and letters, reading papers and books on the subway. You can't imagine what they are doing or learning or experiencing. People talk about news they have read, or advertisements or research results they have mysteriously acquired from some peculiar marks on paper, but they mean nothing to you. You are excluded. You are given forms to fill out but you can't read them. You can't read manuals for the equipment you buy. You can't join committees because you can't read agendas or minutes. You can't read the letters people send you. You can't even read prescriptions on the medicines you are obliged to take, or food labels, or airport regulations, or maps. You feel utterly alone, stupid, but you can't get back to your own planet. Despair now becomes more understandable, does it not?

The ability to decipher the ordinary print of our everyday lives — food labels, maps, prescriptions and the like — is called functional literacy. The very modest aim of adult literacy programs is to teach people a functional literacy so they can cope in our world on a daily basis. This is of course important. It is also, in my view, very dangerous to keep such limited goals as the motivators for teaching people to read. This desire to have everybody functionally literate easily becomes an attitude, a concession to basic reading and a limitation on teaching and learning. People know why they need to read warning labels on poisons, but they do not know why they need to read *Genesis*, *Hamlet* or *Jane Eyre*. We have to be careful then not to feel too good about having a population that is only basically literate. Of course this would be better than what we have now, with rates of illiteracy being variously estimated at between twenty and forty percent. But it would be more likely that everyone was literate if we had national goals of full literacy and were prepared to do whatever it takes to attain them. If reading were our national and cultural priority, we would not have measurable illiteracy. Such a political or cultural policy is not imaginable however, nor justifiable, if our goal is merely to teach people to read poison labels.

It is important to remember that children learn language and reading very easily because their brains are forming as they acquire these human attributes. American neuroscientist Antonio Damasio tells us that "experience shapes the designs of circuits."[9] Reading is not picked up by mimicry and repetition as is speech, which is learned just by listening from birth and at home. We don't have to go to school to learn to speak. Instead we must be taught by those who know the code. Since reading is a key to all academic learning, to science, social science, history, philosophy etc. we surround it heavily with both praise and dismay. To read is to be "clever." To be unable to read is to be "stupid." I had a patient who was severely emotionally abused as a child, a classic family scapegoat familiar to all family therapists. He came to believe himself stupid. In fact he is very intelligent, but he decided he could not learn to read and so would not even try, which was a clear attempt to avoid further humiliation. In fact, this path of least resistance lead to decades of torment, shame, secrecy and self doubt. His decision to learn to read following therapy produced a challenge infinitely more formidable than the one he faced as a child. To lose thirty years of reading practice is no joke.

Once a child is well launched into reading there is a good chance, in the right circumstances, that she can achieve complex reading, and acquire the formative works of the language and culture, which is the real goal of reading. All reading is important because it is always a potential exercise in the training for more language and more complex reading. My patient was taught as a child that he was a bad (stupid) person. Therefore, he could not learn to read. And because he could not read as an adult he still thought he was a bad (stupid) person. It is true that if he had learned to read, he could have avoided major social handicaps and huge self-esteem problems that plagued him for many years. He knew this. What he couldn't know, and what I couldn't begin to tell him at the time, was that in the very act of reading Literature lay the antidote to his personal history. He, like most other people, thought reading was a means to mastering some very modest and practical tasks. He would have to discover for himself that the fully functional identity that he needed to construct could best be achieved by reading complex and appropriate fiction and poetry.[10]

Human beings are supposed to use Literature to assist them in the creation of a personal identity and to help them manage this identity's encounter with the world. That is what evolution is telling us. The human brain, the Literature it writes and the Literature it reads are a systemic feedback loop, continuously self-generating and cumulatively growing. If we deprive children of Literature we mentally and emotionally handicap them. If we reduce the goal of reading to functional literacy, it becomes dysfunctional literacy and plays directly into the hands of whatever forces are at work in the world to limit and control freedom and imagination. The attitude of those who wish to help form whole, confident, aware individuals who care for themselves, and who in turn will form educated, conscious, aware and caring societies, must be one of respect for the most ambitious forms of reading. To belittle, ignore or despise the culture's Literature is to despise ourselves. If we have contempt for the three or four million years of evolution that led to Lao Tzu and Shakespeare, yes, then by all means let's forget the difficult books and just amuse ourselves to death, to borrow Postman's phase. No person is neutral in this struggle. You either read and advocate reading or you join in the great suicide of planetary despair.

I have tried to explain in this chapter how we have gradually lost access to full universal literacy; how various forces have conspired, albeit unwittingly, to keep Literature from the great majority of people. No sooner did the promise of universal education for literacy seem poised to become available than electronic media shifted our focus of attention. Full literacy, in spite of widespread reading, remained the preserve of the few. This has never altered.

We can no longer afford the luxury of this ignorance. We would be loath to accept that only a few privileged people have access to antibiotics. We must cultivate the same respectful attitude to Literature. We are being subjected to the *disintegration of information.* Literature is experienced in the brain as a virtual model of coherence, wholeness. In no regard is this more obvious or more necessary than in the power of Literature to unite emotion and thought. We are now at risk of emotional impoverishment and cognitive numbing. We need Literature to help us be fully human and we must never again allow it to be hijacked.

Notes to Chapter 10
Get An Attitude: The Fight of Your Reading Life

1. See my article, "Recombinant Language: The Biological Imperative," *English Studies in Canada*, Vol. VII (1981) 4: 473-482. Twenty years later I have to believe that if you drop water on a stone long enough it will eventually make an impression.
2. Postman, 1985, p. 27.
3. Miller, 2000. Miller's work emphasizes the important role of language in human sexual courtship. But in at least two famous cases of successful verbal courtship, Othello's wooing of Desdemona, and Sheherazade's overcoming the murderous insecurity of King Shahriyar, it is not merely that they talk a lot that ensures success. The two heroes tell marvellous *stories* with their language skills. It is the story that seduces. I am interested in what the story does for the brain of the listener. We marry the storyteller in order to hear more stories, or we marry the listener because we need to tell stories. Writers and readers certainly need each other and become bonded.
4. "Affective Reading and its Life Applications" (with Fred Gloade), *The Arts in Psychotherapy* Vol. 15 (1988): 235-244.
5. Ian Watt, *The Rise of the Novel.*
6. This pattern of hysterical defense by "establishments," facing a challenge to their "truths" at the threshold of a paradigm or model shift, is well recognized and understood. (see Kuhn, 1970). A current example is the nutritionists' reaction to the scientific evidence that high carbohydrate consumption, not fat, is damaging the health of millions of people. See Eades, 2000.
7. I am of course in favour of a theory of Literature. Indeed this entire book tries to embark on such a theory, and I address the issue head on in Appendix 3. What is peculiar about Postmodernist theory and its deconstructive methods was that it did not see itself as a theory, but a subject, or study, an alternative to Literature itself. As it grew it removed itself further and further from Literature and the grounding of Literature in human experience. "Theory" meant one theory only and gradually elbowed Literature aside in Academic departments of English. I cannot speak for

what happened in other language departments. The kind of theory I envisage as necessary would be called something like Systemic Criticism or Holistic Theory of Literature.

8. My essay can be found in the proceedings of the conference: *Why the Novel Matters, 1990.*

9. Damasio, 1994, p. 112.

10. In contrast to what we have to learn in Literature, we are often socially aware that with someone we know extremely well on many levels, an intuitive glance or gesture can convey a wealth of meaning that is instantly understood. All of the associations and record of meanings embedded in that glance are synthesized and coalesced into a node of meaning that somehow "illuminates," informs our central nervous system for and in a moment. But it would be a mistake to think that this nonverbal instant of "knowing," of consciousness, is somehow free of learning and time. In fact it is founded upon a superstructure of verbal information and exchange previously established over years. We are just unaware of the learning because we paid no attention to it. And if we did not pay enough attention we are in for some nasty shocks as we misinterpret the intimate glance. Everything has to do with consciousness, with awareness of our own "knowing." I point this out because the current Holy Grail of neuroscience is consciousness. The search for its source in human brains or wherever is the hottest race around. This is not really surprising because the more we learn about brain processes the more frustrating and teasing, the more challenging loom the questions of how and where lies the sense of awareness that takes human minds beyond the robotic collection of data that our brains accumulate. How do we know that we know? How do we know how we feel?

CHAPTER ELEVEN

Thinking Makes It So

Our story begins with degradation; our telling ends with glory.

— The Illustrated Haggadah

I say again that daily to discourse about virtue, and of those other things about which you hear me examining myself and others, is the greatest good of man, and that the unexamined life is not worth living....

— Socrates

At any rate, I am taking it for granted that the novel is worth salvaging and that in order to salvage it you have got to persuade intelligent people to take it seriously.

— George Orwell

TIME IS SEQUENCE; SPACE IS DIMENSION. The human brain evolved to reconcile these two ways of perceiving. This was necessary because the world exists for living organisms in these two simultaneous ways. Everything we encounter has both a directional, positioned situation, and is also ordered into a temporal sequence as event. Dimension becomes sequence when it is recorded as event; sequence becomes spatial when it has to be recalled. This may seem a bit complicated at first but it will become very simple to understand in a minute, once we introduce human brains into the equation. To cope with a world experienced as dimensional and sequential, we evolved two major parts to our brains, each with some degree of bias. The left half, or hemisphere, normally specializes in sequence. The right half normally specializes in dimension. They are bound together by a large bundle of neural pathways that facilitate the exchange of information between them about the relation of sequence and dimension. When I broke my glass in the bedroom (Chapter 4), it was an event in a particular space. It registered in my brain as a sequence of events and as spatial coordinates. My brain made it into story. It did this for the purposes of mental organization. The human brain is continually looping back and forth between time and space by means of story. So it is that event turns into space and space turns into sequence. This is how human brains think.

Literature is the human diary or log of experience of time and space. It is a collection of stories and commentaries that constitutes a species memory. Thought of in this way it becomes immediately obvious that without Literature we are limited to our own memory and have to reinvent the wheel, so to speak, with every new encounter. Other people's stories assist us by a form of immunization and rehearsal for events that have not yet happened to us, or help us organize, that is think about, events in memory, not yet understood; and stories that we read help us practice the story-making skill we need to make events into organized units for future use. Grammars and systems of alphabetic signs and words themselves may vary around the globe, from tribe to tribe, but "storying" does not. Story is the fundamental biological characteristic of human thinking.

We have reached a point in our evolution where we not only need to read Literature and to understand why we need to do so, but we must now develop self-awareness, consciousness of our own part in the creation of our reality. We need to become aware of our own brains and what makes us healthy. We must stop acting and thinking as though we have no control over our thinking, or over the products, the technology that our brains have produced. The entire purpose of the time-space brain loop is adaptation, but we have been singularly inept at adapting to what our own species produces. We seem to regard our products as though they were products of nature itself, but for managing them we lack the long evolved adaptive skills that were honed on working in the natural world. This seems to have engendered a kind of despair. We know how to plant gardens, and cut wood and feed chickens. In those survival tasks we feel in control. But in the world of electronics, of voice mail and banking, of the mass media I have described in previous chapters, we have surrendered our minds and turned passive. We settle for being controlled instead of taking charge and thinking about the effects of what we accept upon our health and welfare. We are giving up consciousness at the very time we need to be more conscious than ever. Like Frankenstein, we have created monsters just because we can, and because we do so without self-knowledge or awareness, they can destroy us.

The other day I heard a radio interview with a man who researches artificial intelligence. He is working on a computer program to write fairy tales and news stories. He says it will be ready in five years. Good luck! When he has a machine that can feel the rain in its face, interact with family and friends and cope with all the complications of joy and disappointment, marriage and desire, and feel hunger and thirst and ambition, then he will have created a human machine, and we won't be able to tell the difference. I have helped to create several such machines and they are called children. Oh, the mad arrogance of modern man! What worries me about this is not that computers will write stories. It is that we will come to accept and be satisfied with the stories they will write. What a state we will have reached when we don't even know any more what went into the making of a story! Meanwhile the survival of the species is threatened by the species.

Stories, Schemes and Scripts

There is no getting away from story. It is part of being human, like our skin and bones. Human brains have an evolved preference for narrative forms of information gathering and storage. When Gregory Bateson tells us that our propensity for story construction is shared by "redwood forests and sea anemones," he is telling us about his own brain and how it thinks. Human brains see stories everywhere, even in starfish and stones. Schema is a term from psychology, and refers to the most basic structure of story elements. We begin at birth with a brain ready to complete itself by taking in, I will call it sucking in, information. We also begin to gather that information from the centre of what will become a set of widening circles, like the pebble thrown into the pond, our world. We start the sucking with our bodies, with physical contact, and end with reading Literature. We are given a sucking reflex so that we can survive.[1] The newborn will suck anything, but she quickly learns that some sucking is rewarded and some isn't. So survival reflex turns quickly into survival information. Sucking is rapidly followed by grasping and things grasped go straight to the mouth, where satisfaction has been learned. So we begin to see how schema are simple patterns of learned information, where one thing follows another in a rewarding sequence, rewarding to our survival, that is. This learning is aided and abetted by pleasure.

Scripts is a term used widely in psychotherapy, and refers to roles or parts learned in social interactions. "Please" and "thank you" learned at mealtimes are simple scripts. They never leave us and they get much more complicated. In a collusive marriage, for instance, the husband might have the script of being the harassed, misunderstood, stressed-out alcoholic, and his wife might have the script of being the saviour martyr who begs him to change and nags him to quit drinking. If neither changes, they can stick to these matching scripts like glue. Here again, we see behaviour based on a simple form of learned story that defines and serves as identity. True, these stories are not very functional and not very adaptive, but they are made by the same structuring process in the brain as we employ in more complex story skills. Stories expressed in language share some of the sequential features of schemes and scripts but are much more inclusive and elaborated, and eventually signify self-awareness and conscious construction. The relations between all three forms of story reveal how basic this pattern is to human development.

I have tried everywhere in this book to suggest that the story-making predisposition of human brains is mainly occupied in the service of creating identity and, in a circular way, identity is necessary to the effective continuance of story making. Identity is dedicated to enhancing human adaptability, and therefore human survival, by enlarging and integrating the brain's repertoire of stories. The "I" becomes the central theme of a large story to which are fitted thousands of little stories. This process is interpreted by humans as "making sense of experience." From the earliest infant behaviour we can see this process setting to work. It is not much of a stretch, to my mind at least, to see the development from sucking, then putting things in the mouth, to putting information in the brain, by whatever means work. The goal is to *acquire* the world outside and store it inside us, in our brains, where we have to organize it. We go to school to learn stories, stories about the world, from maps and globes, models of the planet; about history from stories constructed out of records and bits of the past; stories about cells and matter, about social structures and how machines work. We start by learning how to read and write so that we can improve our story-making skills. We read Literature to expand our own physically limited experience by decoding the experience of others and to learn the models of story making from the best storytellers available to us. The teachers and preachers we like best and remember best are those who tell the best stories.

The Pleasure Principle

The brain quest for more stories is encouraged and rewarded by sensations of pleasure: the satisfaction of "making sense," understanding and mastering the relationships of data, which is the essential characteristic of stories. This experience of "I've got it," which elsewhere I call the Eureka or "Aha" effect, is accompanied by the sense of well-being that comes with the feeling of self efficacy, the realization of control over information that we need in order to cope, adapt, and move on to planning and action, in the service of our health and happiness. The feeling of pleasure is managed by a hormonal process in the central nervous system by means of the release of endorphins, groups of naturally occurring hormones that are released from the pituitary gland and hypothalamus in the brain and spinal chord, to various receptors in the nervous system. They are natural opiates or narcotics that reward various efforts or experiences which the survival drive of humans wishes to encourage. Those who experience the "high" following vigorous exercise will readily recognize the presence of endorphins in their brains and bodies. These people report a reduction of pain and a sense of euphoria. Those same feelings of pleasure are reported in natural vaginal childbirth, and in orgasms. Increased levels of such hormones can be found in the mother's blood up to two weeks following childbirth, and they are shown to increase lactation. They can also be produced following successful public speaking, drama performances, winning prizes, and from singing, music and art, both producing it and enjoying it. Laughter, smiling, drumming, and birdsong can all produce endorphin secretion in humans.

The Roman poet Horace said that "Poets would either delight or enlighten the reader." Sir Philip Sidney echoed this in his famous *Defense*, saying that the purpose of poetry is to "instruct and delight." I think we can change this for our time to "construct and delight." Wordsworth said that the key motivating result of reading Literature is "pleasure." What do these poets mean? What can account for the testimony to some almost indefinable satisfaction from decoding words, the tears and laughter of millions of readers over centuries of reading poems, plays and novels? I believe that the same physiological reward systems are operating for those who put down a novel or poem, saying to themselves, "Wonderful, that expresses it exactly. How satisfying! How grateful I am to the writer!" All these rewards are addictive, and our survival drive is designed to "believe" that we should return again and again to these activities. For each activity that is rewarded by endorphin release there are special benefits: for exercise, physical health; for orgasm, reproduction; for laughter, peace and harmony; and for Literature, the increase in identity formation.

The most useful pleasures leave a residue of meaning and knowledge that can be applied to the mind's organization of the world perceived. This was the point of Greek tragedy and comedy, of epic poetry and of religious story. These "feel good" sensations are experienced in the mind as control, enlightenment, resolution, understanding, security, calm, invulnerability, strength, energy, liberation, completion, expectation of benign outcomes, courage, heightened sensory response, stimulation and wholeness. When Wordsworth speaks of "pleasure," and Sidney speaks of "delight," they are, I believe, referring to the sense of satisfaction that endorphins produce upon reading Literature.

The Continuity Principle

Humans experience themselves taking action in the world as "I's." The irreducible defining feature of this identity is its continuity. The "I" must be able to rely on adding constantly to a known story. There must be stability and faith in both the process of building and the structure as it is assembled. We see all too often the very painful consequences of the loss of this story, either in pieces or entirely, as in advanced cases of senility, brain damage by accident or injury, or by psychological trauma, resulting for instance in severe dissociative disorder. We need to be able to construct an autobiography, the story of ourselves and we do this in normal circumstances continuously, retaining an amazing thread, a lifeline that guides us through the mazes, like the string that helped Perseus return from his adventure with the dreaded Minotaur. We have something to learn about this seemingly unconscious skill from studying the writings of those who actually write their life into a story for others to read.

The most obvious example of an "I" constructing itself is in the composition of autobiography, not the entire life story itself, which is of course impossible to tell, but the artfully designed version the "I" chooses to write about its life story.[2] In the case of all biography, of another or of oneself, it is a mistake to think in terms of the "truth." All such writing is a version of story designed by the brain writing it.[3] This is why there are many biographies of someone like Charles Dickens, none of them the same, and I am sure we are not done yet.

People write memoirs because they want to tell the version of themselves that *they want others to remember*. Most people don't put pen to paper to produce autobiographies for others to read. In fact, most people are not even aware that they are constructing their own story day by day, moment to moment. We have not yet embraced the life-story-making paradigm as the normal way of thinking about ourselves. I think it would be a very good thing for us to become much more conscious and active in forming our life stories. It is easy to see how you can write about something out there, something you can see to describe, but it is much more difficult to see how the same person can write about the person doing the writing. You can get a bit dizzy thinking about this, for it takes us close to the heart of the problem of understanding consciousness itself, something we are a very long way from doing, in spite of the optimism of various neuroscientists (or what one such scientist, John Taylor, calls with admirable understatement, the "hard problem").

There is a Zen saying: "The finger cannot point at itself." Yet the "I" appears to be able to write about the "I." This becomes more readily understandable, without being neurally explained, if one accepts that the "I" is not really writing about itself, but about a construct of itself *from which it can be detached.* The astronaut leaves the space ship and, attached only by a cord, repairs or changes the ship from the outside. In our case, the case of self-construction or story repair, *the astronaut/writer is outside and still inside at the same time.* The writing done by the "I" demonstrates the continuous process of self-construction. In a minute I will explain how the "I" achieves this feedback loop between an actual and a virtual self, by which it can continuously revise itself; moving out into the world like a space probe, sending back messages about the Earth that sent it forth, so that the Earth can revise itself in the light of these messages.

What are the tools by which biography is assembled? There are three parts: memory, the content; language, the tool for handling memory; story, the operating principle, or instruction manual, the program for the tool of language. All of these devices are innate in brain development. However, the content of memory, on which all other adaptive behaviours depend, is learned from experience in the world, as the brain is forming and ever afterwards as long as life continues. The writer calls upon stored memory to construct a life story out of language. Damage to memory interferes with this construction to a greater or lesser degree. For humans, memory is accessed primarily, though not exclusively, through the language store, and by pictures usually accompanied by language labels. We take photos as an aid to memory, but without a language guide to what the photos mean they don't mean much. (We do not have much interest in photos of other people's friends and relatives if we don't know them.) There are also aids to memory in the form of object cues. On my bookshelf is a small bust of Shakespeare, reminding me of my pilgrimage from London to Stratford-upon-Avon, when I was seventeen and proudly purchased this trophy of my trip to the shrine of Shakespeare's birthplace. On my desk is a mug embossed with the characters from the song "Widdecombe Fair," which my parents brought back to me from a holiday they took in Cornwall, or thereabouts. A stream of associated memories is triggered by such cues, with all kinds of accompanying emotions lurking nearby. So we see why people cling to the bits and pieces accumulated during a lifetime. These are the props to their very identity.

Among all the aids to memory, none is more stimulating than reading Literature, though of course such reading does much more than that. Literature requires all three components of biography formation to be active. It activates the reader's storied experience even as it provides new experience and editing of the past. Reading a novel requires memory of the text's meaning itself, in the form of story sequence of events and characters and so provides story-making training for the brain. We have to remember what we have read to make sense of what is to come next. Such training is essential for skilled identity formation, which in turn is necessary to active functioning and adaptive behaviour and reliable continuity in life management.

John Taylor believes: "The "I" consists of the set of autobiographic memories developed up to now. Such memories serve the important function of being a repository of response patterns." He says that "the level of conscious experience is determined by the level of past memories ...."

Taylor even goes much further: "We can define the level of consciousness as the average daily number of past memories... evoked in a person over a day."[4] But after the age of fifty, brain cells begin to die and consciousness decreases, so that laying down new memories diminishes. If neonates acquire memory and therefore consciousness from experience as their brains form, then the reverse is true for those entering the aging phase after fifty. And not only is the brain losing cells, but new life experiences are more rare, energy for learning and travel decrease and using the past replaces learning the present. This suggests that reading Literature can provide huge benefits in the aging process, by activating and evoking past memories and providing surrogate experience to shore up consciousness as first-hand experience diminishes. This amazing resource will however only be available to those who have laid down a lifetime habit of reading, a powerful inducement to teach Literature and its benefits at an early age.

Sending out Feelers

I have described how we use Literature as a source for constructing our identities and forming our stories as we live through life experience. Sometimes our stories get broken and then Literature becomes a repair kit. We need to know when that happens, what has gone wrong, and it is precisely at that time that we need to know more than ever that we are story creatures. To make the repairs we have to temporarily leave the story. But you cannot leave or change a story that you are still locked inside. What this means is that you can't change it if you don't know you are in it, and you don't know you are in it if you can't get outside it. Let me explain this by analogy. How can you see what the damage is to the hull of a boat if you remain inside it? I'm afraid you will have to get it ashore or get wet, but either way you will have to get outside the boat. The boat is your story; if that story is dysfunctional, that is, if it makes the believer unhappy, inactive, non-adaptive, then it is necessary to leave or change it. It is harder to get outside a story than out of a boat. How do you get outside of a story in order to see what needs changing and how it can be changed? How do I alter my brain and change how it perceives the world it inhabits and my perceived relation to that world? Since the "I" does all the looking, from the inside out as it were, like the fish in the fishbowl, it must be a pretty neat trick to remove itself from the bowl long enough to see its own perspective from an alternative perspective. This is the goal of all successful therapy. The "I" has constructed a story, yet it must somehow leave that story in order to change it and before it can resume the story composition. How can the "I" be in two places at the same time? The fate of those who cannot do this is explained, perhaps, by the story of Narcissus, who drowned in the attempt to embrace his own image in a pool. Whether it is self-love or self-dislike that traps the perceiver into one inescapable story, the outlook for such a person is not promising.

What sort of magic enables me to leave myself, look at my story, and then return to myself in a wiser state? One clue can be obtained from mirrors. No one expects to shop for clothes today without the help of mirrors. If you want a new look, you try on different outfits and see yourself in mirrors until you see what you like, and then you adopt it as part of your wardrobe. The same is true of versions of yourself. The one you try on and like is the one that becomes part of the continuing "I." To fix something you must see how it works. You would not, could not, replace a tire on your car if you did not know that tires can be removed and repaired. To repair a broken story, you must first see what prevents it working. The "I" exists in a story and has some freedom in constructing this story. But it is not sufficient for me to assert this. The "I" that will change itself must believe in this ability to construct itself before it can take action.

My Apple computer generates something it calls "Aliases." An alias is an icon which can be created for use as a substitute for the real file or document, while never losing its connection or reference to the original. An alias is a very useful device. I want to borrow the term Alias to describe the brain's magic in making it possible to be in two places at the same time. But the alias my brain produces is much more than an icon or sign of the original; it is a virtual "I" which the brain creates out of memory, language and emotion to be an imagined self. My alias can feel, think and quit. The writer of a novel imagines a character out of parts of her own experience and gives it language form. The reader creates a matching, imagined character made up of his experience and language that gives temporary life and energy, to the character in the novel. This reader-animated character now lives in the brain of the reader. Writers say the characters they create take on lives of their own and leave the writer, like children leave home, and do what they want. Not so for the alias created by the reader, who always returns to and merges with the original, like the blobs in my lava lamp that bubble up and then settle down again into the mass at the bottom. The life of the alias is a temporary construct, assembled to live in the Literature only as long as it is being read.

I believe that children who invent imaginary friends are doing something very similar. They create an alias who appears to be a separate imaginary character, but in fact is a surrogate self who can explore and test the world leaving his creator to be safe while sending back crucial information about encounters with a confusing and often scary world. The more intelligent and imaginative the child, the more complicated the world he lives in and the more necessary becomes an assistant explorer, surrogate self or alias.

The reader of fiction always walks the fence line between pretend and reality, but the fence never disappears. Readers create aliases, versions of the "I," that are temporary and occasional, representatives or emissaries for the primary identity. This hologram-like alter ego acts as an explorer, a projected self that goes forth to various adventures or situations, while the actual "I" remains safely at home base receiving reports. The information sent back by the alias is screened, filtered, rejected or integrated into the life experience of the alias creator, depending upon judgments that the alias creator makes at lightning speed. Every alias is new and is created for the occasion and fades back into the original when not needed. The original "I," the alias creator itself, has of course changed since the last alias was created. While the very life energy and skills of the alias depend on the

"I," the alias, like the hologram on the holodeck of the *Enterprise,* is the one who goes over the rapids, endures the torture, wanders through the desert, while the "I" sits in the Lazyboy knowing that there is cold beer in the fridge and his son is doing homework in the den.

I don't pretend to know what are the actual neural processes that achieve this very high level of symbolic consciousness. If these have been explained somewhere, I have not read about it. If they have not, I have no doubt that one day we will understand the molecular neurochemistry that makes aliases possible. For now I need a model to explain the feel and the outcomes of the experience that takes place in reading Literature. This model must account for what actually happens to readers as a result of the reading process in their lives. We have to imagine a process by which readers can plug the reading module, the novel, into their brains, take on a virtual or simulated life from the module, stay grounded in the security of their own identity at the same time, and unplug the module having extracted from it whatever the "I" felt appropriate for its own enhancement.

Sir Philip Sidney said in his most quoted line that poetry holds a "mirror up to nature." In book therapy, bibliotherapy, it is said that Literature holds a mirror up to the reader's self. This is not to the surface self, the beauty that deceived and doomed Narcissus, but to the inner self, the self made up of thoughts, beliefs and feelings. I think it would be much clearer and more accurate to say that Literature holds a mirror up to the reader's story, and compels the reader's gaze to linger on, ponder and feel his way through masses of stored, long forgotten, even suppressed elements of the story record, along with all the associated emotion that accompanied the laying down of memory. Literature can liberate us from what can become a story prison, or a sinking ship. It does, however, take a certain amount of courage to step outside to do the repairs.

The Clash of Stories

I have argued in this book that for contemporary humans, Literature is an indispensable aid in the formation of identity. Pre-agricultural societies operated in small groups, in cultures that shared the same connections to nature and shared the same threats and rewards. Hunter-gatherer peoples communicated within the limitations of information obtainable by physical proximity. Today, we must form individual identities out of an unlimited amount of information, without religious certainty, without cultural boundaries, and without dominant stories and myths that determine belief systems. Any attempt to sustain such myths and beliefs takes place today in the context of resistance to alternative beliefs that are highly challenging. (A simple example is the conflict between creationists and evolutionists.) All conflicts between opposing stories that are seen as mutually exclusive, for instance the "pro-life" versus "pro-choice" battle, represent attempts to sustain a world-explaining story in the face of an alternative and apparently contradictory story, and the determined attachment to one of these stories makes dialogue with the other story impossible. Only opposition to and even destruction of the alternative story can sustain the confidence of the believer. Denial of alternative stories must follow a necessarily "blind" belief in one story only, for in such cases we have committed our identities to the one story to which we have pledged our allegiance.

The most widespread source of "I" information, in a non-reading population, would appear to be derived from institutionalized religions, or various clubs or cults, Catholic, Jehovah's Witness, Anglican, Jewish, Islam, Rotarian, Mason, Lion etc. To varying degrees, being born into or joining these organizations involves surrendering personal identity and submerging the "I" into the collective identity, which by its dogmas supplies answers and instructions that obviate the need for continuous thought and decision making. New information that would require of the individual continuous adaptation and adjustment, is largely eliminated by the authoritarian templates of behaviour and belief, which are applied to all such information on behalf of the members. There is always a trade-off in such arrangements and it is never easy to agree to adopt a "blind" belief or allegiance without a struggle that continues as life goes on. Those who don't fit or want to flout the group rules are exiled, shunned or excommunicated. The story of the dominant institution is unalterable.

The history of humankind is of course a record of the bloodbath resulting from the conflict of such stories and the goals and interests of the combatants. Obviously, if a religion claims for itself priority for its story over all the separate stories of individuals in the group, then it must also claim its superiority over the stories of whole other groups and their beliefs, this in order to justify the demands it places on its own adherents. If another group has a better story, why should people stay in this one? Religious conversion is the choosing of a story one prefers. When the citizens of Athens turned down St. Paul (as he would later become), they were saying that his story seemed less convincing to them than their own. This "superiority" of story, be it religious, historical, national, racial or gender based, has been used to justify any kind of atrocity, and every kind of rape and pillage, including the theft of entire continents.[5] When only one story can be "true," others can be compelled to succumb.[6]

What is called "tolerance" in political or religious language is really the agreement that stories other than our own are also valid and permissible alongside our own. To attack and kill people who live inside stories that differ from our own stories is not only and not principally an attack on flesh and blood, on buildings, churches, mosques, synagogues, but an attack on stories. The bodies, buildings, and flags of other people are merely the signs and symbols of the stories that gave birth to them. Today, the grand narratives or world stories that are in conflict are intensely confused and interfused. Since boundaries have been erased by communication and transport systems on a global scale, and since nation states are at the mercy of multinational and transnational corporations, the clash of stories can be more destructive than formerly. The capitalist story, having defeated the communist story, seeks to achieve a hegemony of homogeny, spreading the gospel of consumerism, materialism, and the pursuit of profit globally. In the service of this economic goal the language of ideology and religion are used, so that a "manifest destiny," religious fundamentalism, and xenophobia have slipped over into economic imperatives. Similarly, a religious fundamentalism that embraces repression of women, censorship of speech and writing, and endorsement of Jihads and Fatwas, must oppose by all means those stories that threaten its "one true story." So we witness acts of mass killing, such as the suicide assaults on people and buildings in New York City on September 11, 2001.

The cycles of violence perpetrated by various ideologies, religious wars, political wars, territorial wars, can never be broken until human beings abandon their attachment to "rightness," the inevitability, the supremacy of one story only. Whether we speak of domestic violence, spousal abuse, or wars between states or movements, the same rule applies: the conflict is the result of one story trying to dominate and displace another. Neither fathers, gods or God, nor governments or institutions, be they commercial, political or religious, that is, no one authority in our world, however powerful in the scale of rhetoric, will change the biological truth that in a human world we are all actors in human stories. We invent them. We learn them. We invoke them. And we use them to impose our will on others by any means available and at any cost. We will never live in peace until we come to terms with our own story-making brains, from the processes of which there is no escape. We are afflicted with the most massive case of denial of our own nature as story species. In a world now capable of destructive acts on a scale never before imagined, this denial, this global psychosis, must be broken.

If Literature can illuminate our world and help us to shape it, enhancing our autonomy and identity, we would expect totalitarian movements to be hostile to it. Literature is always a casualty of totalitarianism. There is no historic exception to the rule that those who wish to impose their own "rightness" on others must, if they can, ban writings that are believed to express ideas contrary to the interests of the dominant belief system. Censorship is the single most powerful piece of evidence that Literature liberates individuals and threatens tyranny, of every kind.

The Age of Despair

In 1854, Henry David Thoreau offered his view in *Walden* that, "The mass of men lead lives of quiet desperation." In 1850, Wordsworth reissued his Preface, containing many indispensable explanations of the power of Literature, and made this comment: "For a multitude of causes, unknown to former times, are now acting with a combined force to blunt the discriminating powers of the mind, and unfitting it for all voluntary exertion...and, reflecting upon the magnitude of the general evil, I should be oppressed...had I not a deep impression of certain inherent and indestructible qualities of the human mind...." Were both of these writers commenting on the degradation brought about by the industrial revolution, on the "increasing accumulation of men in cities, where the uniformity of their occupations produces a craving for extraordinary incident...."? Or were they observing some fundamental change in human perception and behaviour, an ushering in of an era much longer lasting than they could possibly have foreseen? Have things improved, and can we see signs of a return to enlightenment, or are we doomed to a playing out of the destructive forces of greed and immediacy? What has happened to our minds?

Any analysis of trends around the world, be they economic, social, sexual, environmental, or health or education based, must convince us that we are on a course of global destruction. We are losing the power to think and feel. We take no time for thought or discourse. We find it harder to amuse ourselves without exogenous (taken in from outside as opposed to endogenous, naturally produced in our bodies by activity), narcotics and stimulants. We are obsessed with sex, and sex crimes are among the most common.[7] Health problems proliferate. We build prisons not schools. We elect uneducated men to govern us. We are deceived by image and slogan. We have begun to think of ourselves as helpless and perhaps hopeless. Can this world epidemic of mindlessness be reversed? A thoughtful answer to this question would require another book, and it would have to be an economic/political book, that begins with an investigation of values. I have, in discussing the role of Literature, returned to some of the tenets of the great defenders of Literature, who saw in reading the cultivation of thought and feeling, of individual autonomy and brain development, that can be encouraged with the pleasures of making sense of whole constructs by which to manage perceptions of the world that we must inhabit. Such reading is necessarily political. To read Literature is to arm ourselves against the mind-numbing messages, commercial in motivation, that would turn us into autistic consuming robots, with minds trained only to respond to those messages. But the trends are against us.

I have argued in this book that Literature is a natural, useful and safe biological product of human brains, a specially constructed form of accessible information. Literature is *functional.* We need it. We might well ask at this point what else is there that we could substitute for what Literature does? How else do people enhance their functionality, learn to form identity, and live happy, healthy, and satisfying lives in a literate culture? I cannot see any activity still available to us in the world we have created that will help us become aware enough to make the necessary changes, if it is not Literature. We cannot return to the environment and lifestyle of the hunter-gatherer, whose lives were so filled with survival-oriented action that endorphins were in plentiful supply and life was too busy and people too unsettled to invent print. Literature has to be seen as an evolved antidote to the other dangers to our minds and lives that post-agricultural society has created.

We are certainly surrounded by evidence, on a global scale, of how *dysfunction* is working. The use of addictive narcotics, carbohydrates, alcohol, caffeine and prescription drugs has reached epidemic proportions. People want to escape, not experience their world and its multiplying problems. They want ever more immediate and easily acquired stimulation and sedation. This suggests a vast plague of tedium and ennui, and the need for flight from an intolerable reality. And this reality consists of a planet in the throes of serious disease, with air and water being poisoned at an unsustainable rate, resources being ruthlessly squandered in a kind of frenzied greed, and crime statistics so staggering that it is hard to imagine that we tolerate it all so uncaringly. In North America at least, there is no sign of political will to examine the root causes of crime and act upon them. Everything has been reduced to the dualism of good and evil, those with money and power being the good, of course. From petty theft to mega fraud by giant corporations, from stupidity and corruption in our political leaders and business icons, we seem to have accepted with a zombie-like tolerance a global reality that we feel helpless to change, unable to understand and are indifferent to morally.

Our coping choices seem to be mindless, numbing, trivial entertainment, more theme parks, more Disney sentiment, more spectator sports, the more violent the better. Transitory amusement breeds a need for ever more fleeting sensation. None of these do very much for the construction of identities, of the deep and lasting satisfactions of feeling that the world makes sense to our brains, and that we have a role in controlling it by means of constructed stories or schema, stories that produce equilibrium and adaptive strategies. On the contrary, we seem to be determined to splinter and bewilder our perceptions, living moment by moment in a nauseating kaleidoscope of incomprehensible fragments of unrelatable data.

We are mostly living by habit, reaction, rules, or learned programs, in all cases passively. What did Thoreau mean by "quiet desperation"? I interpret this as meaning a failure to live metaphorically, failure to live in an actively constructed story, failure to see the complexity of meanings in metaphoric language. We are desperate by being reduced to iconical and indexical language, by losing the symbolic power that is our human evolutionary birthright.[8] It is, for instance, amazing to me to encounter those who would literalize and historicize the Bible, stripping its wonderful linguistic richness of all metaphor and symbol. Such metaphoric layering is after all the very characteristic of complex writing. Those who aver that God wrote the Bible should also, surely, admit that God would be at least as skilled at creating symbol and metaphor as was Shakespeare!

Everything is being simplified, even the Mind of God, to the level that literalist believers can manage to understand. The politics of the extreme Right that has hijacked our world is founded on simplification, on literalization. We are being encouraged to live as though everything is a "fact," rather than a constructed perception over which we have some control. And we are being brainwashed into believing that what is happening is "inevitable," when in fact it is being perpetrated by a philosophy of greed, using strategies of persuasion far more powerful than anything ever seen before. We will have to change our thinking. What I am trying to describe in this book is not merely a theory but a way of living, for the making of story is a human behaviour that we must come to understand more and more if we are not to doom ourselves to extinction.

Are people who don't read Literature at some disadvantage in managing their lives? My experience with patients who do not read fiction is that personal change and adaptation are much more difficult for them. I have said that the thinking of non-readers is literal. They live in one story only, and more problematically they do not recognize that it is a story. They have a harder time leaving the fishbowl. This means they do not think of their lives as active or in their control. They have not learned their own brainpower. They seem to live inside one, unalterable "truth," on one dimension, and it is a truth that seems to come from some unexplained non-human place. Their lives just happened; they feel trapped in some unexamined destiny or doom; they are less aware than readers and more passive and helpless. They have more difficulty looking around and examining the events and feelings of memory in conjunction with the time and space of their current lives. Non-readers have more difficulty with relativity and context. They have a shortage of variable perspectives and cannot leave themselves to look at themselves. Non-readers have great difficulty examining and reflecting upon their origins and their own thinking and behaviours. They lack, I believe, the practice and training of examining their own feelings in response to characters in fiction, the skill of judging, weighing, playing out what they read as they read, a training that becomes customary to readers of Literature. Non-readers are impoverished in the alias-making skill.

So the practice of reading and talking about Literature is crucial life training for young people. As the schools become training programs to serve the short-term needs of corporate managers, Literature in education will go the way of music and art and physical education. Literature will be brushed aside as an expensive frill, under the present ideological regime. Those who share my convictions must ensure that their children read Literature to learn how to form successful, thoughtful, autonomous, functional identities.

Recycling Literature

If Literature is a biological imperative,[9] it may be viewed as an extension of mind, and a presence of mind; it is sent out, read, received, turned into mind content, and so affects the life of the mind possessing it and the behaviours that mind dictates. Literature is like a benign virus that we catch from each other and which helps our autoimmune systems. I have recently been asking myself another question. Can the Literature we already possess be recycled and reused by means of new life experience reactivating and reapplying stories from memory? Can Literature be resurrected from the archives of memory when needed and retrofitted by new and unaccustomed events? And can this retrofitted reading then be used to assist the mind's coping needs for the new circumstances? Is Literature like some little, modest Swiss Army knife, that grows organically from two small blades to a huge collection of useful tools, as the needs of life encounters demand more tools to do the jobs? To apply this metaphor to remembered Literature would be to find newly applicable meanings in it. It would mean not discarding old meanings, but adding to them. And only new experiences would prompt the need to make this happen. The readings are stored resources for life management. Can they be brought up to date in the mind, or are they locked into place with the meaning and application they represented at the time of reading? Do our stored readings grow and get revised with us?

The world I grew up in required me to seek a different set of possibilities from the life I was living, an alternative from bombing, from fear, from illness, from limitation and powerlessness. Through Biggles, and the heroes in Rider Haggard, Zane Grey, the courage and self-reliance of Joshua Slocum and the wild world of Grey Owl, I learned not only about different worlds I could imagine and inhabit. I played mental roles; I became bigger, smarter, braver than myself and I used these experiences of mind to construct my identity. Through every stage of development I have learned from reading what others could teach me about love, deception, disappointment, sex, greed, hope, endurance and survival, about what is moral and what is cruel, about being kind and being frightened. And as I learned about all these qualities of mind and emotion, about being human, I saw abstract concepts like love and fear turned into words and actions that I could concretely construct and understand, make part of my map making of the world I inhabited. Metaphors explained abstractions, abstract concepts gave order and meaning to word models. I was also learning the language itself that made this miracle possible. I learned that language was magic and that mere data, frequencies, light waves, sensations could be transformed by language into meaning, into a whole life. From where else, and how else, could I have learned all these things, some at school, most from the books in the library.

Last year a very strange set of events that I alluded to earlier, got me caught up in social action and I learned something completely new to me about my reading life. I live in a small town in a somewhat remote region of Northern Ontario, along with about thirty-five thousand people in the whole district. We are situated on the border with our neighbouring province of Quebec. My town and a few others sit on the shores of a jewel of a lake, a very large body of water that forms the headwaters of the Ottawa River which flows to Canada's capital. Toronto is Canada's largest city and needs to dispose of a million tons of household garbage each year, having failed to take steps to divert or reprocess seventy-five percent of this. About an hour's drive north of my home there sits a series of abandoned iron ore open-pit mine holes, man-made lakes in the rock, and into these, which have become beautiful lakes, Toronto planned to deposit urban waste for a minimum of twenty years. An historic battle covering a period of eleven years developed between local residents and the corporate and political powers to the south, who relentlessly pursued this scheme. I found myself among the group of organizers opposing it and urging the local population to protest and action.

During this very difficult, and sometimes frightening time, I discovered that I was sustained by my recall of Literature that I had read and knew well, but which now took on new and profound meaning for me as I applied it to the situation I was living through. The conflict seemed to me to be between a small group of relatively powerless people, dependent on their own skills and resources, but who had a right to defend their homes, jobs and water supply against a powerful group of elites who had unlimited funding and control of the political structure, and who cared about nothing but profit. The scheme to create one of the largest dump sites in North America, in an unspoiled watershed, and so threaten everything in its impact zone and ecosystem, seemed to me so wrong and so threatening to my own habitat that I came to view the struggle in universal terms. It was not just this group of known and named business people and politicians that we opposed. They represented some larger principle of indifferent destruction to everything I cared about.

Within this framework, many stories I had read suddenly and surprisingly loomed into focus for me from my memory. I thought of Flem Snopes, in Faulkner's *Hamlet*, and of Ratliffe's dream. Flem is the quintessential banker, entrepreneur, capitalist, ruthless in pursuit of money, exploiting the poorest people, somehow free of feeling or compassion, which turns him into a partially human monster. His principle and self-appointed opponent, Ratliffe, has a dream in which Flem goes to Hell and demands his soul, which embarrasses Satan who confesses that this soul was so small he mislaid or lost it. Because we were dealing with individuals who, in the pursuit of tens of millions of dollars in profits, managed to free themselves of compassion, responsibility, connection to the Earth or to their neighbours' fears, I came to a new, a "real" understanding of Flem and what he means. Before, Flem had been an idea, an abstraction, that I understood only intellectually.[10] Now the novel, the allegory, ceased to be an allegory for me and took on flesh. In turn, the story helped me to frame, understand and recognize the forces we opposed. There was power in this new "sight" because it helped me not to be confused by the indifference to reason and compassion and the single-minded pursuit of profit that drove the uncaring behaviour of those forcing this scheme. It also freed me from hate of individuals, who could and would be replaced if we could not withstand the wrong-headed plan itself which drove them blindly on. I was and am grateful to a writer who could show me that our conflict was not unique and not unforeseen.

I also recalled stories I grew up on in my cultural background and to my amazement these stories suddenly became living explanations of life, strangely emerging in my memory out of the mists of history and myth and taking detailed, concrete human form. We were David, fighting the odds against the giant Philistine bully, Goliath. We were the children of Israel fleeing the wicked Pharaoh in our quest for freedom. As the enemy spent huge dollar amounts on radio and newspaper propaganda to further its interests, I thought of *1984* and what Orwell meant by "Newspeak" and "Doublethink." This novel, too, became "real." I thought of Tolkien and the lowly rural Hobbit fighting the dark powers. I came to new respect for J.K. Rowling, who said in a recent interview that readers can expect her Harry Potter books to get darker as the series progressed because the world is getting darker. I found myself longing for a Dumbledore to save us, until I realized that the magic had to emerge from our own brains, our honesty and our convictions and hard work, and most of all from our language. And I was profoundly moved by my recent reading of the great Chinese Classic, *Journey to the West*, which records the adventures of the Tang priest in search of the true scriptures and the eighty-one ordeals he must undergo, as he meets evil after evil, monster after monster, trying to hinder his journey. That was an endorphin feast, without weight gain.

Without all this Literature my courage and my understanding might have failed. I don't really know how to describe this process. I had always said the right things about Literature in my classes. I had persistently conveyed my enthusiasms to my students. But for some reason I had never fully crossed the boundary between Literature and life so completely as I did during those difficult days. My discovery that my reading was a living part of my character, my identity, struck me with the force of revelation. My stored reading had somehow become part of who I am and rose up as a source of meaning and strength when I needed it. I was usefully interpreting the world through Literature, as though in some extraordinary clinical experiment. The line between fiction and life dissolved. I had discovered personally what it meant to say that great writing is timeless. The stories gave shape, order, meaning, and manageability to the struggle. My remembered stories took on a new and more trenchant life than they ever had when I read them. They connected me to past and future, to other human beings. Surprisingly, they connected me to other people, mostly older people, when I used references to them, and the language and characters from them, in public speeches. My audience understood me through these stories. They reawakened my links to the past and to my traditions. They helped me see why I was in the struggle, why I cared, how I had formed my identity, my values, my beliefs, my professional commitment, what I really care about.

So now I know that what we read and enjoy and admire is stored in us for our use and reuse. We cannot always know and see how our reading will serve us in our lives and in all the unpredictable eventualities that we will encounter. In hardship, in grief, in joy and sadness, our management of our experience will be informed and modulated by the reading that mattered to us and helped form who we are. If we have the reading to call upon, of course. The stories that mattered to us become part of our brains, and it is our brains that make us human and arrange for our adaptation and survival. We desperately need our Literature. There are more riches in the pages of books than in all the treasuries of the world. We have no time to lose in coming to this realization.

Readers know that the life-transforming magic of the novel's words are a mystery. They know that what they have read has somehow entered into their consciousness in a transforming way. Sometimes they hope that by seeing the author in person, or asking the author questions, they will solve the mystery of how this happened. This is why authors are always being interviewed. But this hope of solution to the mystery is no more likely, at this point anyway, than a bird being able to explain how it flies. Even if the bird could speak, it would have to know that it flies in context. Flight requires air, heat, wind, current, diet, muscle, vision, smell, training and practice, modelling, and rest. Writers, even if they were neuroscientists, could not know, as things stand, how they compose narrative out of the materials of their experience. Nor do we know precisely how an audience of readers determines and selects what to make uniquely their own. Nor do we know how readers or writers can or can't separate what they have composed in their minds from their own unique life experience. We just know that some profound exchange of coded information is shared in reading and that writers and readers become bonded in ways that are inextricable; and that communities are formed from these connections. We know that life and Literature are part of one biological process. To separate them is to distort reality and impoverish ourselves.

I have tried to indicate in this book that there are forces at work in the world that seem to be moving our energies toward destroying the planet and reducing the majority of the world's people to slave wage earners and helpless participants in their own disempowerment. The principle weapon in the hands of the privileged few is mind control, through media control. Those who control wealth and governments can easily control education or its elimination. *They can control our minds.*

Only our minds will make us free. Our minds require information and the benefits deriving from reading Literature. We need a public education system, adequately funded through taxation, and dedicated to teaching full literacy above all things. We need a public library system dedicated to reading and not sidetracked by the promise of survival through technology and machinery. We need media that fully represent all viewpoints and is dedicated to providing essential political and science information to everyone, not in bits and bites but in detailed analysis. Literature is a biological aid to keeping the human organism alive and well.

We have been asleep far too long. I think we need to turn our attention to things that matter. Like our survival; not as slaves or zombies, but as fully human, fully conscious, creative, compassionate and connected, whole Human Beings.

Notes for Chapter 11
Thinking Makes It So

1. I am borrowing the "sucking" schema example here from John Taylor (1999), who follows Jean Piaget in his thinking. I interpret the significance of this reflex quite differently however, and I disagree with his proposition that sucking in the newborn becomes "generalized" to sucking on other objects. Sucking the nipple does not generalize to sucking other things. Sucking in general precedes the preferences for what to suck.
2. Perhaps the most intelligent commentary on the complexity of story, reality and autobiography can be found in the play by Luigi Pirandello, *Six Characters in Search of an Author*. I believe the paradox he posits can be resolved by the inclusion of the audience, who provide by means of their own stories the link between art and life, real emotion, pain and pleasure, which cannot be adequately represented by the author. The author supplies cues only, which the audience uses to flesh out the drama from their own experience. A process described originally by Aristotle.
3. For a more elaborate discussion of the constructivist character of biography, see Gold, 1988.
4. Taylor, pp. 331, 332.
5. See Wright, 1992.
6. This seems to be true of Christianity which has been frantic to convert others and is responsible for the Inquisition and concepts like Heretic, Infidel, and Savage, who all had to be converted and/or killed. This may be colouring my view of history. Some stories like Buddhism and Judaism have been noticeably uninterested in large scale conversions of others, even as they maintain the supremacy of their stories. It depends on what instruction is in the story itself as to its own evangelical stance.
7. Our media and advertising is saturated with the temptations of sex. Sex has become an addiction like other quick fixes to not feeling good. We are offered a variety of exorphins, chemical remedies for what ails us, and similarly we are offered sex. The use of sex as an exploitive universal promise of reward for consumerism has an unexamined but vastly destructive impact on our society. Huxley clearly foresaw this coming in his prophetic novel, *Brave New World*, where Soma is the drug of choice, available in unlimited supply and approved by the authorities as a way of keeping everyone stoned with pleasure, and so compliant.
8. As described by Deacon, 1997.
9. See Gold, 1981.
10. See Gold, 1966.

Part Five

Appendixes

Appendix I

Life Losses and Literature

Feedback is a loop in which experience of stimuli in the present environment is registered by the brain, and recognized as either conforming to what we already know or as new information that in some way modifies our record of past experience. This past experience has been organized into our life story, from which we form our "I." But we don't just live in the past, always looking backwards. We also live in the future. We plan, we predict, we anticipate and we do all this on the basis of past experience, the organization of this experience and the "I" that is formed from these. This process is called "feed forward." This "I" becomes more and more active and controlling in seeking experiences that increase the pleasure and security that it wishes for itself. It also becomes more selective and discriminating about what it accepts or rejects from the smorgasbord of life. The use of the past to plan and execute behaviour in the future may be regarded as a sign of mental health, when such planning is not "over determined" or dominated by the past in spite of the patient's desire to be free of it. When we speak of older people being set in their ways we are referring to their extended experience of themselves, their well-established record of tastes and expectations and their diminished willingness to take risks that might threaten the security of their knowledge of themselves in relation to their environment.

The simplest example of feed forward is the decision that having read one book by Dick Francis or Reginald Hill I want to read another. It is as though, having hiked various paths in varied terrains, some through difficult or ugly surroundings, others through beautiful and yielding settings, we choose to seek out those routes that have given us most pleasure, to choose lifelines that have pleased us best. Habit is based much more on choices firmly laid down than we normally think. We are not completely free, of course, to live exactly as we wish. The plans and choices that we make are relative to necessity and, as such, are based on adaptation. Some of us are forced to live and work where income is available, not where we would prefer to be, where, for instance, we speak the language spoken around us, or where our family resides. Even in these cases unacknowledged choices may be operating — the desire for enough money to do other things we want to do, the wish to please or care for others, or an unwillingness to learn another language.

It is important to know as much about ourselves as possible in order to extend the freedom to choose. It is also necessary to see how our life stories can be violated by events that change and disrupt our plans and expectations. We have already talked about trauma events, abuse, injury or violence. But we must not overlook ordinary and inevitable life events like divorce, death, job loss, war, disease and other system altering events. We refer to all such events as losses, because they represent the departure of a component of the story that was integral to some stage of the formation of the "I," an "I" that planned its future on the continuing presence of the lost component. The simplest and most common example of this today is divorce.

When people choose to marry they take the "I" lifeline and construct a second theme to their story called "we." For some couples, the joined, parallel "we" narrative becomes dominant and actually merges into a single, wider, more complex composition. For others, the two stories merge rarely or not at all and simply run more or less side by side. For now I want to emphasize that the personal "I" story is to one or another degree radically altered by accommodation to a "we" story that has to be created by joint authorship.

The loss of a marriage partner, through death or divorce, necessitates a return to the creation of an "I" story and for many reasons, a great many or perhaps most people find this extremely difficult and painful. For one thing, it is impossible to return to where the "I" story left off and became "we" because that "I" ended at that point and a different "I" has been created through the agency of "we." People don't want to start over again. Then again, the individual may not have been very fond of the "I" and liked the person they became as part of "we" much better. In fact, the departure of the partner, especially in divorce, may confirm the unsatisfactoriness of the "I" that was brought to the marriage. The marriage, the choice and acceptance of the "I" by another, was an affirming and healing process. The suppressed dislike of the self now surfaces again with greater emphasis and becomes the basis of the feeling of rejection and causes much anger. This anger can become violent and produces the many news stories that confront us daily in our media, where assault and murder of a former spouse or lover, now "estranged," is commonplace.

How can reading help people overcome the pain of various losses and disappointments to the point where they can resume constructing their life-narratives? In *Read For Your Life* I suggested several novels that could help in the healing process of divorce and loss. *Jane's House* by Robert K. Smith, *Ordinary People* and *Second Heaven* by Judith Guest, various stories by Katherine Anne Porter and Doris Lessing, *Fear of Flying* by Erica Jong and *Heartburn* by Nora Ephron, to name but a few. I based this list on clinical work and cases where patients had found such reading helpful. Today, however, I would be much more eclectic and inclusive, for I have learned that relevance to people's own situations is found in all kinds of stories by patients seeking ways to understand what has happened to them. Nor would I confine my reading suggestions to fictions. When a life-narrative is broken, patients may find it very difficult to enter a narrative. This is often explained as a problem with concentration. In fact, it is entirely possible that people do best with fiction when their own life-narrative is proceeding well. It is as though they are grounded in a secure place from which they can venture into other "not I" narratives, safe in the knowledge that at any moment they can return to knowing who they are and what they are doing. When this path is lost it may be necessary to reorganize and redirect the life journey by bringing into mind new information not necessary before the loss. For instance, I have found that reading about grief processes as described by Therese Rando is very helpful to patients feeling lost and confused by the emotions and circumstances of grief.

We must remind ourselves that we are dealing here with brains. As I said before, brains are formed in conjunction with the world in which they learn. Brains have context, both internal — the bodies they inhabit, what they are fed — and external, what information the senses provide them. In the case of grief, trauma or serious injury there is a shutting down process, a withdrawing from stimuli that is experienced as a feeling of numbness. This numbing that blocks stimuli can be viewed in a number of ways. Certainly it is achieved biochemically. What is its purpose? It is tempting to think of this biological response as a form of self-protection. It seems like a form of neural anesthetic, a fear of further harm and pain. I am tempted to understand this withdrawal from the "not-I" world input as a consequence of the inability to integrate new information into a broken-off story. The filing system has broken down. There is nowhere to put new information, no way to understand it in terms of a story that once made sense but is no longer viable. The survivor of deep grief has to some degree herself died. She no longer makes sense of the world, of her own feelings or her role in life arrangements, work, family, love. She may go through the motions of work and food preparation but her heart and mind are not "in it."

We must remind ourselves at this point that serious loss, grief and harm are a new reality to the sufferer, and they are not part of her customary experience. Such experience and surviving it are not part of her narrative history and she has no life-training in finding a narrative place in her brain for these emotionally explosive blows. She feels as though she has been swept onto a strange and incomprehensible planet. The emergency ward physician, or even more the battlefield surgeon, becomes used to blood, death and horror. They form part of his narrative of life, part of his own continuing story and his view of the world and if he gets surprises, they are not from the horror, but from the responses of others to the horror. Normally, a patient has no such experience and many people are fortunate enough to go through their entire lives without experiencing untimely loss of child, spouse, home or limbs. For our patient, then, we must re-contextualize the loss experience. We must assist her in rejoining the world. We must get the cortical part of her brain active and interested again. We must reintroduce the sense of control over data and sensory input and so, using this control, begin the long process of reconstructing a self-narrative. This self-narrative, as I point out to grieving patients, will never be one of forgetting the lost loved one, or even permanently eliminating pain of the lost past itself. It is best not to expect that and certainly best not to try to look very far ahead. Remember that feed forward depends on a coherent past and intact self-narrative — so that until the "I" is reconstructed the future cannot be constructed.

The survivor who can find appropriate and manageable reading will be helped to begin the process of reassuming control. Information about new and terrible experiences is crucial to this task. Where else can the patient get this information, this understanding of her situation that the book, fiction or non-fiction reflects back to her? Not only is the book the summary of other experiences, personal or clinical "research" into how humans grieve and survive, but this information is entering the reader's brain and being coded there into the reader's own personal storying structure. The reader is making implicit comparisons to her own experience and is able to revisit and revise her own experience, indirectly and therefore less painfully. She is less alone and more detached at the same time. So reading has process side benefits in grief and loss beyond mere content information. It stimulates visual, speech and auditory cortex. It demands attention which distracts from paralyzing emotion and circular thinking. It produces thought about the reading self. It is available when and as needed by the controlling reader. It provides an escape from the prison of self-absorbed emotional pain and withdrawal. The reading begins to reunite the brain of the reader with the world outside that brain.

At first glance, reading would seem to be least relevant to the healing process following grief and loss. After all, the survivor is too sad, too angry, too hurt, too shut down to focus on anything as demanding as reading. The silence, the loss of appetite, the lack of motivation are all signs of such withdrawal that focusing on words and decoding them hardly seems possible. And yet, soon after the first shock of loss wears off, and as soon as reality and acceptance of the loss fact takes hold, the survivor begins to ask a stream of questions. Why me? How could I or others have prevented this? What did I do wrong? Why do I feel so lost or confused? And on and on. Who can answer these questions? What doctor, friend, therapist or family member has the time, the language, the wit, the patience, the knowledge, the strength to explain any part of it, let alone most of it? And who can be trusted? Aren't any of these people "interested" parties with a stake in making the questioner feel better?

Once again, and in this instance very dramatically, we see how reading is a special survival tool of extraordinary power. Some very gifted and very dedicated people order their experience in the service of the tribe. Even when writers claim or confess to be writing for their own survival, if they have the talent, their behaviour is, I believe, species directed, and their personal experience and knowledge is compelled by forces far beyond individual goals to assist the adaptation and health of their kind.

In the case of overcoming the painful disruption of one's own story, reading is an act of personal courage. Therapists must have and use their knowledge of Literature with discretion and they must support and encourage readers struggling with the task of reconstruction, recognizing that this is no small feat. Therapists must be trained to recognize the complexity of the patient's healing process. Any response that is glib or impatient is harmful, insulting and unethical.

Appendix II

The Writer's "I"

I have said that reading Literature is the most important tool in the kit for constructing identity and building the whole story that connects the "I" to the "not-I" across space and time. In the case of healing broken stories, traumatic wounds, painful memories and experiences, it is probable that nothing is more effective than writing as part of therapy. Talking has been the preferred and basic, universal medium of therapy. It will remain basic because it is easier for most people to talk than write. Talking covers a lot of ground fast, and produces immediate back-and-forth looping between patient and therapist. But writing does something that cannot be achieved in any other way.

Constructing ourselves is like building a comfortable, convenient, pleasing, durable, safe house from the materials available to us. Literature is a major source of building materials, the Home Hardware or Beaver Lumber of human culture. But imagine that our house, so lovingly constructed and so very much ours, is so badly damaged or disordered by vandals, thieves, or by hurricane or earthquake that our task is not to build, but to rebuild. First we must overcome denial and despair before we can even rise from the debris or clean up the mess. Then we must sift through, salvage, and inventory what we can. Only then can we know what we have lost, what we must replace, what we don't want anymore, what matters to us now and how we want our new construction to be. This process of reconstruction is how writing functions in the healing process.

It is not possible to write from and about our experience, and see and read what we have written, without seeing it with new eyes. The brain cannot process the reading of material we have written in the same way as it processes the writing of the material in the first place. *Outside-in* is not the same to brains as *Inside-out.*

Pennebaker describes an experiment (op. cit. p. 199) in which comparisons were made of outcomes in groups of trauma patients who engaged in self-expression through dance movement and those who combined such movement with writing. Only the group who wrote showed objective improvement in health and academic performance. I believe that "self-expression," whatever that means, does not provide a sufficient description for what is going on when we write. A satisfactory explanation must account for the employment of language as an organizing principle. The writer uses language to take control of previously unmanaged, emotionally intrusive data, experience that creates the sense of helpless suffering, victimization in the writer. Language can be the tool that produces the controlling activity experienced in story formation by the writer.

Pennebaker calls his book *Opening Up*, but the relief of verbalizing provides not only the comfort of sharing and being heard. Primarily and more importantly writing creates a brain association that was not there before and enables the writer to see, understand and manage data in a new form. When we express in words some secret that burdens us we speak of getting it off our chests. We are describing a sense of relief because the heart and lungs, in a state of fear, when breathing is not relaxed, are in tension, and throw us off balance; the heart rate increases uncomfortably and breath becomes rapid or held. We feel better when we can breathe freely, be relaxed and regain control. In other words, we feel better when we move emotion from the place in the brain where it controls us, and certainly disregulates our heart rate and our breathing, to the place in the brain, our language centre, where we can name it and control it. The act of composing words to achieve this shift is a demonstration of control and is in itself an accomplishment that provides us with the knowledge that we can do this, that this is possible. The self-as-control reinforcement that writing produces spills over to other aspects of our lives and improves our autoimmune systems, makes us more resistant to disease and imbalance. We must also remember that writing is active. It is doing something. Taking action overcomes feelings of weakness and being victimized. Writing also requires putting thoughts in order, organizing them and actualizing oneself. It is being heard, but even more surprisingly, it is being seen.

To understand why writing makes us visible, we must return to the concept of feedback. An inevitable component of writing is that as we write we are forced to read our writing, recognize, interpret, decode and install it, even though we generated it ourselves. Reading what we write completes the looping process that is required to ensure the transmission and conversion of information between parts of the brain. When we look at ourselves silently in the mirror we see a stranger: the face may be familiar but it does not mean anything. I may say "You look tired Joe," or "You need a shave," but I may as well be talking to a friend. When I write about my feelings, my thoughts, my emotions I am both learning and clarifying how I feel — because I am forced to use the top level of consciousness available through the language centres of the neocortex and I am also reading myself back into my brain and identity — forming a neural network. *I am practicing self-knowledge as I create myself.* I am increasing my sense of self-efficacy. At the same time I have crossed some kind of social threshold because while I am now feeling relief, someone else may be forced to deal with what I write. Some people write letters to the editor and feel better, while others cannot imagine being so exposed.

When we read fiction, a description of a character tells us little about him, but when the author tells us about what the character is thinking or feeling we begin to know who he really is. When we write about ourselves we are *both author and reader.* We create ourselves. We learn who we are, who we have created out of our feelings, thoughts and emotions. Obviously, the more language we have, the better we are able to do this.

Consider that each of the following steps in writing is a conscious act of control: we make a decision to find words for our incoherent feelings; we analyze and track down sources and associations lying around these feelings;

we search for and organize our word store for appropriate arrangements, often a taxing and challenging task; we write these words into sentences and read them, thus confirming their objective reality and storing the resulting organized information into our newly arranged life story.

Let me illustrate the effect of this by reference to other human activity. We can all identify the security and satisfaction that comes from making lists we can read, instead of trying to remember everything we have to do or get at the grocery store. With the list tucked into a pocket we don't have to think or worry about all these items again. The same is true of filing systems that work, helping us to know where to find information, to live in order, not chaos. In fact a great deal of human activity is focused on achieving just such organization. As we saw much earlier, no sooner had life become settled, urban and complex than writing was invented in the form of book keeping. The human brain functions as an organizing tool. Most of the electronic tools we have invented — calculators, computers, data processors, automated machinery — are all aids to the brain's need for organizing information. Databases are merely brain extensions. It is hardly surprising, therefore, that health and balance urge the human organism to move from the non-linguistic toxicity of overwhelming emotions like fear and anger, as in trauma, to the organizable and organizing language store. When emotions and their registration into feeling are translated, converted into language that can be read and stored, they retreat into personal history. As with the items on our shopping list, through the medium of language, the chaos and confusion of emotion can be stored, tamed, used as information to be retrieved when needed as a manageable reference tool. Converted to language, negative or unbalancing emotion can be put in its place as a troubled piece of our life history.

The value of writing in therapy lies in *the process itself.* Most writing by patients in the clinical setting is done by people who are not especially gifted writers. That does not matter. As Johnson told Boswell, the remarkable thing about the circus dog walking on its hind legs is not that he does it badly but that he does it at all. Self-therapeutic writing is not of much interest to anyone other than the writer and his therapist. And even the writer quickly looses interest in the written text itself. The effect of such writing is immediate and it produces immediate change, even though the results and import of the change may not be clear until weeks or months later, when the changes have become observable in the writer's behaviours, feelings, thoughts and relationships. The changed writer will therefore look upon the writing, from a later perspective, as done by someone else, by an earlier version of the self, and often with surprise and perhaps dismay at recalling how badly she felt then. It is important, I think, that those doing this writing be assisted in understanding clearly that they will not be judged on their writing skills. They are not composing art. They are not writing for others. The process itself is important and that is all.

I have also found it extremely helpful to writers and readers in therapy to explain patiently and carefully some rudiments of the brain processes I have outlined above. I find it necessary to tell patients that writing about feelings and experiences may free them from carrying in their bodies unacknowledged and unnamed thought and emotion. It will do this by a series of mental steps. Finding the words moves the emotion from one part of the brain to different language and storying parts. Seeing the words written will give them an objective reality, an "otherness" that creates distance from what the words convey. And having them written will create a sense of record, of history, as reference that eases the struggle to remember and retain everything in the head. People have a right to know and a need to know that there is a rationale behind processes that we say are beneficial, yet which may be very difficult for them to accomplish.

The process of writing will of course be much easier for those who are accustomed to writing and/or to reading Literature than for those who are not. This is one more advantage for readers. The reasons for this increased facility in language and story making for those who have been readers of Literature have been discussed throughout this book and to a large extent constitute its contents.

Appendix III

For Teachers of Literature: Reading Brain and Theory Vacuum

The old debate between nature and nurture has outlived its usefulness and is now a distraction, a hindrance to our knowledge of human behaviour. Obviously we are dealing with systems and subsystems of enormous complexity. It is the very interconnectedness of human brains with bodies, of individual humans with the group, of groups with the Earth, and the whole with the efficiency of all its components that must concern us. We won't get very far in any kind of inquiry without a theory, and you may be surprised to learn that as regards the existence of Literature as a human behaviour, no such theory exists.

Formulating a theory that will account for the organic unity of the triad—brain, Literature and reader—will take time and a lot of work by a variety of people. All I can do here is point the way to a theory that will have to explain the production of the Literature: why the human brain should evolve its peculiar compulsion to produce language models of its world in written form and why our brains seem insatiably hungry to absorb such models; why readers want to read; and what is the neural and social outcome of the energy exchange when the writer's language enters the reader's brain.

What is the purpose of this writing and reading behaviour of humans? So far, professors have not been notably successful in explaining the origins and purposes of Literature, the very basic features that you might expect to find in beginning approaches of any discipline to its subject. I have vague memories of countless occasions when my announcement that I taught

English at a university was greeted by carefully veiled looks of puzzlement. Didn't students already know English by the time they got that far? Could they not already read? Were these foreign students? All these unasked questions hovered just below the polite social surface.

University of Columbia English Professor Carolyn M. Heilbrun seems troubled by the same need for self-justification. Perhaps these never-answered questions about what they have been doing nag at retired English professors emeriti, a post-occupational hazard. My guess is that Ms. Heilbrun, in her novel discussed below, is trying to justify a lifetime spent with books, with the joys of reading and the security of being paid for it. If you have the best job in the world you may be forgiven for being a bit tortured about it. Would that all God's children could be English professors. Writing under the name Amanda Cross, in *An Imperfect Spy* (1995), Heilbrun attempts somewhat cautiously to approach the problem. Her hero Kate Fansler is teaching a literature course in a law school. A hostile male law student rudely confronts professor Fansler during a class on *Jane Eyre*. He asks, "What makes you think you know more about literature than we do?" Kate counters with a defensive question, "What makes you think you know more about law than I do?" This is evasive of course; she is not there to learn law, but to teach Literature. But Ted, the student, ignores this irrelevance and replies with a more troubling response. "We've studied law. Anyone can read. As it happens I've read a lot." All teachers of vernacular Literature will have to address this student objection, I think. It could easily be argued that ever since the vernacular replaced the Classics as the foundation humanist education, academics have been wrestling with the problem.[1]

Kate goes on to expose the student's lack of knowledge of *Jane Eyre*, but this put-down is a further evasion. She, or rather her creator, misses a golden opportunity to struggle with the real question being posed: "What knowledge do you have that makes your opinions superior to my opinions?" This is a good question, and troubles me long after I have finished reading this little power struggle. For the life of me I can't remember ever having had to pass an exam on this question to qualify as a teacher. The reason we have difficulty dealing with this question is that we have no *theory* upon which to base a reasonable answer, one that will help us define a clear role for ourselves. Most historical answers have been based on non-literary assumptions that always smack of philosophy or are otherwise swathed in mystification.

I do not doubt that teachers of Literature have a very important role to play in the world of learning, but how can they articulate it? How can they get beyond transmitting persuasion, opinion and prejudice? With texts full of notes and glosses, biographies and sources, could we not leave the job to librarians? A greater repertoire of Literature and critiques is a matter of age, is it not? What exactly do teachers know that students don't? Perhaps their main function is to provide the opportunity, the excuse if you like, for students to read Literature. I would not dismiss such a social purpose as unworthy, merely as a bit expedient. We might do much worse than have teachers simply to explain at the start, "I am here to provide you with the opportunity to read wonderful words and you will see the benefits for yourselves." Can they get funding to do this? What happens instead is that considerable energy is spent seeking justification for doing what teachers want to do for a living. That is part of it. The other part is the need to justify the personal conviction that somehow, in some way, Literature is good for people and they should acquire it. Teachers will be the providers, the middle persons, who will retail, or even wholesale, Literature to consumers. But have they ever been clear about what *makes* it good for them? How good are they as salespersons?

The history of academic literary studies is a tour of monuments to the theories that had their day and passed on. They passed into weighty tomes with titles like *The Critical Tradition* or *Criticism: The Major Texts*,[2] one after the other lined up on our office shelves. They record no cumulative progression of theory. What is the student to make of such texts, how is she expected to assemble this smorgasbord of fashions into a coherent banquet that will end with a sigh of satisfaction and a sense of completion, a celebration of wholeness, from hors d'oeuvres to cigars? We have histories of criticism, but we do not have a history of developing theory that describes the whole human behaviour of making Literature and its purpose.

In my view, the succession of theories in literary studies has, with a few notable exceptions, lamentably failed to lead us to secure ground from which to launch our Literature enterprise. They have left the discipline more and more naked and insecure, and more vulnerable to the attacks of those who see in Literature a threat to the expansion of their materialist empire. Our theories have increasingly removed us from the real strengths and functions of Literature. They have made us less and less comprehensible to the people we need to educate. Credibility has diminished rather than increased. Critics have looked elsewhere and borrowed models to apply to Literature, from moral philosophy and logical positivism, from religion and historicism, from social science and art. Literature has become an "object" so that it could be studied. Theorists have most recently invented impenetrable language and driven a wedge between ourselves, who profess to value and transmit the benefits of reading, and readers who want to experience stories and poems and integrate them into their personal and social lives. Professors have become scholasts that nobody listens to, but they still have not asked the hard questions. Feminist criticism and Reader Response came closest to helping us, since they frankly brought the reader into the picture and admitted the structuralist and political dimensions of reading, but they too balked at embarking on a full-scale theory that would see Literature as a human behaviour with all its biological implications. How can we get back on track — and what is the track?

There are a few important seeds in all the chaff of literary criticism, as we have called it, the notable exceptions mentioned above. Let us revisit them. One is Aristotle's theory of catharsis. It addresses several crucial components of theory that we must re-establish. It speaks of poetry as an imitation of life, the audience as emotionally affected by seeing it, and the purpose as having health benefits. If we are honest, we will admit that we have hardly come any distance at all to improve on this and we have failed to do the research to test, reject, or elaborate on this theory. Horace's *Ars Poetica* gave us another important clue, picked up by Sidney in his famous defense, that poetry "instructs and delights," a comment on the uses to which readers put Literature that I will return to shortly. Wordsworth told us that the key to the power of poetry is "pleasure," but we hardly paid that any attention, when in fact it is crucial. He also drew our attention to memory, mood, utility, and thought, but the profundity of this seems to have slipped by us. Shelley explained with some care that poetry is essentially political, that "poets are the unacknowledged legislators of the world," and we took this for hyperbole and wishful thinking. We might as well have borrowed that dismissive teenage put-down of things adult: "Whatever!" T.S. Eliot said that Literature is cumulative and builds upon itself, so the more we read the more we know of whatever we read, but we kind of said, "so what?" From these masters who have gone before we can, I think, distill five principles that could lead us to a comprehensive theory of Literature, or at least they can show us for what our theory must account.

One is that Literature provides important information about life, about the reader and the reader's relation to the world, and this information is embodied in Literature in ways that are unique to language and apprehensible to readers in a peculiarly congenial and accessible form.

Two is that the pleasures derived from reading Literature are certainly addictive and must therefore be related to other pleasure experiences in the central nervous system, using the Dopamine pathway. From this we can theorize that the neural rewards of reading are sufficient to keep us reading and the purpose of this must be biologically evolved; reading must somehow enhance our survival.[3]

The third is that Literature is a cumulative resource that is a stage in the evolution of story making, and can usefully be regarded as necessary to human survival. Following the breakdown of highly integrated hunter-gatherer societies and the disappearance of oral cultures, written stories form the principle repository of human wisdom and instruction. In other words, Literature is a cumulative and unparalleled reservoir of continually updated human interactive information.

Four is that emotion and thought are integrally related in the brain; that thought leads to emotion and emotion to thought in a looping effect described by Wordsworth. This theory is confirmed by the brain research of the last ten years. It is now obvious that serious discussions of Literature will have to be cognizant of the role of emotion in forming responses to what we read.

The fifth is that human behaviour and action is significantly affected by reading and that the political consequences of access to Literature are socially profound, and very threatening to the hegemony of homogeny that now represents the establishment commercial goal of shaping the world as a commercial machine.

These five principles enable us to see the crucial elements that will have to be accounted for in any theory that would attempt to explain the existence, the purpose and the uses of Literature in human life. It will have to account for the symbiotic connection between the writer and the reader. It will have to explain the neural processing of Literature in the human brain. It will have to assess the role Literature plays in the experience and behaviour of the reader affected by reading. And it will have to assess the social and political consequences of Literature as a component of human cultural organization. This is a large task, but I don't think we should be daunted. Half the battle is confronting the reality of what is required and not hiding away in denial and cowardice, or feeling unworthy or unequal to the challenge. We will start with the bits of evidence that lie around us—the testimony of readers, the anthropology of reading, storytelling and song and poetry, the knowledge of brain processes that has followed the researches of recent years.

Let us remind ourselves that a theory is a story that explains the relations of the bits of evidence. It binds together disparate elements into a whole. Stories explaining the thunder and lightning, the common cold or love at first sight may vary, but they all gain dignity from being focused on what they have to explain. I don't think we have reached common ground yet on what we are theorizing *about*, so that is where we have to start. In science these stories are called models and the history of scientific theory appears to have unity and continuity because it returns to models that it can modify and adjust. The human brain requires models to organize and so make sense of otherwise incoherent data.

Stories give pleasure because they organize information into manageable and applicable units of connected information out of a symbolic code, for storage and integration, one story joining with another and growing into a larger whole, but detachable as a distinct unit when needed. This is a bit like an Alice Munro novel, where each chapter can stand alone but also can be plugged back into the larger story to be part of a whole.

I believe virtually all teachers of Literature entered the profession because they loved to read, wanted to keep reading and wanted to share their enthusiasm. That is what happened to me. I did not want to work, I wanted to read. And if they would not pay me to read by myself, I was prepared to talk about reading to groups of other humans assigned to me.

I think we have to ask ourselves what happened when we became professionalized. Any theory of Literature will have to make explicit to students how rewards for reading work. Learning, resolving, adapting and organizing life experience data come from reading Literature and are reinforced by the endorphin effect, what I call the "Aha" effect elsewhere in this book. Following closely upon this outcome is the construction of the reader's identity. Each reader is unique for two reasons. One is genetic, given the permutation of genetic factors in non-cloned humans. The other is the infinitely variable life circumstances of each individual at every moment and with every sense-stimulus/brain response, in a continuous flow, a process that must produce more individuation along with aging. The identity is formed by the acquisition and the integration of experiences into the personal story record of the "I" meeting the World. Literature produces an inexhaustible reservoir of models of experience that can be brain-accrued for use in the encounter with life experience. Novels provide training in storymaking skills necessary for identity formation. Literature is the primary tool for language enrichment and data management. We must think of Literature as sets of symbolic modules designed by an adaptive organism hungry to expand the capabilities of its limited first-hand life experience. I think we have no time to lose in sharing some of these ideas with our students. We need them to listen and respond because when they all turn away, like the law student Ted in Amanda Cross's novel, it will be too late.

But there is another and very urgent reason for engaging our students in our quest for the applicability of Literature, a reason that is political and takes us back to Shelley, the key to our fifth principle, and forward to globalization. Literature is a brain-altering stimulant and promotes action and change. Literature shapes reality and redesigns perception. We need to get this clear in our minds. Literature is an active agent in human experience and flourishes where freedom of thought and expression flourish. It finds fertile ground in a population of practiced and addicted readers hooked on books. As Orwell pointed out, novels are produced by autonomous individuals out of personal experience, experience which they can think about freely and metaphorically. To quote Orwell exactly, "The novel is...a product of the free mind, of the autonomous individual...," and again, "Good novels are not written by orthodoxy-sniffers, nor by people who are conscience-stricken about their own unorthodoxy. Good novels are written by people who are *not frightened*."

Likewise, novels speak most strongly to other autonomous, unfrightened readers, who use what they read to enhance their independence of thought and feeling. At the same time these autonomies are joined in intimate ways, precisely because Literature links person to person by means of forms of language that evoke thought and feeling common to human brains. Literature creates a symbiotic membrane through which human energy flows back and forth. Literature develops the humanness of readers. Just as the best marriages occur between autonomous individuals, so the most dynamic and creative societies arise from the bonding of empowered, mutually respectful and secure individuals. The classroom is such a society in miniature and works most fruitfully where it is recognized as a safe and compassionate place for the expression of each participant's individuality. This will be especially applicable to the student responses to Literature. If Literature is a powerful agent in developing reader autonomy and social bonding through free and open thought and discussion, then its political dimension becomes immediately obvious. For these reasons, Literature will always find itself at war with totalitarian regimes of all kinds and in all social spheres, be they religious, economic or governmental.

Teaching Literature, and especially teaching it on the foundation of appropriate theory, will necessarily be a subversive activity in a culture dedicated to the reduction of independent thought and feeling. It would be at best ignorant, and at worst cowardly, not to recognize that we are advocates of a powerful weapon for undermining tyrannies. The time has come to show our faith in the powerful human resource that I am trying to describe. If teachers have convictions, if you share my views, show these convictions now. If teachers lose faith in the power of Literature they become its enemies. Those who teach, read, publish or review books got into this by trusting their own responses to the pleasures, beliefs and ideas found in reading. We must return to that trust and share it. If poets are so good at legislating, why are they unable to end child poverty and violence against women and men? Because as Shelley noted, they are *unacknowledged.* And who should acknowledge them if not teachers, readers and writers?

In 1975 Walter Jackson Bate questioned whether any advances had been made on the work of Wordsworth and Coleridge, who began to look intently at the human mind, the imagination, and the production of Literature. Still very little has changed. To make the necessary advances will require our joining forces with psychologists, therapists, anthropologists, neuroscientists, biologists, and many others we are not accustomed to seeking out. Our theory will have to explain the role of Literature in brain formation, and how brains can and do use Literature to improve their vision and understanding of the organic connectedness of the world that sustains us.

Literature can provide human brains with two primary tools that it is biologically designed to use, in order to overcome despair, isolation and powerlessness. One is metaphor. Its opposite is the literal. The literal simplifies. The literal enslaves. When the world is simplified it can be destroyed much more quickly and easily. The "Symbolic Species" grew its brain adapting to the complexity of its environment. If it now insists on the literal, it must necessarily simplify that environment and in doing so threaten its own survival. Nathaniel Hawthorne gives us many apt examples of where we are headed if we persist in our current thinking. Peter Goldthwaite *literally* brings his whole house down around his ears as he systematically pulls it apart searching for illusory riches buried in its walls. Aylmer the alchemist *literally* kills his wife Georgiana in his obsession to remove her birthmark and so render her beauty perfect. Literature provides us with brain-shaping metaphors to fit us for a healthy mutual symbiosis with our elegantly complicated world.

The other tool congenial to human brains is story. How we represent the world is a story, and many stories are possible. We can choose among them, or be doomed to one story only, and it may be and often is someone else's story imposed upon us. As Blake said, "I must invent my own system or be enslaved to another man's." At the moment we are living in the story of "market forces," which is the gospel according to Greed. We have been offered this gospel as a divine, unalterable destiny, Margaret Thatcher being the first, apparently, to apply the word "inevitable" to our current market credo. This is the kind of economic terrorism that comes from submitting to one story. We are empowered by story selection and story combining. Growing up, being an adult, means writing one's own story, and the best training for this is reading Literature.

NOTES TO APPENDIX III
FOR TEACHERS OF LITERATURE:
READING BRAIN AND THEORY VACUUM

1. In fact, this problem was addressed by the Bishops who opposed the translation of the Bible into the vernacular, prior to the issuance of the Authorized Version of the Bible under King James the First of England. They argued that if everyone could read the Bible, each citizen would become his own priest. Precisely Ted's claim to "priesthood" in this novel almost four hundred years later.
2. Richter, 1989; Bate, 1970.
3. The best modern essay I know on becoming joyously addicted to reading is by Lynn Sharon Schwartz, *Ruined By Reading*, which in spite of its over subtle and misleadingly apologetic title, should be on every English curriculum.

Selected References

Albert, M. and Obler, L., *The Bilingual Brain*. New York: Academic Press, 1978.

Allen, Charlotte Vale, *Daddy's Girl* . Toronto: McClelland & Stewart, 1980.

Atkinson, Paul, Davies, Brian and Delamont, Sara, eds., *Discourse and Reproduction: Essays in Honour of Basil Bernstein*. New Jersey: Hampton Press Inc., 1995.

Baars, Bernard J., *A Cognitive Theory of Consciousness*. Cambridge, England: Cambridge University Press, 1988.

Baars, Bernard J., "Interview with Walter Weiner," in *The Cognitive Revolution in Psychology*. New York; London: Guildford Press, 1986.

Baddeley, Alan, *Human Memory*. Hove, England: Psychology Press, 1997.

Bandura, Albert, *Self-Efficacy: The Exercise of Control*. New York: W.H. Bremen & Co., 1997.

Bandura, Albert, *Social Foundations of Thought and Action*. New Jersey: Prentice Hall, Inc., 1986.

Bate, Walter Jackson, ed., *Criticism: The Major Texts*. New York: Harcourt Brace Jovanovich, 1970.

Bateson, Gregory, *Mind and Nature: A Necessary Unity*. New York: Bantam, 1980.

Bernstein, Basil, *Class, Codes and Control*. St. Albans, United Kingdom: Granada Publishing, 1973.

Bernstein, Basil, *Pedagogy, Symbolic Control, and Identity*. Lanham, Md.: Rowman and Littlefield, 2000.

Birkerts, Sven, *The Gutenberg Elegies*. Boston, London: Faber & Faber, 1994.

Bonnycastle, Stephen, *In Search of Authority*, 2nd Ed. Peterborough, Canada: Broadview Press, 1996.

Bowers, Kenneth S., "On Being Unconsciously Influenced and Informed," in *The Unconscious reconsidered*, ed. K. S. Bowers and Donald Meichenbaum, New York: Wiley, 1984.

Bowers, Kenneth S. and Meichenbaum, Donald, *The Unconscious reconsidered*. New York: Wiley, 1984.

Brody, Hugh, *The Other Side of Eden*. Vancouver: Douglas & McIntyre, 2000.

Cairns-Smith, A.G., *Evolving the Mind.* Cambridge, England: Cambridge University Press, 1996.

Chatwin, Bruce, *The Songlines.* New York: Penguin, 1988.

Cheng'En, Wu, *Journey to the West*, trans. F. Jenning, 3 Vols. Beijing: Foreign Language Press, 1982.

Chomsky, Noam and Herman, Edwards S., *Manufacturing Consent: The Political Economy of the Mass Media.* New York: Pantheon, 1988.

Cook, Guy, *Discourse and Literature: The Interplay of Form and Mind.* Oxford: Oxford University Press, 1994.

Corballis, Michael C., *The Lopsided Ape.* New York: Oxford University Press, 1991.

Damasio, Antonio R., *Descartes' Error.* New York: Grosset Putnam, 1994.

Damasio, Antonio R., *The Feeling of What Happens: Body and Emotion in the Making of Consciousness.* New York: Harcourt Brace & Co., 1999.

Damasio, Antonio R. and Damasio, Hannah, "Brain and Language," in *Scientific American Book of the Brain*, pp. 29-41. New York: Lyons Press, 1999.

Danica, Elly, *Don't: A Woman's Word.* Charlottetown, PEI: Gynery Books, 1988.

Davidson, I. and Noble, W., "The Archeology of Perception: Traces of Depiction and Language," in *Current Anthropology*, Vol. 30, pp. 125-155. 1989.

Deacon, Terrence W., *The Symbolic Species: The Co-Evolution of Language and the Brain.* New York: W.W. Norton, 1997.

Demett, Daniel, *Consciousness Explained.* Boston: Little, Brown & Co., 1991.

Dooling, D.M. and Jordan-Smith, Paul, eds., *I Become Part of It.* New York: Parabola Books, 1989.

Dow, Miriam and Regan, Jennifer, eds., *The Invisible Enemy.* St. Paul, Minn.: Gray Wolf Press, 1989.

Eades, Michael R., M.D. and Eades, Mary Dan, M.D., *The Protein Power Life Plan.* New York: Warner Books, 2000.

Fine, Lawrence, "The Unwritten Torah," in *Parabola*, Vol. XVII, no. 3, pp. 65-70. Fall 1992.

Forster, E.M., *Alexandria: A History And A Guide.* Garden City, N.Y.: Anchor Books, Doubleday & Company, Inc., 1961.

Frank, Anne, *Diary of a Young Girl: The definitive edition.* Trans., Susan Massotty, New York: Doubleday, 1995.

Galbraith, John Kenneth, *A Tenured Professor.* Boston: Houghton Mifflin, 1990.

Gold, Joseph, "Biography as Fiction: The Art of Invisible Authorship," in *Reflections: Autobiography and Canadian Literature*, ed. Klaus Stich, pp. 131-139. University of Ottawa Press, 1988.

Gold, Joseph, ed., *In the Name of Language.* Toronto: MacMillan, 1975.

Gold, Joseph, "Recombinant Language: The Biological Imperative," *English Studies in Canada*, Vol. VII (1981) no. 4, pp. 473-482.

Gold, Joseph, *Read For Your Life: Literature as a Life Support System*, 2nd Ed. Markham, Ont.: Fitzhenry and Whiteside, 2001.

Gold, Joseph, *William Faulkner: A Study in Humanism, From Metaphor to Discourse*. University of Oklahoma Press, 1966.

Gold, Joseph, "The Function of Fiction: A Biological Model," in *Why the Novel Matters*, ed. Caroline McCracken-Flesher and Mark Spilka, pp. 270-279. Indiana University Press, 1990.

Gow, Miriam and Regan, Jennifer, eds., *The Invisible Enemy*. St. Paul, Minn.: Gray Wolf Press, 1989.

Hackett, Robert A. and Yuezhi Zhao, *Sustaining Democracy*. Toronto: Garamond Press, 1998.

Hawkin, Paul, Lovins, Amory and Lovins, L. Hunter, *Natural Capitalism*. Boston: Little, Brown & Co., 1999.

Healy, Jane M., *Endangered Minds. Why Our Children Don't Think*. New York: Simon & Schuster, 1990.

Healy, Jane M., *Failure to Connect: How Computers Affect Our Children's Minds — For Better or Worse*. New York: Simon & Schuster, 1998.

Healy, Jane M., *Your Child's Growing Mind.* New York: Doubleday, 1996.

Hillman, James, *Healing Fiction.* Barrytown, NY: Station Hill Press, 1983.

Hofstadter, Douglas R., *Godel, Escher, Bach*. New York: Vintage, 1989.

Holgren, Eric, "Human Hippocampel and Amygdala Recording and Stimulation: Evidence for a Neural Model of Recent Memory," in *Neuro-Psychology of Memory*, ed. Larry R. Squire and Nelson Butters. New York and London: Guilford Press, 1984.

Homer-Dixon, Thomas, *The Ingenuity Gap*. New York; Toronto: Alfred A. Knopf, 2000.

Hughes, Robert, *Culture of Complaint: The Fraying of America.* New York, Oxford: Oxford University Press, 1993.

Izard, Carroll E., "Four Systems for Emotion Activation: Cognitive and Noncognitive Processes," in *Psychological Review*, Vol. 100, no. 1, pp. 68-90. 1993.

Jacoby, Larry L., "Incidental Versus Intentional Retrieval Remembering and Awareness as Separate Issues," in *Neuro-Psychology of Memory*, ed. Larry R. Squire and Nelson Butters. New York and London: Guilford Press, 1984.

Jaynes, Julian, *The Origin of Consciousness in the Breakdown of the Bicameral Mind*. Boston: Houghton Mifflin Co., 1990, [1976].

Kapp, Bruce S., et al, "The Amygdala: A Neurological System Approach to Its Contribution to Aversive Conditioning," in *Neuro-Psychology of Memory*, ed. Larry R. Squire and Nelson Butters. New York and London: Guilford Press, 1992.

Keller, Helen, *The Story of My Life*. New York: Signet Classics, Penguin Group, 1988.

Kihlstrom, John F., "Conscious, Subconscious, Unconscious: A Cognitive Perspective," pp. 149-211, in *The Unconscious Reconsidered*, ed. Kenneth S. Bowers and Donald Meichenbaum. NY: Wiley, 1984.

Klein, Naomi, *No Logo*. Toronto: Vintage, 2000.

Koestler, Arthur, *Darkness at Noon*. Harmondsworth, Eng: Penguin, 1964.

Krashen, Stephen, *The Power of Reading*. Englewood, Colorado: Libraries Unlimited, 1993.

Kuhn, Thomas, *The Structure of Scientific Revolutions*. Chicago: University of Chicago Press, 1970 [1961].

L'Engle, Madeleine, *A Wrinkle in Time*. Farrar Straus Giroux, 1962.

LeDoux, Joseph, *The Emotional Brain*. New York: Simon & Schuster, 1996.

Lenneberg, Eric H., *Biological Foundations of Language*. New York: Wiley, 1967.

Lewontin, R.C., Rose, Steven and Kamin, Leon J., *Not in Our Genes*. New York: Pantheon Books, 1984.

Macioca, Giovanni, *The Foundations of Chinese Medicine*. Edinburgh; New York: Churchill Livingstone, 1989.

Mander, Jerry, *Four Arguments for the Elimination of Television*. New York: First Morrow Quill Paperback, 1997.

Marsh, Ngaio, *Grave Mistake And Other Mysteries*. Boston: Little, Brown, 1978.

Meleoltheart, M., Sartonis, G. and Tob, R., eds., *The Cognitive Neurophysiology of Language*. London, New Jersey: Erblaum Ass., 1987.

Miller, Geoffrey F., *The Mating Mind*. New York: Doubleday, 2000.

Nathanson, Donald, *Shame and Pride: Affect, Sex, and the Birth of the Self.* New York: W.W. Norton, 1992.

Niagara — River of Fame. Kiwanis Club of Stamford, Ontario, 1968.

Orwell, George, *Inside the Whale and other essays*. London, England: Penguin, 1962.

O'Sullivan, Julia and Howe, Mark L., *Overcoming Poverty: Promoting Literacy in Children From Low Income Families.* Thunder Bay: Lakehead University, 1999.

Pennebaker, James, *Opening Up: The Healing Power of Expressing Emotions.* New York: Guilford, 1997.

Piaget, Jean, *The Child's Conception of The World.* Lanham, Md.: Littlefield Adams, 1951, [1929].

Pinker, Steven, *The Language Instinct*. New York: Harper Collins, 1995.

Pirandello, Luigi, *Six Characters in Search of an Author*. London: Heineman, 1954.

Postman, Neil, *Amusing Ourselves to Death: Public Discourse in the Age of Show Business.* New York: Penguin Viking, 1985.

Postman, Neil, *Technopoly.* New York: Vintage Books, 1993.

Postman, Neil and Weingartner, C., *Teaching as a Subversive Activity.* New York: Dell, Inc., 1969.

Rapson, Linda M. "Acupuncture: A Useful Treatment Modality," In *Canadian Family Physician*, Vol. 30, January, 1984.

Rauch, S.L., Van der Kolk, B., et al, "A Symptom Provocation Study of Postraumatic Stress Disorder Using Positron Emission Tomography and Script-driven Imagery," in *Archives of General Psychiatry*, pp. 380-391. May 1996.

Richter, David H., ed., *The Critical Tradition*. New York: St. Martin's Press, 1989.

Rose, Steven, *Lifelines: Biology beyond Determinism.* New York: Oxford University Press, 1998.

Rosenblatt, Louise M., *The Reader, The Text, The Poem*. Carbondale: Southern Illinois University Press, 1978.

Rostand, Edmond. *Cyrano de Bergerac*. Winnipeg: Blizzard Publishing, 1995.

Sacks, Oliver, *The Man Who Mistook His Wife for A Hat and Other Clinical Tales.* New York: Summit Books, 1985.

Saul, John Ralston, *The Unconscious Civilization*. Toronto: Anansi, 1995.

Scheff, Thomas J., *Catharsis in Healing, Ritual and Drama.* Berkeley: University of California Press, 1979.

Schmandt-Besserat, Denise, *Before Writing.* Austin: University of Texas Press, 1992.

Schwartz, Lynne Sharon, *Ruined by Reading.* Boston: Beacon Press, 1996.

Shapiro, Dean M., *Blondin.* St. Catharines, Ontario: Vanwell Pub., 1990.

Shattuck, Roger, *The Forbidden Experiment: The Story of the Boy of Aveyron.* New York: Farrar Straus Giroux, 1980.

Showalter, Elaine, *Inventing Herself.* New York, London: Scribner, 2000.

Siegler, Robert S., *Children's Thinking.* New Jersey: Prentice Hall, 1998.

Spreen, Otfried, Risser, Anthony H. and Edgell, Dorothy, "Neglect of the 'feeling' brain/emotion/ [Simulated Aggressive Expression]" in *Developmental Neuropsychology* New York: Oxford University Press, 1995.

Spretnak, Charlene and Fritjof, Capra, *Green Politics.* Sante Fe, New Mexico: Bear & Co., 1986.

Studdert-Kennedy, Michael, ed., "Language and Social Connectivity," in *Psychobiology of Language.* Cambridge, Mass.; London, England: MIT Press, 1983.

Tawney, R.H., *Religion and the Rise of Capitalism.* New York: New American Library, 1954.

Taylor, John, *The Race* for *Consciousness.* Cambridge, Mass.: MIT Press, 1999.

Timerman, Jacobo, *Prisoner Without A Name, Cell Without a Number.* New York: Knopf, 1981.

Vanderhaeghe, Guy, *The Englishman's Boy.* Toronto: McClelland & Stewart, 1996.

Wade, Nicholas, ed., *The Science Times Book of the Brain.* New York: The Lyons Press, 1998.

Watson, James D., *The Double Helix.* New York: Atheneum, 1968.

Watt, Ian, *The Rise of the Novel.* Berkely: University of California Press, 1965, [1957].

Webster, Douglas B., *Neuroscience of Communication*, second ed. San Diego, London: Singular Publishing Group, Inc., 1999.

Wharton, Thomas, *Salamander.* Toronto: McClelland and Stewart, 2001.

Winkeljohann, Rosemary, ed., *The Politics of Reading.* Newark, Delaware: International Reading Association, 1973.

White, Michael and Epston, David, *Narrative Means to Therapeutic Ends,* New York: Norton 1990.

Wolf, Michael J., *The Entertainment Economy*. New York: Times Books, 1999.

Wood, David, *How Children Think And Learn*. Oxford, England: Blackwell, 1998.

Wright, Ronald, *Stolen Continents*. New York: Houghton Mifflin, 1993.

Wynot, Christopher Allen, "Hearing Metaphor: A study of Clients' use of Language in a Family Therapy Situation." Unpublished Masters Thesis, Wilfrid Laurier University, 1994.

Zipes, Jack, ed., *Tales of Enchantment*. New York: Penguin, 1991.

Credits

We thank the following for graciously granting permission to incorporate copyrighted material:

Excerpt from AMUSING OURSELVES TO DEATH by Neil Postman. Copyright © 1985 by Neil Postman. Used by permission of Viking Penguin, a Division of Penguin Putnam Inc.

Excerpt from BLONDIN by Dean Shapiro. Copyright © 1990. Used by permission of Vanwell Publishing.

Excerpt reprinted with permission of Simon & Schuster from THE MAN WHO MISTOOK HIS WIFE FOR A HAT AND OTHER CLINICAL TALES by Oliver Sacks. Copyright © 1970, 1981, 1983, 1984, 1985, by Oliver Sacks.

Excerpt from THE SCIENCE TIMES BOOK OF THE BRAIN published by The Lyons Press © 1998 by Nicholas Wade. Used by permission of The New York Times.

Excerpt from MIND AND NATURE: A NECESSARY UNITY Copyright © 1979 by Gregory Bateson, published by EP Dutton. Used by permission of the Institute for Intercultural Studies, New York City.

Excerpt from THE ENGLISHMAN'S BOY by Guy Vanderhaeghe. Used by permission, McClelland & Stewart Ltd., *The Canadian Publishers.*

Excerpt from LIFELINES: BIOLOGY BEYOND DETERMINISM by Steven Rose. Used by permission of Oxford University Press.

Excerpt from ENCYCLOPÆDIA BRITANNICA reprinted with permission of Encyclopædea Britannica © 2002 Britannica.com, Inc.

Excerpt from THE SYMBOLIC SPECIES: CO-EVOLUTION OF LANGUAGE AND THE BRAIN by Terrence W. Deacon. Copyright © 1997 by Terrence W. Deacon. Used by permission of W. W. Norton & Company, Inc.

Excerpt from "The Transparent Column" from A WRINKLE IN TIME by Madeleine L'Engle. Copyright © 1962, renewed 1990 by Madeleine L'Engle Franklin. Reprinted by permission of Farrar, Straus and Giroux, LLC.

Excerpt from GRAVE MISTAKE by Ngaio Marsh. Copyright © 1978. Reprinted by permission of Little, Brown and Company

Index